T0309906

Social Media Management

PERSUASION IN NETWORKED CULTURE

Social Media Management

PERSUASION IN NETWORKED CULTURE

Ben Shields

NEW YORK | OXFORD
Oxford University Press

Oxford University Press is a department of the University of Oxford.
It furthers the University's objective of excellence in research, scholarship,
and education by publishing worldwide. Oxford is a registered trade mark
of Oxford University Press in the UK and certain other countries.

Published in the United States of America by Oxford University Press
198 Madison Avenue, New York, NY 10016, United States of America.

© 2017 by Oxford University Press

For titles covered by Section 112 of the US Higher Education
Opportunity Act, please visit www.oup.com/us/he for the
latest information about pricing and alternate formats.

All rights reserved. No part of this publication may be reproduced, stored
in a retrieval system, or transmitted, in any form or by any means, without
the prior permission in writing of Oxford University Press, or as expressly
permitted by law, by license, or under terms agreed with the appropriate
reproduction rights organization. Inquiries concerning reproduction outside
the scope of the above should be sent to the Rights Department, Oxford University
Press, at the address above.

You must not circulate this work in any other form
and you must impose this same condition on any acquirer.

Library of Congress Cataloging-in-Publication Data

Names: Shields, Ben Ryan, author.
Title: Social media management : persuasion in networked culture / Ben
Shields.
Description: 1 Edition. | New York : Oxford University Press, 2016.
Identifiers: LCCN 2016045125| ISBN 9780190296339 (paperback) | ISBN
9780190296346 (e-ISBN)
Subjects: LCSH: Internet marketing. | Social media--Marketing. | Mass media
and business. | Public relations--Management. | BISAC: BUSINESS &
ECONOMICS / General. | BUSINESS & ECONOMICS / Marketing / General.
Classification: LCC HF5415.1265 .S5334 2016 | DDC 658.8/72--dc23 LC record available at
https://lccn.loc.gov/2016045125

Love to Misha

Contents

About the Author

Ben Shields is a Lecturer in Managerial Communication at the MIT Sloan School of Management. He served previously as the Director of Social Media and Marketing at ESPN. He is the coauthor of two other books: *The Sports Strategist: Developing Leaders for a High-Performance Industry* (Oxford University Press, 2015) and *The Elusive Fan: Reinventing Sports in a Crowded Marketplace* (McGraw-Hill, 2006). He holds a B.S. and M.A. in Communication Studies and a Ph.D. in Media, Technology, and Society, all from Northwestern University.

Preface

You may be wondering, "Social media is changing so rapidly. Why would I use this textbook to teach such a dynamic subject?" Regardless of the platform du jour, I believe there are fundamental concepts, strategies, and best practices to maximizing the business value of social media. The platforms may change, but the underlying social media management principles still apply.

Based on this premise, I wrote *Social Media Management* to give you and your students a common approach and language to study this emerging field. The book has the following features and benefits:

1. *Comprehensive text. Social Media Management* addresses key topic areas in this evolving field, providing you with a comprehensive textbook to serve as the foundation of your course. In one book, students learn how to develop, integrate, and implement social media strategy. The book also pairs well with supplementary articles and the latest industry news.
2. *Focused framework*. The social media management framework is a model to help your students acquire the skills and knowledge to become more effective managers and executives. The elements of the framework (goal, audience, platform, brand, content, distribution, and measurement) pose core questions that are relevant to any leader or organization pursuing a social media strategy.

3. *Diverse cases. Social Media Management* explores a wide range of examples from different industries (e.g., finance, commercial engineering, entertainment), different organizations (e.g., startups, big brands, medium-sized companies), and different disciplines (e.g., marketing, sales, supply chain, human resources). It gives your students practical cases of how others have leveraged social media platforms to derive business benefits.
4. *Accessible style.* To connect with your students, *Social Media Management* is written with the intent of being an accessible read, emphasizing comprehension and engagement. The use of visuals throughout the book is also designed to enhance readability.
5. *Complementary teaching materials.* Each chapter has a "Your Turn" exercise that encourages students to apply what they have learned in an exercise. PowerPoint presentations are also available for each chapter on the book website, which includes other resources to help with the teaching of social media management. If you are in an organization and looking to train employees or a team to think differently about social media, I encourage you to use the website material as well.
6. *Academic and practitioner perspective.* To write this book, I have applied my experiences as a practitioner, researcher, and professor in the field of social media management. As director of social media and marketing at ESPN, a unit of the Walt Disney Company, I was on the ground level at ESPN developing, leading, and implementing their social media strategy for five years. As a researcher, I have studied online communities and social technologies for more than a decade, and I have written about the topic within the sports media context in two previous books. As a professor, I developed the Social Media Management MBA course at the MIT Sloan School of Management, upon which this book is based. I have also taught numerous executives in the MIT Sloan Executive Education program. The students in the MBA and Executive Education programs have successfully applied the framework and best practices to their roles as entrepreneurs, consultants, marketers, and other executive leadership positions.

Organization and Chapter Preview

The social media management framework serves as the organizational structure for this book. Chapter 1 reviews the first component of the framework: setting goals. The remaining chapters are divided into two parts. Chapters 2–7 flesh out the framework, breaking down each component, discussing key strategies and tactics, and reviewing best practices and case studies that illustrate the theories and principles of social media management. Chapters 8–10 apply the social media management framework to specific situations. Following is a brief preview of the coverage in chapters 2 through 10.

Chapter 2, Targeting Social Audiences, details the components of the social media audience analysis, which is a critical exercise in devising social media strategy. We examine such questions as: Who are your audiences in social media? What are the characteristics of your audiences? And what are the social media goals of your audience? We also cover methods of audience research specific to the social media space.

Chapter 3, Adopting Social Platforms, explores the platform decision-making process and the strategies and tactics to arrive at the appropriate platform choices for an organization, regardless of what's trending at the moment.

Launching and managing a social presence is in many ways an exercise in brand strategy. Chapter 4, Developing Social Brand Strategy, discusses how to brand social platforms, extend a brand personality into the space, and organize and arrange social media platforms into a coherent brand portfolio.

Chapter 5, Designing Social Content, covers the building blocks of social content, addresses important lessons about tailoring content to the platform, and reviews key content development approaches in social media.

The mantra "if you build it, they will come" does not apply in the social media space. Because the frequency of a campaign or initiative going viral is fairly low, successful social media management often requires a strategic marketing and promotion approach to distribution. These distribution options and choices are covered in chapter 6, Distributing Social Content.

How should organizations define success in the social media space? By examining the various components of the social media management framework in chapter 7, we identify a measurement approach that helps organizations understand whether their social media management efforts are achieving business goals over the short and long term.

Chapter 8, Managing Crisis in Social Media, applies the social media management framework to crisis management. In the social media era, crisis management strategy has become an unavoidable discipline for most organizations. We share concepts and tools to prepare for and navigate these difficult, but inevitable situations.

In chapter 9, Building a Social Culture, we turn our lens inward and, using the book's framework, examine how organizations can implement social media platforms internally to develop stronger, more productive and engaged employees. Leaders often point to culture as a competitive advantage. If deployed effectively, social media can be a helpful tool in growing that culture.

We explore in chapter 10, Defining Your Personal Brand in Social Media, why and how you can apply the framework to your own personal brand. Regardless of where you are in your career, developing a strategy for your own social media can help you become a more effective leader, desirable employee, and better professional.

The Epilogue issues a challenge to all firms and business people to take a leadership position on balancing people's privacy and business interests in social media.

Last but not least, we have a number of resources for both instructors and students available online at www.oup.com/us/shields. Instructors can find PowerPoint slides and an Instructor's Manual for teaching with this book. Students can access a companion site with relevant materials and links to enhance the learning experience.

Your students demand (and need) social media management skills and experiences in today's marketplace. Students may be looking to pursue a career as a social media professional or a role in communications or marketing that requires aptitude in social media. They may also be leading a team or organization that includes a social media function, as many now do. Or perhaps they are interested in studying this topic to find new ideas to inform their work in a different discipline. Whatever their motivation, this book will help you teach students how to develop, implement, and measure an effective social media strategy that drives business value. Let's get started.

Acknowledgments

I could not have written this book without the inspiration and support of those around me. First, I want to thank my family—my relentlessly positive wife and teammate, Misha; my incomparably fun parents, Ben and Ginny; my loving sister, Heather, and loyal brother-in-law, Mike; my adorable nieces, Julia and Ava; and my technology-savvy Grandpa Don. I'm also extremely grateful to Mark, Arlene, Whitney, Wesley, Bubba, Gramsy, Rene, Peggy, Sara, and Daniel. My family gave me the strength and resolve to write—and finish—this book.

I want to thank Irv Rein, my mentor, coauthor, and friend. Irv taught me how to research, write, and work. I can only hope to influence one of my students as much as he has influenced me.

I am indebted to my editor, Ann West, for her initial vision for this project and her constant support and guidance throughout every phase. Thank you for everything you've done to make this book a reality. I am also grateful to the rest of the Oxford team, including Abigail Roberts and Christian Holdener, for your work on this book.

And a special thanks to my reviewers: Ko Kuwabara, Columbia Business School, Columbia University; Colin Campbell, Kent State University; Yasuaki Sakamoto, Stevens Institute of Technology; Daniel M. Ladik, Seton Hall University; Tracy A Cosenza, Fogelman College of Business, University of Memphis; Charles Besio, Cox School of Business, Southern Methodist University; Eric Brey, University of Wisconsin; Mindy McAdams, University of Florida; Mohammed Nadeem, National University; Kirsten Whitten, Curry College; Lawrence

K. Duke, LeBow School of Business, Drexel University; Michael Germano, California State University, Los Angeles; David J. Faulds, University of Louisville; Eric J. Karson, Villanova University; and Mary C. Martin, Fort Hays State University. I very much appreciate the time you spent reviewing this book and all your helpful suggestions to improve it.

I am extremely appreciative of the MIT Sloan community for their belief in me. Neal Hartman, JoAnne Yates, Virginia Healy-Tangney, Kara Blackburn, Roberta Pittore, Miro Kazakoff, and Chris Kelly are some of the best colleagues I could imagine. Thank you also to my key research assistants throughout this process. Rachael Plitch was instrumental during the writing phases of the project and was a constant supporter and invaluable sounding board. Sarah MacMillan also played a very useful role at the beginning research stages of the process. I'm indebted to my students in Social Media Management both in spring 2015 and spring 2016. You clarified my thinking and understanding of how to best teach social media management. And to my exceptional teaching assistants, Zachary Levine and Sarah Callaway, I will always be grateful for your unconditional support and enduring contributions to our class and this book.

My six years at ESPN were invaluable to my research and practice in social media management. My heartfelt gratitude to my executive leadership of George Bodenheimer, Sean Bratches, Katie Lacey, Chris Brush, Aaron Taylor, Moira Davis, Carol Kruse, and my direct bosses, Hayes Tauber, Kevin Kirksey, and Jeff Gonyo, for believing in me and supporting me along the way. And to my ESPN social media team, I am beyond grateful for how much you taught me during our time working together. Gabe Rose is one of the smartest, most creative social media minds I know and was instrumental to everything we did at ESPN Social. Tim Hubbell brought tremendous business sense, excellent leadership, and passionate curiosity to our team as well. Sara Gitig, Steve Braband, Won Kim, John Twomey, Riki McDermott, Michael Giblin, and Julian Gompertz rounded out an extraordinary group that I had the pleasure of having on my team during my time at the company. Not only did they produce best-in-class work day in and day out, but they also treated one another with respect, kindness, and admiration. And to my many other ESPN social media colleagues, including Gabe Goodwin, Glenn Jacobs, Chris Sheridan, Kevin Butler, Mike Bucklin, Mary Sheehan, Sarah Tanner, Victoria Vaynberg, David LiCalzi, Ian Lasher, and Raphael Poplock, I am grateful for your partnership and proud of all the work we did together.

Finally, thank you to Jeremy, Michael, Matt, Mic, Dan, Evan, Adam, Johnny, Jerm, Joe, Ben, Jay, Chris, and Jon, my loyal friends who keep me laughing.

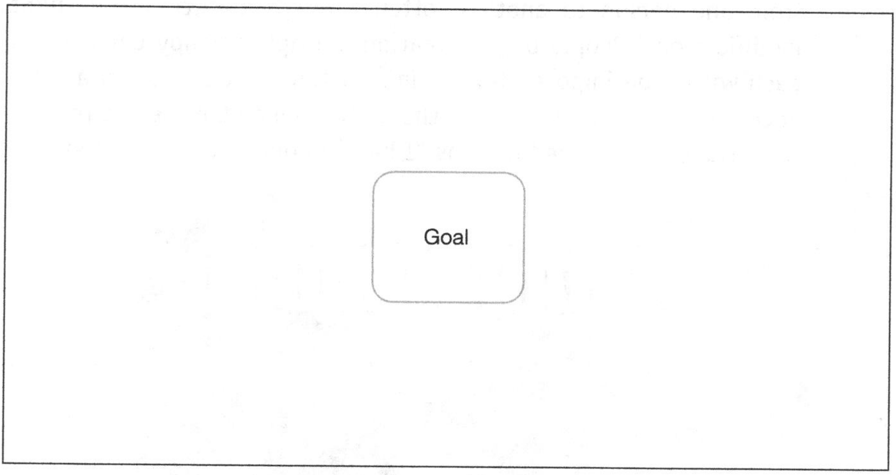

1 Maximizing Business Value

Tardar Sauce was only five months old when her life changed forever. In September 2012, Bryan Bundesen visited his sister Tabatha and saw her new cat. This feline was like nothing he had ever encountered. Although she was healthy and normal by most accounts, she had feline dwarfism and an underbite that etched a frown permanently on her face.

Bryan decided to post a picture of Tard on Reddit, the social platform known by some as the "front page of the Internet." Redditors were both in awe and perplexed by this peculiar kitty. After views of the original photo soared, a number of people questioned whether Bundesen Photoshopped the cat's smile upside down. To prove the naysayers wrong, he followed up with YouTube video evidence that quickly went viral.[1] An Internet star, who now goes by the name of Grumpy Cat, was born.

If her look attracted the intrigue, the community ignited the phenomenon. Grumpy Cat's image became a *meme*, an idea that spreads from one person to another, often through imitation and slight modification.[2] People began creating multiple Grumpy Cat memes, each with superimposed text in impact font that expressed annoyance and disapproval.[3] One of the early Grumpy Cat memes to gain wide traction, pictured here, is "I had fun once . . . It was awful."[4]

The community also created other versions of the meme. For example, "There are two kinds of people in this world . . . And I don't like them." "If you're happy and you know it . . . I don't care." "Of all nine lives I've lived . . . This is the worst."[5] On one level, the juxtaposition of Grumpy Cat with a simple setup and disdainful payoff became a reliable source of humor for many. On another level, some posit that Grumpy Cat reflected society's collective stresses about the state of the economy and geopolitical issues at the time.[6] Either way, Grumpy Cat became one of the most popular search terms on Google in both 2013 and 2014.[7]

The surging popularity of Grumpy Cat presented business opportunities. "I was able to quit my job as a waitress within days of her first appearance on social media and the phone simply hasn't stopped ringing since," Tabatha said in December 2014.[8] To harness and capitalize on the interest, she and Bryan began working with talent manager Ben Lashes, who had already established himself as a "meme manager," guiding the careers of other Internet celebrities like Keyboard Cat, Success Kid, and Ridiculously Photogenic Guy.[9]

Grumpy Cat became a multiplatform brand franchise. For example, her frowning image was emblazoned on t-shirts for her legion of fans to wear proudly and ironically. She inspired the creation of the Grumppuccino, a frappuccino-like drink with the slogan "It's Awfully Good."[10] Like politicians preparing for a presidential run, Grumpy Cat also "wrote" a *New York Times* bestselling book and embarked on a countrywide book tour. She was the most popular attendee at the social media star–studded South By Southwest (SXSW) in 2013, posing for photos all day with conference goers courtesy of her sponsor, Friskies, who also awarded her a "Lifetime Achievement Award" that year. Capping off a busy twenty-four-month stretch, she starred in her own Christmas movie on the Lifetime Network in December 2014.[11]

Meanwhile, the Grumpy Cat "empire" grew into its own media company. In just two years, she had amassed more than 7 million Facebook likes, 275,000 Twitter followers, 500,000 Instagram followers, and 30 million views on YouTube. Directly through social media platforms, Grumpy Cat attracted, engaged, and monetized an audience in ways that would not be possible through "traditional" media.

• • •

After two years as a celebrity, Grumpy Cat reportedly made upward of $100 million in revenue.[12] Tabatha denied the report (which set off a wave of criticism about owners profiting off their cats), but at the time she also declined to correct it.[13] Because Grumpy Cat is not a public company (at least not yet), we may never know the actual financial details. But if you consider her sprawling social media presence and diverse brand extensions, the social media–fueled transformation of Tardar Sauce to Grumpy Cat was an undeniable business success.

Social Media Equals Business Opportunity (and Not Just for Cats)

Grumpy Cat's ascendancy from a Reddit post to an internationally renowned brand is just one example of the business potential of social media. Organizations and leaders now approach social media in different and creative ways and are achieving a variety of results. Consider the following:

- Organizations are using social media to help transform their internal cultures. Computer software storage company EMC, traditionally a top-down, command-and-control hierarchy, launched EMC One, an internal social network, which has helped the company become more "open, inclusive, and transparent."[14] This shift has paid dividends, particularly in times of crisis. During the economic recession of 2008, EMC faced significant financial pressure and needed to cut costs considerably. Through their EMC One internal social media network, employees engaged in a dialogue about money-saving solutions and executives listened and participated. One of the suggestions was a pay cut across the board (including executives), an inherently unwelcome policy but one that would not result in any lost jobs. The executive team acted on the idea. When the memo announcing the change from Joe Tucci, EMC president, was sent to EMC's thousands of employees, the message was received positively (or as positively as a pay cut could be) due in large part to employees feeling involved in the decision-making process. The use of EMC One not only helped implement a difficult policy change but also stabilized employee morale during a tumultuous period.[15]
- Social media is not just the domain of business-to-consumer companies. As organizations of all stripes are integrating social media to drive business value, a large and influential business-to-business support industry has also spawned. Hubspot is a prime example. It built a platform that helps organizations develop an "inbound marketing" approach, which seeks to reach people where they spend time online, increasingly on social media, and attract them with interesting and relevant content. For example, Thermo Fisher Scientific, a company specializing in supporting scientific research, used Hubspot and within 8 months saw their Twitter following grow by 154% and website traffic increase by 182%.[16] Because of success stories like Thermo Fisher and many others, the demand for Hubspot's platform and services became so high that the company went public in 2014 at an $880 million valuation[17] Hubspot grew successfully alongside social platforms like Facebook and Twitter, capitalizing on the fundamental changes in how people are now interacting with businesses online and through social media.

- Social media has also proven to be a valuable tool for nonprofits. The ALS Ice Bucket Challenge dominated the summer of 2014, generating $220 million in donations worldwide to the organization.[18] Powering this global phenomenon was social media. Thousands of people made videos of themselves getting doused by ice water and then nominating three friends (often through Facebook tagging) to either do the same or donate $100 to the ALS (Amyotrophic Lateral Sclerosis) Association. Many decided to do both. In fact, numerous celebrity influencers from Facebook's Mark Zuckerberg to social media maven Katy Perry to basketball star LeBron James contributed to and accelerated this social movement. In a pre–social era, the ALS simply would not have had the word-of-mouth mechanisms to raise awareness and donations at the scale of the Ice Bucket Challenge. Although the phenomena was criticized at times because some participants seemingly lost sight of the real cause of fighting ALS, the money raised has reportedly helped advance scientific discoveries of possible cures to the disease.[19]

These are just a few examples. We will explore many more in the coming pages. What you will notice is that the strategic use of social media is expanding across a variety of industries, at organizations large and small, and within a number of disciplines, from communication and marketing to supply chain and sales. And yet despite the disparate business uses of social media, those that are having success in this space share one commonality: they practice sound social media management.

What Is Social Media Management?

Our work together in this book will address this central question: *How can organizations and leaders maximize the business value of social media platforms?*

To begin, it is important that we operate from a common definition of social media. Let's use this one: "Social media are computer-mediated tools that allow people to create, share or exchange information, ideas, and pictures/videos in virtual communities and networks."[20] This definition is intentionally broad and for our purposes will help shape and focus the discussion. (We will address in detail the various types of social platforms and the differences between them in chapter 3.)

Now, the question of maximizing business value of social platforms can be approached from multiple angles and methodologies. To be fair, organizations and leaders of all sectors and sizes have been asking it for the better part of a decade, leading many to experiment with different approaches. However, as the industry matures and organizations increasingly seek to realize benefits from their social media investments, taking a more systematic management approach to the social media space is both an opportunity and a necessity.

The discipline of social media management is designed to help organizations and leaders meet this increasingly important need. What is social media management? We define it as:

The ongoing practice of adopting, managing, and measuring social media platforms to achieve business goals.

Social media management is built on three guiding principles. Adhering to these principles can spell the difference between success and failure with your social media initiatives.

Connection to Overall Firm Strategy

Social media management should be driven by the high-level strategy at the firm. It is imperative that the organization understands the role of social media relative to its goals. If a social media strategy is not aligned with the organization's strategy, it will usually not be worth pursuing.

Integration across the Enterprise

Social media management promotes the cohesive integration of social media across the enterprise. This discipline cannot be practiced effectively in a silo of an organization. It must be a tool for various departments to use depending on the business challenge at hand. Increasingly, the organizations that are deriving the most benefit from social media are the ones that have integrated it across all relevant business units and/or functions.[21]

Iteration over Time

Social media management is an iterative process, informed by rigorous monitoring and measurement. It requires constant evaluation of how and when a social media strategy should be adjusted to align with firm strategy to achieve its goals and better integrate across the enterprise.

Guided by these key principles, the theory and practice of social media management will equip you with a framework, strategies, and best practices to capitalize on the business potential of the social media. The first step in that process is becoming more goal-centric in your approach.

Evolving from a Platform-Driven to a Goal-Centric Approach

The history of the social media industry may not be long in years, but we have already witnessed an evolution in how businesses are approaching the space. Take Facebook, for example. When the platform rolled out brand pages in 2007, businesses and celebrities began building presences on the platform. The key strategic question driving their efforts: "How do we acquire as many Facebook fans as possible?"

Brands approached fan acquisition in a number of ways. Many focused on posting engaging content that existing fans would "like" and comment on, actions that could then be seen in Facebook's "News Feed" by their friends, who might be persuaded to become a fan as well. Some bought Facebook advertisements that targeted potential fans and enabled people to "fan" the page within the advertisement. Others installed a Facebook "become a fan" button on their own website, a tactic that often targeted existing customers. Developing applications on Facebook that were "fan-gated," which restricted access to a promotion or interactive experience until you fanned the page, was another tactic.

Seemingly all social media efforts among these early-adopting organizations were directed toward attracting Facebook fans. And the more fans, the better. In many ways, it mattered little who your fans were or whether they might buy your product. If you had what was perceived to be a healthy number, then you were a success.

At a certain point, however, many organizations began asking the question, "Now what?" From the big brand with 5 million fans to the small business with 5,000, understanding the value of the fan became an industry-wide pursuit, as did measurement strategies for return on investment. Gaining fans just for the sake of it was increasingly becoming a less defensible activity. Executives demanded more accountability, and rightfully so. The industry started evolving as a result.

The story of Facebook fans (and the feverish quest to acquire them) illustrates a key historical shift in the industry: many organizations were once platform driven in their approach. They focused on achieving success as defined by the platform itself. In the case of Facebook, success meant fans, likes, and comments. On Twitter, followers, retweets, and favorites were the coin of the realm. And for YouTube, it was all about the view counts.

Today, organizations are becoming more goal centered in their approach, seeking to tie their efforts on social media platforms more directly to their business performance. A study by the *MIT Sloan Management Review* and Deloitte Consulting found that as companies mature in their social media efforts, they evolve beyond a platform-driven approach and develop a social media strategy within the context of their organization's goals.[22] To be clear, platform metrics remain relevant. However, the organization's goals and corresponding success metrics (not the platform's metrics) should inform its social media strategy. After all, "How can we acquire Facebook fans?" is a different and ultimately less productive question than "How can we use Facebook to help us accomplish our business goals?"

A goal-centric approach to social media has a number of benefits:

1. *Better for strategy development.* A goal-centric approach forces an organization to devise a focused strategy. In a new space with countless platforms and ideas, it is impossible to do everything. Goals help prioritize what's important.
2. *Better for measurement.* A goal-centric approach helps organizations measure the effectiveness of their social media strategy. Without clearly defined goals, it will be more difficult to determine which metrics to use to understand the business impact of social media on your organization.
3. *Better for resource allocation.* A goal-centric approach helps clarify where and how to invest resources. By focusing on achieving goals through social media, organizations avoid spending time and money on social media strategies that are not aligned with their overall approach.

Does adopting a goal-centric approach mean organizations should avoid experimentation? No. Quite the contrary, in fact. Testing and learning are central to successful social media management. You should experiment, but with an overarching goal in mind. Launching a presence just to have one is not a winning strategy. Launching a presence centered on a goal is. In the next section, to help you think about possible goals, we examine the types of business value organizations can derive from social media.

Setting Goals to Drive Value

Before developing your social media management strategy, a critical initial step is to explore the potential outcomes your organization might achieve. By first

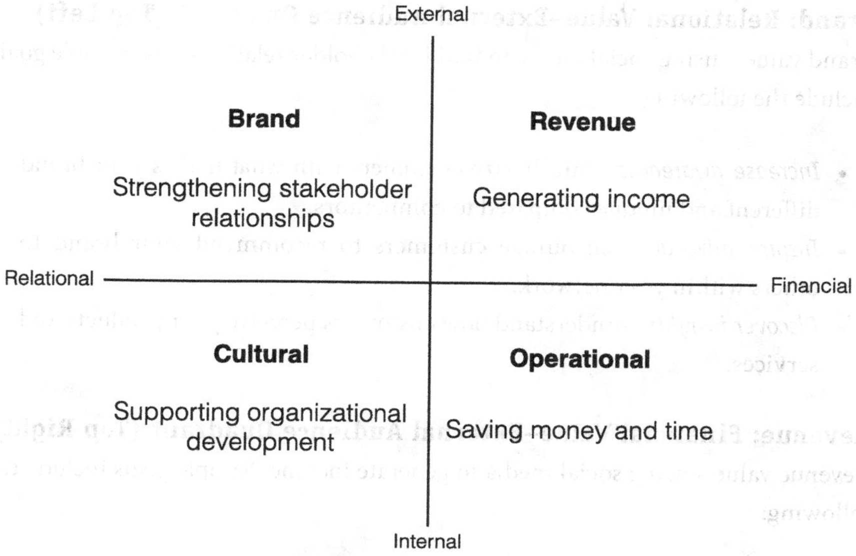

FIGURE 1.1 **Business Value of Social Media**

knowing what is possible via social media and then reflecting on your own priorities, you will be in a better position to decide on realistic goals and actionable strategies.

Business value in social media can come in a variety of forms. Figure 1.1 outlines a range of social business possibilities. It is divided by two axes:

- The horizontal axis includes relational value on the left and financial value on the right. For most organizations a measured combination of the two is ideal.
- The vertical axis represents possible audiences, accounting for both external and internal stakeholders. External can refer to customers, shareholders, the media, government, and other outside constituents. Internal refers primarily to employees or other people affiliated with the operations of an organization.

Corresponding to the four quadrants these axes create, there are four main types of social media business value: brand, revenue, operational, and cultural. Let's look at definitions and potential business goals for each.

Brand: Relational Value–External Audience Quadrant (Top Left)

Brand value—using social media to build stakeholder relationships. Sample goals include the following:

- *Increase awareness*—familiarize customers with what makes your brand different and unique compared to competitors.
- *Inspire advocacy*—encourage customers to recommend your brand to others within your network.
- *Discover insights*—understand how customers perceive your products and services.

Revenue: Financial Value–External Audience Quadrant (Top Right)

Revenue value—using social media to generate income. Sample goals include the following:

- *Create demand*—generate leads for potential purchases.
- *Increase sales*—convert leads into paying customers.
- *Increase repeat purchases*—drive additional spending from existing customers.

Operational: Financial Value–Internal Audience Quadrant (Bottom Right)

Operational value—using social media to save money and time. Sample goals include the following:

- *Lower costs*—accomplish the same (or more) with less money.
- *Increase productivity*—accomplish the same (or more) in less time.

Cultural: Relational Value–Internal Audience Quadrant (Bottom Left)

Cultural value—using social media to support organizational development. Sample goals include the following:

- *Increase qualified applicants*—find and recruit prospective employees with strong potential fit.
- *Improve employee engagement*—create opportunities for empowerment and impact.
- *Lower retention rates*—drive employee satisfaction and likelihood to stay.

The four quadrants of brand, revenue, operational, and cultural are comprehensive, but not exhaustive of the potential business value of social media. In addition, the sample goals in each quadrant are suggestive. Depending on the organization, other goals may be more relevant to the firm's overall strategy. Whether you draft off these or use others, the key in goal setting is being specific, realistic, and actionable with each goal you set.

In addition, not every social media strategy can—or should—achieve all four types of value. Sometimes the scope of a strategy is inherently narrow and focused solely on, for example, improving operations through social media. This outcome is normal. What these categories offer is a starting point in designing social media strategy.

Let's now look at an example of an organization that set clear business goals and achieved value in a number of ways through social media. The company is Maersk Line, part of the Danish conglomerate Maersk Group.

CASE STUDY: MAERSK LINE B2B: FROM BORING TO BRILLIANT

As the world's largest business-to-business shipping company, Maersk Line on the surface does not appear to be tailor-made for an industry where the Harlem Shake, blue and white dress, and Old Spice Guy live and thrive. In fact, prior to entering into the social media space, there was a feeling within the company that they were simply too "boring" to succeed. They were wrong.

The story starts in 2011 with Jonathan Wichmann, who eventually became head of social media at Maersk Line. He saw opportunity for the brand in the new and exciting social space and pulled together a proposed approach for experimentation, persuaded a couple executives to support his efforts, and started moving quickly. "Our initial goals for social media were to raise brand awareness, increase customer loyalty, improve employee engagement, develop customer insights, and control news flow," Wichmann said.[23] He also decided to execute his plan with minimal in-house resources rather than outsource it to an agency, a move that would be more cost effective and enable him to operate quickly and nimbly.

CONTINUED

CASE STUDY: MAERSK LINE B2B: FROM BORING TO BRILLIANT *CONTINUED*

Contrary to other B2B companies, which gravitated toward LinkedIn, the first initiative for Wichmann was to build out the company's Facebook presence to reach a core target audience: Maersk Line employees.[24] There were both practical and strategic reasons for this approach. Practically, many of Maersk Line's 25,000 employees were located all over the world, given the nature of work in the maritime industry; most were already on Facebook, and launching a brand page would be an easy way to connect them. Strategically, to grow the page organically, employees would be an efficient place to start; they were strong candidates to "like" the page and spread the word that it existed to their networks, which included customers, prospective customers, shipping experts, and others in the shipping industry.

Maersk Line's content strategy was instrumental to the launch of the Maersk Line Facebook page. Rather than send promotional posts about the company, Wichmann and team capitalized on Maersk Line's historical archive of 14,000 images.[25] In the first post reproduced here, Maersk Line posted a seminal photo in the company's history, the first steamship Captain Maersk-Moller acquired. The black-and-white photo reinforced the longevity of Maersk Line, suggesting that the brand is strong and has stood the test of time. Importantly, the post is also written in a conversational, human style with less of a corporate tone.

Maersk Line shared their photo.
November 27, 2012
Where it all began. In 1886, Captain Peter Mærsk-Møller bought his first steamship, the British-built S.S. Laura.
Maersk Line with Mark Lisicky and 6 others.
October 17, 2011
In 1886, Captain Peter Mærsk-Møller bought his first steamship, the British-built S.S. Laura.
1.3K Likes 31 Comments 167 Shares
Share

The Maersk Line team also welcomed user-generated content from fans, employees, and customers who loved their ships. This next post is from a photographer in Hamburg who "loves" Maersk and spotted one of its vessels in his hometown. As we will discuss in depth, working with user-generated content not only opens up an additional content source for a brand but also can strengthen relationships with key stakeholders.

Maersk Line shared Jan Sieg Photographie's photo.
December 7, 2012
Maersk Essen surrounded by tugboats and cranes in the Port of Hamburg. Kindly shared by Jan Sieg. Discover more of his photos here: http://maerskl.in/TM870o
Jan Sieg Photographie ▸ Maersk Line
December 6, 2012
I LOVE MAERSK
1.2K Likes 24 Comments 144 Shares
Share

By all accounts, Maersk Line developed a content strategy that highlighted what was unique about the brand and remained consistent in executing on this strategy.

While building the Maersk Line Facebook page, Wichmann and team began moving strategically into other platforms. Approaching each platform differently, they expanded into LinkedIn, Twitter, Pinterest, and others. Each had a different audience they were trying to connect with and unique content as well. For example, Twitter was targeted directly to customers who were looking for the latest news about the company.[26] Moreover, Maersk Line surveyed and received feedback from its multiple audiences about what content they wanted and on which platforms.

After eighteen months of this strategy, the results—purely from a numbers standpoint—were impressive for a B2B shipping company: 800,000 Facebook fans, of which 15%–20% were customers, 40,000 Twitter

CONTINUED

CASE STUDY: MAERSK LINE B2B: FROM BORING TO BRILLIANT *CONTINUED*

followers, and 22,000 Instagram followers, all with a budget of $100,000.[27] Yet a peek behind the numbers tells an even more meaningful story. To do so, let's return to the four business benefits of social media to summarize the results:

- *Brand.* Maersk Line did a survey with customers and found that 68% said Maersk Line's social media initiatives improved their perception of the company, whether they followed the company on social media or not.[28]
- *Revenue.* Because the company had connected with customers, its social media efforts helped influence the sales cycle and result in additional sales leads.[29]
- *Operational.* The company emphasized customer service through social media and was able to reduce the time spent on resolving such matters.[30] In addition, the media relations function also benefited from increased social media activity, as the Maersk Line brand was praised in multiple press outlets for its social media presence. Without social media, the cost to achieve similar awareness and recognition would likely be considerable.[31]
- *Cultural.* Finally, as a result of the social media initiatives, Maersk Line saw improvements in employee empowerment. Social media not only helped connect a globally disparate group of employees but also changed the way some of them performed their jobs and viewed the company culture.[32]

Maersk Line was an early, if surprising, benefactor of social media. Importantly, Wichmann and team did not just build a following on Facebook, Twitter, LinkedIn, and other platforms. They used social media to further the goals of the organization. In doing so, Maersk Line derived brand, revenue, operational, and cultural benefits as a result.

Now, as we move toward your own social media management efforts, let's turn to the social media management framework, which is a blueprint for maximizing the business value of social media.

Social Media Management Framework

The social media management framework is intended to help organizations and leaders adopt, manage, and measure social media platforms to achieve business goals. Consistent with the guiding principles of social media management mentioned earlier, it helps you (1) connect your social media initiatives to your firm's overall business goals and strategies, (2) integrate your social media initiatives into key disciplines and processes throughout your organization, and (3) set up iteration mechanisms to measure and improve your social media initiatives in real time and over the long term.

Most, if not all, of the components of the framework will likely be familiar. This is by design. Success in social media management should not require a never-before-seen magic formula. Instead, leaning on and synthesizing fundamental concepts in management, strategy, and communication, as this book's framework does, can be especially valuable in the buzzword-heavy, hype-filled social media space. If little else, the framework should help you take a more measured, realistic approach to defining what social media can (and cannot) do for your organization.

There are seven components to the social media management framework: goal, audience, platform, brand, content, distribution, and measurement. All components are interrelated and interdependent. For example, the choice of goal informs what audiences an organization should target and the platforms through which to reach them. Meanwhile, platform choice also helps an organization tailor its brand, content, and distribution strategies. The measurement function evaluates the effectiveness of each component in accomplishing the organization's goals.

Let's walk through the social media management framework as illustrated in figure 1.2.

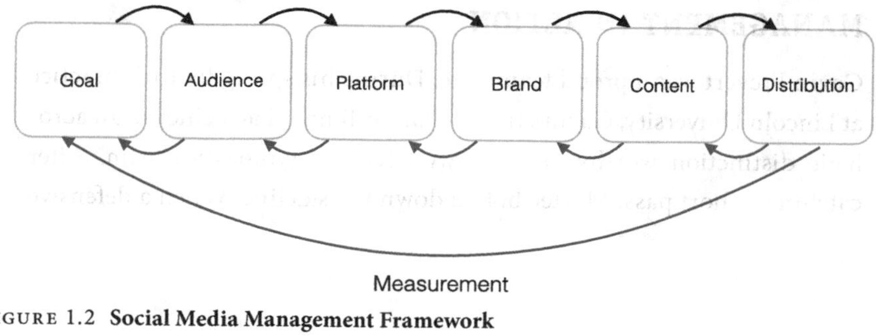

FIGURE 1.2 **Social Media Management Framework**

- *Goal.* Define your business objective(s). Are they brand, revenue, operational, and/or cultural?
- *Audience.* Based on your goal(s), determine your target audiences.
- *Platform.* Based on your audiences, identify the social media platforms to reach and engage them.
- *Brand.* Decide the brand(s) that will engage with your audiences on your selected social platforms.
- *Content.* Design a messaging strategy and creative content appropriate to your audience, platform, and brand.
- *Distribution.* Organize and execute a marketing strategy to increase the engagement and reach of your content.
- *Measurement.* Relative to your goal, measure the results of the social media initiative.

Because each component of the framework is interrelated, iteration is a key tenet of success. If the initiative does not achieve the desired results, perhaps the content or distribution strategy should be adjusted. If not, are there ways to alter the brand strategy? Is the platform choice appropriate? Or if the platform is not the issue, you might reconsider whether you are targeting the appropriate audiences. If changes or modifications to any of these elements do not result in achieving your goal, then it will be necessary to reevaluate the goal.

How does the social media management framework function in practice? Consider this example from ESPN's SportsCenter.

CASE STUDY: #SCTOP10: SOCIAL MEDIA MANAGEMENT IN ACTION

Gavin Frevert was a proud teammate. During his spring football practice at Lincoln University, Gavin's friend Martee Tenner had achieved an acrobatic distinction worthy of the USA Olympic gymnastics team. After catching a short pass, Martee bolted down the sideline. When a defensive player attempted to tackle him, he did a full frontal flip, landing cleanly on his feet and running for a touchdown.

In another era, few outside of the local community would ever know of Mr. Tenner's feat. After all, the Jefferson City, Missouri-based Division II football team was hardly a national powerhouse. If it weren't for the camera at the top of the bleachers, used by the coaches to diagnose their team's progress, Tenner's spontaneous trick would have become part of the Peacocks' lore and nothing more.

Thanks to social media, the video had new life. The entrepreneurial Frevert got his hands on the raw footage, cut together a highlight of the play, set it to a jolting soundtrack, and uploaded it to YouTube.[33] On a crowded platform with over a billion users and an endless stream of content, he would need a little help to get the play the attention he felt his teammate deserved.

Gavin decided to reach out to the company that effectively invented and popularized "the highlight," ESPN. Posting the highlight to the "wall" of the ESPN Facebook page, Gavin pleaded that the company consider it for that night's SportsCenter Top 10, historically the show's most revered segment. He probably thought it was a long shot, but figured it was worth the effort.

When the ESPN social media team received Gavin's request on Facebook, they were awed by the crazy play and tried to help him accomplish his goal. The first move was to post the video to the rest of the ESPN Facebook community, with an h/t to Gavin. Then the team shared the highlight with the SportsCenter producers. After vetting it for authenticity, the producers decided to put the editorial decision in the hands of fans via Twitter. On the SportsCenter Twitter feed, they asked fans to tweet using the hashtag #SCTop10 to help them decide whether the play was worthy of being on the SportsCenter Top 10. The play received enough positive endorsement that it became the number 1 play on the Top 10 that night, an achievement befitting of Martee's daredevil approach.

To close the loop, SportsCenter's Twitter feed congratulated Martee publicly for his noteworthy play.

CONTINUED

CASE STUDY: #SCTOP10: SOCIAL MEDIA MANAGEMENT IN ACTION *CONTINUED*

The ESPN social media team then went back to where the story began and thanked Gavin for submitting the video and saying that his dream came true. Gavin's response: "omg I'm crying I'm so happy."

Because of this use case and others like it, SportsCenter producers saw potential in fans nominating plays for the Top 10 via Twitter. In turn, the ESPN sales marketing team created a new #SCTop10 sponsorship package that attracted interest from various advertisers. Mazda USA eventually agreed to sponsor the segment, which resulted in additional advertising dollars for the company. With this program and others like it, social media–driven advertising became a viable source of revenue.

The #SCTop10 initiative developed over time into a consistent social media initiative that delivered value to the company. Let's break it down with the social media management framework to see how all the components work together.

- *Goals.* Connected to the firm strategy, the main goals for #SCTop10 were twofold: (1) Brand—strengthen fan relationships with viewers; (2) Revenue—generate ad sales.

- *Audience.* The core target was avid SportsCenter viewers; these were the fans that were watching the show already and wanted to contribute. A secondary audience was casual SportsCenter viewers who may need a reason to tune in to the show rather than watch it out of habit. The "tertiary" audience, a concept we will discuss in chapter 2, was the advertising sales community, who might be interested in sponsoring the initiative, and the media, who might publicize this innovative new SportsCenter segment.
- *Platform.* To reach both avid and casual SportsCenter viewers, Twitter was an appropriate platform choice. From an audience standpoint, it proved to be a platform where fans watch and comment on live sports in real time.
- *Brand.* There were several choices in brand selection for this initiative. SportsCenter anchors on Twitter could have spearheaded it, or perhaps the @ESPN flagship brand on Twitter might have made sense. But the logical branding choice was SportsCenter, as it would offer direct fan access and engagement with the show.
- *Content.* The hashtag #SCTop10 was shorthand for the greatest moments and plays in sports. In addition, the use of the hashtag communicated that fans would have a role in helping decide the content.
- *Distribution.* Because the initiative took place during live games, the #SCTop10 initiative was marketed in real time on Twitter and through live "cut-in" promotions during games from SportsCenter.
- *Measurement.* To measure the success of this initiative, let's examine performance relative to the two key goals:
  - *Brand.* SportsCenter was able to connect one to one with its fans and inspire fan advocacy for the show, as fans participated in, contributed content to, and promoted #SCTop10. This activity was quantified by tracking viewer #SCTop10 submissions and the number of people #SCTop10 tweets engaged and reached.
  - *Revenue.* Mazda sponsored the #SCTop10 segment, which resulted in additional advertising revenue for ESPN.

This #SCTop10 initiative was an important turning point for ESPN in the social media space. The company had moved beyond amassing

CONTINUED

CASE STUDY: #SCTOP10: SOCIAL MEDIA MANAGEMENT IN ACTION *CONTINUED*

Facebook fans and Twitter followers and began to consider how social media platforms could be integrated into various functions of the organization and meaningfully support the business. #SCTop10 was a direct manifestation of this effort, and it symbolized the start of a more strategic social media management approach.

This is just one example of how the social media management framework can help structure a social media strategy, with all the elements working in concert to accomplish business goals. This framework is not the only way of developing, organizing, and implementing social media strategy. But it is a proven strategic template that encourages goal-centric thinking on how to harness social media platforms for maximum business impact.

Recap: Platforms May Change, but the Industry Will Still Grow

In 2013, an Internet archaeologist discovered a long-lost social network, Friendster—at least according to the satirical, farcical Onion News Network. In a parody news report, this researcher explained how Friendster had once lived a healthy life with over 50 million members, only to be largely deserted in what seemed like an overnight exodus. He compared the civilization to another once-popular community, AOL, which he thought might have been pronounced "all."[34]

Whether it's Friendster, AOL, or a platform to be named later, there will always be change in the social media industry. Platforms will come and go, but the social media industry is growing and here to stay. Social technologies that people use to create, share, and exchange information are now embedded as part of our society and are a dominant mode of communication.

The question of how organizations and leaders can maximize the business value of social media platforms will remain pressing as well. The discipline of social media management gives you the tools to connect your social media strategy to your firm's objectives, integrate it across the enterprise, and iterate based on rigorous monitoring and measurement. As we discussed in this chapter, the first step in this process is setting clear goals, whether they are brand, revenue, operational, and/or cultural in nature. Next up is analyzing and selecting your target audiences.

Your Turn: A Goal-Setting Exercise for Your School

The dean has challenged your class to develop a social media strategy for the school. She said, "I know we need to be doing something in social media, but I don't know what. Can you help me figure it out?" Being the bright and ambitious students that you are, you accept the challenge. Now what?

As we discussed in this chapter, the first and most critical step in social media management is setting clear, specific, and actionable goals. Before you begin to devise a social media strategy, aligning your team and key decision makers on the goals you are trying to achieve is essential.

Your challenge: identify the business goal(s) that are instrumental to the school and that a social media strategy might be uniquely positioned to help achieve. To inform your choices, reference the four different sources of business value: brand, revenue, operational, and cultural. Importantly, a key component of social media management is choosing what to do and what not to do. You should deliberate your goals carefully.

You will have to recommend to the dean the key goals your social media strategy will address, so be sure to include a rationale for each goal you select. Good luck.

Notes

1. Cataliades, "Meet Grumpy Cat," *Reddit*, September 23, 2012, https://www.reddit.com/r/pics/comments/10bu17/meet_grumpy_cat/c6c8hko.
2. James Gleick, "What Defines a Meme?" *Smithsonian Magazine*, May 2011, http://www.smithsonianmag.com/arts-culture/what-defines-a-meme-1904778/.
3. In Internet culture, these images are also called "image macros." See http://knowyourmeme.com/memes/image-macros.
4. Grumpy Cat, *I Had Fun Once—It Was Awful | Grumpy Cat®—The World's Grumpiest Cat!*, accessed May 26, 2015, http://www.grumpycats.com/memes/i-had-fun-once-it-was-awful/.
5. Grumpy Cats, "The 50 Funniest Grumpy Cat Memes," *Complex*, March 4, 2013, http://www.complex.com/style/2013/03/the-50-funniest-grumpy-cat-memes/.
6. Terry Thornton, "Why Do Cats Dominate the Internet?" *PBS Mediashift*, May 13, 2013, http://www.pbs.org/mediashift/2013/05/why-do-cats-dominate-the-internet/.
7. Kelli Bender, "Grumpy Cat and Jennifer Lawrence Are Among Google's Most-Searched GIFs of 2013," *PEOPLE.com*, December 17, 2013, http://www.people.com/people/article/0,,20767123,00.html; Google Trends, "Dogs Rule," Google (2014), https://www.google.com/trends/2014/story/pets.html.

8. Mike Parker, "Cheer Up Grumpy Cat, You've Got a £64million Fortune," *Express.co.uk*, December 7, 2014, http://www.express.co.uk/news/weird/544409/Grumpy-Cat-worth-more-than-Hollywood-stars.
9. Katie Van Syckle, "Grumpy Cat," *NYMag.com*, September 29, 2013, http://nymag.com/news/business/boom-brands/grumpy-cat-ben-lashes-2013-10/.
10. Grumpy Cat, "Grumpy Cat™ Grumppucino™. Available at http://www.drinkgrumpycat.com | Grumpy Cat®—The World's Grumpiest Cat!" accessed January 26, 2016, http://www.grumpycats.com/grumpy-cat-merchandise/grumppuccino/.
11. Daniel McDermon, "You're Getting a Grumpy Cat TV Movie for Christmas," *New York Times*, June 12, 2014, http://artsbeat.blogs.nytimes.com/2014/06/12/youre-getting-a-grumpy-cat-tv-movie-for-christmas/.
12. Alison Griswold, "Has Grumpy Cat Really Earned $100 Million?" *Slate*, December 8, 2014, http://www.slate.com/blogs/moneybox/2014/12/08/what_grumpy_cat_is_worth_did_tabatha_bundesen_s_pet_really_earn_100_million.html.
13. Megan Garber, "Welcome to the Grumpy Cat Industrial Complex," *The Atlantic*, December 8, 2014, http://www.theatlantic.com/technology/archive/2014/12/Welcome-to-the-Grumpy-Cat-Industrial-Complex/383532/.
14. Erin Carson, "How EMC Unleashed a Strategy to Mobilize Its Employees as a Social Media Army," *TechRepublic*, August 5, 2014, http://www.techrepublic.com/article/how-emc-unleashed-a-strategy-that-mobilized-its-employees-as-a-social-media-army/.
15. Thomas H. Davenport and Brook Manville, "EMC: How Can We Cut Our Costs in Tough Times? Using Social Media to Increase Engagement in Key Decisions," in *Judgment Call: Twelve Stories of Big Decisions and the Teams That Got Them Right* (Boston, Mass.: Harvard Business Review Press, 2012), 161–184.
16. HubSpot, "How to Execute Inbound: 3 Lead Generation Success Stories," *Hubspot*, accessed April 18, 2016, http://offers.hubspot.com/case-study-offer-lead-generation-success-stories.
17. Brian Kardon and Lattice Engines, "Why Hubspot's IPO Was More Than Just an IPO," *VentureBeat*, October 11, 2014, http://venturebeat.com/2014/10/11/why-hubspots-ipo-was-more-than-just-an-ipo/.
18. Mark Holan, "Ice Bucket Challenge for ALS Raised $220 Million Globally," *Washington Business Journal*, December 12, 2014, http://www.bizjournals.com/washington/news/2014/12/12/ice-bucket-challenge-has-raised-220-million.html.
19. Nicholas Kristof, "Payday for Ice Bucket Challenge's Mocked Slacktivists," *The New York Times*, September 3, 2015, http://www.nytimes.com/2015/09/03/opinion/nicholas-kristof-payday-for-ice-bucket-challenges-mocked-slacktivists.html?_r=0.
20. Few areas of academic study lend themselves to a definition from Wikipedia, but social media is one of them. This definition is comprehensive and clear, and it was decided upon by a community of people, reflecting the co-created spirit of social media. For the definition, see "Social Media," *Wikipedia, the Free Encyclopedia*, May 22, 2015, http://en.wikipedia.org/w/index.php?title=Social_media&oldid=663553791.
21. Gerald C. Kane et al., "Finding the Value in Social Business," *MIT Sloan Management Review*, Spring 2014, http://sloanreview.mit.edu/article/finding-the-value-in-social-business/.
22. Ibid.
23. "Being B2B Social: A Conversation with Maersk Line's Head of Social Media | McKinsey & Company," *McKinsey.com*, May 2013, http://www.mckinsey.com/insights/marketing_sales/being_b2b_social_a_conversation_with_maersk_lines_head_of_social_media.
24. Zsolt Katona and Miklos Sarvary, "Maersk Line: B2B Social Media—'It's Communication, Not Marketing,'" *Berkley-Haas Case Series* 56, no. 3 (Spring 2014). This case also offers an excellent ROI exercise and organizational decision-making challenge on Maersk Line.
25. "Being B2B Social."
26. Jonathan Wichmann, "Our Social Media Channels: Which One Is Right for You?" *Maersk Line Social*, March 27, 2013, http://maersklinesocial.com/our-social-media-channels-which-one-is-right-for-you/.
27. "Being B2B Social."
28. Ibid.
29. Author interview with Jonathan Wichmann on January 29, 2016.

30. Katona and Sarvary, “Maersk Line: B2B Social Media—‘It’s Communication, Not Marketing.’”
31. “Being B2B Social.”
32. Katona and Sarvary, “Maersk Line: B2B Social Media—‘It’s Communication, Not Marketing.’”
33. Gavin Frevert, “Lincoln University (MO) Football. Amazing Flip by RB Martee Tenner 2012 by Gavin Frevert,” April 23, 2012,” https://www.youtube.com/watch?v=muNGKmrzYi8.
34. The Onion, “Internet Archaeologists Find Ruins of ‘Friendster Civilization,’” 2009, https://www.youtube.com/watch?v=7mFJdOsjJok.

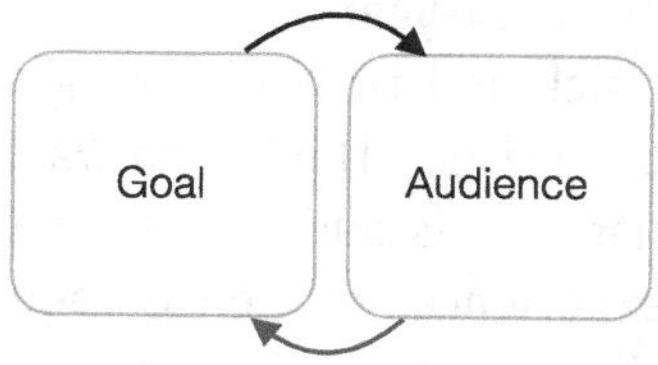

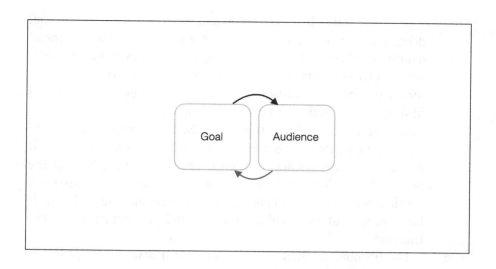

2 Targeting Social Audiences

In the first years of e-commerce, people were comfortable ordering some products online more than others. Getting a DVD shipped to your doorstep rather than visiting a local Blockbuster was an easy proposition. But what about buying eyeglasses on the Internet? For such a personal decision on a highly idiosyncratic accessory, most people preferred to touch and feel the frame and see firsthand how it fit on their face. In the late 2000s, less than 1% of eyeglass sales occurred online.[1]

In this undeveloped market four Wharton MBA students saw opportunity. In 2010, they started Warby Parker, a lifestyle brand centered on low-cost, yet stylish eyeglasses that is also driven by a "get-a-pair, give-a-pair" charitable mission. *GQ* dubbed it at launch the "Netflix of eyewear," and shortly thereafter its growth accelerated rapidly. After just five years it closed an investment round led by T Rowe Price valuing it at $1.2 billion.[2]

Although Warby brought clearer and cheaper vision to everyone, driving the brand's rapid growth was a segment of the Millennial generation that was both fashion and cost conscious. As cofounder and co-CEO Neil Blumenthal once described them, "The sweet spot for us has been 17–34-year-olds: folks who appreciate beautiful design and are sick and tired of paying $500 for a product that should be 1/5 the price."[3] The key to Warby's success was not only that they persuaded this audience to buy its glasses, but that it also designed experiences that encouraged them to talk about the brand with their friends and family. As a result, these personal, credible recommendations helped Warby overcome the challenge it faced at the outset: convincing people to buy eyeglasses over the Internet.

The linchpin of their strategy was the Home Try On program, which redefined online eyeglass purchases into a social experience. It allowed customers to demo the product and encouraged them to solicit feedback from their friends in person and via social media on which pair to choose. This collective decision-making process ensured people bought their frames with confidence.

Here's how the program worked: via the Warby website, customers could select up to five pairs of glasses (without prescription lenses) to try on for five days. The Warby team would then send them free of charge, with no obligation to buy, and paid for shipping them back. The glasses would arrive packed in a sleek and thoughtfully arranged box, like the one shown here, complete with Warby Parker

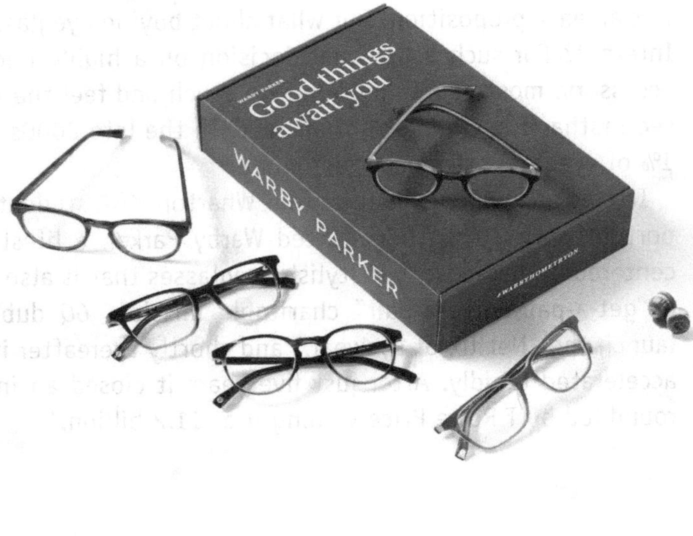

branding and no detail unnoticed. Once they landed on a pair, customers informed Warby of their decision and specific prescription, and the finished product would be sent shortly thereafter.

With five frames to try on, customers naturally needed to consult the opinions of others. Of course, they could ask a friend or roommate in person, but Warby also encouraged them to leverage social media to crowdsource the decision. The hashtag #warbyhometryon was seamlessly included in the Warby packaging, nudging prospective buyers to take selfies with each pair and post them on Twitter, Instagram, or Facebook for thoughts from their network. As it happens, Warby's 17–34-year-old core audience had significant expertise in posting selfies.

The Warby team monitored mentions of @warbyparker and #warbyhometryon and provided feedback to customers periodically. For example, when Twitter user @RobertGilbert tweeted his favorite pair of eyeglasses, @WarbyParkerHelp acknowledged how "fantastic" the glasses looked. Then, with the follow-up shown on the next page, Robert asked for additional recommendations. That's when a Warby representative created a short YouTube video with personalized advice on other styles for him to consider.[4]

Robert Gilbert @RobertGilbert · 7 Jan 2014
I think I'm digging these new @warbyparker glasses I ordered to try.
Warby Parker Help @WarbyParkerHelp · 7 Jan 2014
@RobertGilbert The Thompsons look fantastic, Robert! The shape is very flattering on you. They get our vote!
WP

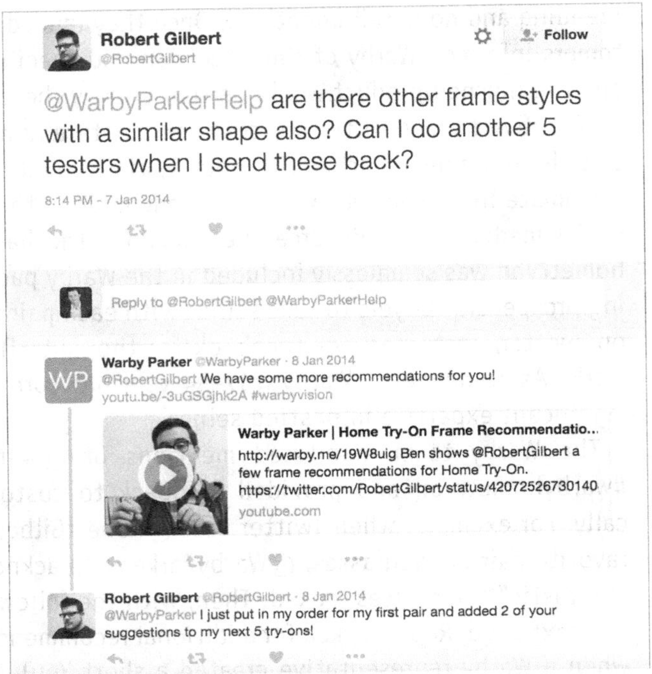
Robert Gilbert
@RobertGilbert
Follow
@WarbyParkerHelp are there other frame styles with a similar shape also? Can I do another 5 testers when I send these back?
8:14 PM - 7 Jan 2014
Reply to @RobertGilbert @WarbyParkerHelp
Warby Parker @WarbyParker · 8 Jan 2014
@RobertGilbert We have some more recommendations for you!
youtu.be/-3uGSGjhk2A #warbyvision
Warby Parker | Home Try-On Frame Recommendatio...
http://warby.me/19W8uig Ben shows @RobertGilbert a few frame recommendations for Home Try-On.
https://twitter.com/RobertGilbert/status/42072526730140
youtube.com
Robert Gilbert @RobertGilbert · 8 Jan 2014
@WarbyParker I just put in my order for my first pair and added 2 of your suggestions to my next 5 try-ons!

YouTube
Warby Parker | Home Try-On Frame Recommendations
WarbyParkerHelp
Subscribe
525 views
Published on Jan 8, 2014
http://warby.me/19W8uig
Ben shows @RobertGilbert a few frame recommendations for Home Try-On.

Over an 18 month period, the brand filmed and distributed more than 2,000 of these personal recommendation videos. Interestingly, the average views for each were not 1 or 2, but 120.[5] On @RobertGilbert's video, for example, the view count was 525 at the time of publication. Individual customers shared the videos with their network, almost as a badge of honor that Warby Parker helped them. Moreover, although it might not pertain specifically to them, other potential customers could glean insights from the advice as well, as the videos were publicly available on the Warby Parker Help YouTube page. By targeting one customer through social media, Warby also reached numerous other prospective customers without any extra effort.

• • •

How could Warby Parker evaluate the business value of all this social activity? To answer this question, let's return to the four quadrants we discussed in the last chapter:

- *Brand: Advocacy and awareness*—When customers share their selfies with the hashtag, it leads to increased awareness for Warby Parker. For example, including the hashtag in the packaging grew social sharing by 40% in one month.[6]
- *Revenue: Sales conversions*—During the initial phases of this initiative, Warby found that on average 50% of people who posted selfies and received advice from the brand via social media converted into paying customers.[7]
- *Operational: Cost savings*—Because customers decided on a frame before the prescription lenses were added, returns of finished glasses with prescription lenses, which can be a significant expense, were low.
- *Cultural: Employee empowerment*—Employees were empowered to interact with customers in an innovative way (and maybe even enjoyed their 15 seconds of social media fame), which could help Warby Parker become a more satisfying and fun place to work.

Warby Parker achieved business value through the #warbyhometryon program because it focused intently on the audience experience. The initiative reflected a strong understanding of Warby's multiple audiences (prospective customers and their networks), the specific characteristics of their audiences (young, tech savvy, design-focused, and price aware), and how and why they use social media (self-expression, connection, and information gathering).

In chapter 1 we covered the initial step in developing a social media strategy: setting goals. This chapter addresses the second component of the social media management framework: targeting social audiences. Decisions on audience are critical because an organization's ability to achieve its goals rests largely on whether it can activate audiences to take action on its behalf.

To help you decide on the most appropriate and valuable target audiences, we will discuss a critical tool in social media management: the social audience analysis. It addresses the following three fundamental questions:

- Who are your audiences?
- What are the characteristics of your audiences?
- What are the social media goals of your audiences?

In the remainder of the chapter, we will examine each of these questions in more detail, giving you concepts and tools along the way to help you conduct your own social audience analysis. We will then close the chapter by reviewing possible approaches to social audience research, which should be the foundation for any audience analysis. By the end of this chapter, you will be in a better position to identify, analyze, and engage the key target audiences for your social media management efforts.

Who are Your Audiences?

Organizations large and small have a wide range of audiences to manage: customers, employees, journalists, bloggers, investors, government regulators, and so on. Because of the ability—and inevitably—of reaching multiple groups through social media, the first step in a social audience analysis is to identify your various stakeholders. Importantly, even though an initiative may be focused on a specific audience type, planning for how other stakeholders will perceive and act on that initiative is essential due diligence.

As a targeting template, consider which audiences for your social media strategy would fall into these three categories:

- *Primary audience*—Your direct target; the audience for which you are designing your social media initiatives. It is central to achieving your business goals.

- *Secondary audience*—Your indirect target; the audience that may share similarities with your primary audience but has its own differentiating characteristics. Engaging a secondary audience can often help scale the success of an initiative.
- *Tertiary audience*—Audiences that are not your direct or indirect targets but can still influence how your initiative is received. While a default answer could be "everyone else," avoid taking the easy road. What are the specific groups that can meaningfully affect your organization? The board of directors? Shareholders? Government agencies? Employees? The media?

Every social media initiative should at least have a primary audience identified. Given the public and networked nature of social media platforms (and the ease of taking screenshots), deciding on a secondary audience, which can often be closely related to your primary audience, is a best practice. While not a direct target per se, tertiary audiences are also important groups to account for in your audience planning. To illustrate the strategic value of developing a multiple-audience strategy, let's look at two examples—one from Sony and another from IBM.

CASE STUDY: SONY'S LAUNCH OF PLAYSTATION 4

Sony is an example of a firm that benefited from focused audience planning with its successful launch of the Playstation 4 (PS4) console. In its market share battle against rival Microsoft XBOX One, Sony made the decision to target hardcore "gamers" (or videogame players) as its primary audience.[8] If it could convince this early-adopting audience to buy the console, it would imbue the product with credibility and desirability that could attract a secondary audience: casual-gamers. This audience may play "casual" games like Angry Birds on their smartphone. They may have also owned a casual games console like the Nintendo Wii, but want to take their gaming activities to another level, or perhaps they are attracted to the console because of the streaming video options, including Netflix. Key tertiary audiences for the PS4 included employees at both Sony and Microsoft, investors in both companies, and the media, all of whom were following the PS4 versus Xbox One showdown like a prizefight.

CONTINUED

CASE STUDY: SONY'S LAUNCH OF PLAYSTATION 4 ***CONTINUED***

Sony's primary audience for the PS4 is exemplified in the YouTube video pictured here. At the time of the PS4's launch, the ability to share used games was a major point of difference between the two consoles. The PS4 allowed it, whereas the XBOX One restricted it. With a target of hardcore gamers in mind, Sony created this low-budget but highly persuasive 21-second video on how to share used games, which amounted to one person giving the game to the other person.

In just a few days, Sony had 8 million views on YouTube, far more than the 460,000 views the official brand TV commercial had accumulated on YouTube at the time.[9] It was a simple message that struck a chord with hardcore gamers who were already disappointed with Microsoft's policy. It also crystallized a key difference quickly and easily for casual gamers considering an upgrade but perhaps had not done in-depth product comparisons. And because it received so much attention across the social sphere, it reached tertiary audiences such as employees, investors, and the media and helped shape the perception of the battle for market share.

The success of this video is one indicator of the PS4's overall launch strategy, which helped it achieve and sustain a lead over Xbox One.[10] Although both have sold well, PS4 has been dominant in part because of its focused primary target of hardcore gamers and efforts to capture the secondary audience of casual gamers. For its part, Microsoft Xbox focused on positioning the console as an all-in-one entertainment device for the living room, a decidedly broad and unfocused approach that the company has since revised. But because the PS4 had a focused audience strategy, it rose above its rival.

Primary and secondary audiences can often come from the same audience group. In the case of the Sony PS4, the audiences were both groups of customers that varied based on their gaming intensity. In the Warby Parker example, the primary target was prospective customers and secondary was their networks. But by no means is this the only possible approach to audience targeting. Sometimes organizations also can get creative with their targeting strategy and activate one audience group to influence another to take an action, as in the case of IBM.

CASE STUDY: IBM'S INNOVATIVE SOCIAL AUDIENCE STRATEGY

As a first mover in the social media space, IBM has been at the forefront of implementing social media to achieve its business goals. When they launched a B2B marketing campaign for the new email service IBM Verse, they continued this tradition with an innovative social audience strategy. Rather than implement an expensive multimedia advertising campaign, they developed an employee advocacy initiative designed to mobilize its employees to use social media to drive clicks and ultimately registrations among IBM customers.

To facilitate the campaign, the IBM team built an internal social media platform with a company called Dynamic Verse. On the platform employees could access stories, other content, and hashtags that they could share via their own social networks to reach customers. Incentivizing them to participate, there was also a leaderboard that tracked the employees with the most activity. Importantly, since IBM was among the first companies to empower its employees to use social media, it already had a strong base of socially active employees on networks like Twitter and LinkedIn.

CONTINUED

CASE STUDY: IBM'S INNOVATIVE SOCIAL AUDIENCE STRATEGY *CONTINUED*

Moreover, these employees built up social media followings that included IBM customers, so they were reaching the key targets of the campaign through their social media communications.

Following are three IBM employees all sharing the link to the same video as well as an image promoting the IBM Verse brand and #NewWayToWork campaign. Like other components of this campaign, the IBM social team created the content and uploaded it to the internal platform that employees could access. Then employees could pick and choose which content to share on their networks and rephrase it, if ever so slightly, in their own voice.

After about a half year of the employee advocacy program, Amber Armstrong, the director of this initiative at IBM, reported that over 1,000 employees had been responsible in large part for more than 120 million digital impressions and 141,000 clicks.[11] In addition, the campaign resulted in operational savings, as the cost of employees driving clicks is far cheaper than buying digital or social advertising on these networks. Finally, the employee advocacy campaign received an American Business Award for viral marketing campaign of the year in 2015.[12] It was a major social media success story for the company.

What was the audience strategy for IBM? In light of the goals to drive clicks and registrations for IBM Verse, the IBM team created an employee advocacy campaign with employees as their primary target. The secondary target were potential IBM Verse customers within the personal and professional networks of their employees. Through this campaign, IBM leveraged employees to reach the end customer, rather than traditional brand advertising techniques targeted directly to customers. This campaign also reinforced IBM's continued legacy of innovation in social media to key tertiary audiences such as technology journalists and industry groups.

An employee advocacy program may not be the right fit for every company. As a software and technology firm, IBM is in a unique position to capitalize on this type of campaign, as its employees may be more enthusiastic about social media. But for firms that do see potential in engaging employees on their behalf, the multiple audience targeting strategy can be a viable and effective approach.

Identifying primary, secondary, and tertiary audiences is a useful best practice in any social audience analysis. As in the Sony PS4 example, it can help you "target narrow" and focus your social media efforts on a primary audience, while also positioning your brand to "catch wide" and connect with secondary audiences. Or it can illuminate other, more creative possibilities to achieve your business goals, as in the IBM employee advocacy program.

The key in audience selection is to prioritize the groups that will be the most valuable to your initiative. Which audiences will help you successfully and efficiently accomplish your goals? For example, if your goal is to drive more revenue, existing clients may be your best and most profitable primary target audience. On the other hand, if your goal is to increase brand awareness, then targeting new customers will likely make the most sense. Or if you are looking to improve internal operations via social media, target the teams or functions that need the most help achieving efficiencies. And finally, a goal of improving employee morale could start with those employees that are the least satisfied. These are all hypothetical goals and audiences. The point is to identify and prioritize target audiences based on what you are trying to achieve.

Now that we've discussed the broad categories of primary, secondary, and tertiary audiences, let's turn our attention to better understanding the characteristics of the audiences you have chosen, which can help you design effective social media strategies to engage them.

What are the Characteristics of Your Audiences?

The digital and social media revolution has led to the emergence of two of the greatest buzzwords of all time: "big data" and "analytics." At the risk of oversimplifying them both, organizations now have large datasets (big data) and are using quantitative tools to uncover and interpret data (analytics) to make better decisions. Because we have more information and smarter analytic tools, the answer to the question, "What are the characteristics of your audiences?" can become more specific and quantifiable than ever before.

As we continue the social audience analysis, you've already identified the general categories of audiences you will be targeting, whether it's customers, employees, journalists, investors, and so on. Now the challenge is to flesh out the characteristics of these various groups. The better you know your audience, the more effective you can be in designing social media strategy.

Understanding audience characteristics is not a new component of audience analysis. In fact, it has been the cornerstone of effective communication and marketing for decades. With the advent of social media, what's different now is the level of detailed information firms have on audience characteristics. In the past, firms may have targeted large and specialized audiences. But now through social media, audience targets can be more specific and individualized. In this section we will review several social audience characteristics to analyze and then look at a case study of how a firm can translate insights about their audiences into action.

Depending on your organization, you may have audience characteristics that matter most to your business goals. But for the purposes of this discussion, fundamental audience analysis categories include the following. With each category social media offers new and expanded capabilities.

- *Demographics*—population data such as age, gender, race, ethnicity, education, income, occupation, and language
  - *What's different in social media?* Social platforms increasingly support hypertargeted messaging to specific demographics. Although reaching 18–49-year-old adults is still possible, a brand could also target 22–24 year-old Hispanic men who work in finance.
- *Location*—where people live and go in real time
  - *What's different in social media?* Location not only refers to a person's place of residence. Because of the global positioning system (GPS), it can also refer to where audiences are located at a certain point in time (e.g. in a neighborhood or at a shopping mall).
- *Interests*—what people like and have an affinity toward
  - *What's different in social media?* People are explicit about what they like and don't like through their social media activity, based on the brands they follow and the content they like, comment on, and share.
- *Behaviors*—actions related to your product
  - *What's different in social media?* With behavioral tracking technology, firms have a better understanding of how people interact with their brand online. They can more easily identify people who have shown interest in a product based on their browsing history. In turn, firms can be more targeted in communicating with people at different stages of a basic purchase funnel, from awareness to consideration to purchase.[13]

- *Influence*—degree to which a person influences the decisions of others
    - *What's different in social media?* In the offline world, finding and targeting influential people that can effectively convince others to try a product or service is a challenging process. On social media, influencer targeting can be more of a reality, as firms have visibility into people's "social graph" and how what one person says or does is received among her network. But as we will see momentarily, having a large number of friends or followers does not necessarily mean one is influential.

By analyzing your possible audiences along these characteristics, you'll be able to develop a deeper understanding of who they are, which will help you devise effective strategies to move them toward your goals. Indeed, knowing your audiences' characteristics is only half the battle. Acting on this knowledge is critical to success. Let's look at an example of how fitness startup ClassPass can analyze the characteristics of its audience in support of a business goal.

CASE STUDY: CLASSPASS KNOWS ITS AUDIENCE

As an alternative to joining a gym, ClassPass is a platform that offers a monthly subscription service that gives customers access to a wide variety of fitness establishments. Studios can benefit because ClassPass increases the number of students taking classes, which can be helpful in filling up excess inventory. Meanwhile, customers can benefit from increased choice at a comparatively lower price than what some gyms and studios cost. Since it was founded, ClassPass has grown considerably, expanding into new cities and raising money at a valuation of $200 million.[14]

One of ClassPass's key business goals is to increase the number of memberships across all of its cities. To achieve this objective, ClassPass is focused on new members as its primary audience. A secondary audience for the brand would be existing members, encouraging them to use the membership more to inspire advocacy among their networks. Key tertiary audiences are employees, who can serve as brand ambassadors, bloggers who may be sources of free publicity for the brand, board members and investors tracking the progress of the company, and other studios that are not on ClassPass but may be looking to join the supply side of the platform.

Let's say ClassPass is expanding into a new city. How about Montreal? It is considered one of the best cities for young people in the world.[15] To gain new members in Montreal, ClassPass will need to make decisions on which audiences to target, as the brand does not have the resources to reach all citizens of Montreal in a strategic way. The brand can consider the following targeting possibilities:

- *Target by Demographics*—Women comprise the majority of ClassPass users in other cities. It is also a younger-skewing audience in the postcollege years of twenties and thirties. ClassPass can start its social media efforts in Montreal with the hypothesis that Millennial women will be a core user base for them in this city as well.
- *Target by Location*—Although ClassPass services the suburbs of a major metropolitan area, targeting the urban areas of Montreal could be a wise first step based on their previous growth strategy. Once solidifying the membership in the urban core, expanding out to the suburbs would be a logical next move. Eventually, ClassPass may be able to target in real time via GPS, reaching someone at her lunchbreak and surfacing possible classes nearby to take.
- *Target by Interests*—For ClassPass to gain new members in Montreal, they can target people who demonstrated affinities for certain fitness activities. For example, they might build an audience target of women who live in Montreal that have posted about doing yoga. Or perhaps the next coming of Zumba (or another fitness craze) is overtaking the city.
- *Target by Behavior*—ClassPass can target Montreal residents that have searched for or visited websites related to fitness. And for prospective members that already have visited ClassPass.com or followed ClassPass on Facebook or Instagram but have not signed up, the brand can follow up with individualized offers.
- *Target by Influence*—ClassPass can also target influencers in the Montreal fitness community, such as fitness bloggers or trainers who have developed loyal followings.

CONTINUED

CASE STUDY: CLASSPASS KNOWS ITS AUDIENCE *CONTINUED*

These are all possible ways ClassPass could analyze and target its primary audience of potential new members in Montreal. To give you a sense of how this analysis can become more than just an exercise, let's look at the following Instagram post from the company.

The post reflects a number of audience characteristics we reviewed: the principal of the post is a woman in her twenties or thirties (demographics); with its use of "city," the post makes clear that it is targeting urban dwellers (location); the image is of a boxing class, which could be targeted to people who have liked similar activities on Instagram or Facebook (interests); and through the "sign up" call-to-action, the post could be directed to people who have already expressed intent to join ClassPass (behavior). As you can see, analyzing audience characteristics not only forces you to better understand your targets but also can also lead to more focused social media outreach.

To accomplish its goals to drive to new memberships, ClassPass could also explore an influencer campaign in Montreal, which would be a different targeting approach from what we have been discussing. Similar to the IBM employee advocacy example, the idea here would be to shift the primary audience to *existing* ClassPass members and incentivize them to engage and persuade prospective customers (now the secondary audience) to join. Taking a cue from its previous strategies, ClassPass has activated an influencer strategy in two ways: celebrity endorsement and peer-to-peer influencer campaigns. First, it has identified well-known people to carry its message for them. For example, actress Lindsey Morgan and others have campaigned on behalf of the brand. Second, it has employed peer-to-peer strategies where any user at any time can refer a friend and receive a credit. Examples of both are shown here.

CONTINUED

CASE STUDY: CLASSPASS KNOWS ITS AUDIENCE *CONTINUED*

When implementing an influencer strategy, ClassPass and others should monitor how influential people actually are. Just because a Twitter superuser has 50,000 followers does not mean an audience will do exactly what she recommends.[16] Giving influencers unique links like the one with Lindsey Morgan will help firms track actual conversions. And the refer-a-friend program also helps quantify "regular" customers and how influential they are in persuading others to become paying customers. For their efforts in Montreal, ClassPass could try the celebrity and peer-to-peer programs to see which resonates more and dial up or down each one depending on the results.

In this example, we addressed two different audience-targeting possibilities for ClassPass to grow in Montreal. In the first we looked at how ClassPass could target prospective new members based on demographics, location, interests, and behaviors. In the second initiative, we examined a potential influencer strategy to incentivize new members to increase ClassPass users. As it seeks to expand its customer base in Montreal and beyond, ClassPass will go through a similar exercise to define the characteristics of its target audiences and develop specific social media strategies to engage them.

Once you have a more detailed understanding of your audience's demographics, location, interests, behaviors, and influence, the final component of the social audience analysis is looking specifically at your targets' goals in social media, which will be critical to effectively engaging them. Let's examine those goals in more detail. Hint: they have little to do with your organization's business goals.

What are the Social Media Goals of Your Audience?

The firms that have maximized social media successfully have a strong understanding and appreciation of why their audiences use these technologies. To be sure, users of each individual platform can have different goals: LinkedIn may be more about self-advancement and networking for some, whereas Twitter is a primary news source for others. But there are broader psychological drivers of social media usage that are important to understand, analyze, and operationalize in your strategy. The bottom line: *To accomplish your goals in social media, you must help your audience accomplish theirs.*

What are those goals? One theory that has been particularly useful in understanding social media is the uses and gratifications theory, popularized largely by Elihu Katz.[17] He and his colleagues examined a number of different media platforms and why people used them. Since then, numerous scholars have also applied this theory to understand modern technologies like the Internet and social media.

To help you establish a baseline understanding of people's social media goals, consider the social media usage model in figure 2.1, which is informed by and builds on the Uses and Gratifications research.[18] Social media fulfills three main categories of individual goals: identity building, social connection, and infotainment. People may use a social media platform to satisfy one, two, or all three of these goals. That is, not all goals must be met in order for a person to adopt and use a social media technology. Understanding these goals can help you develop more effective social media management strategies. Let's look at each in more detail.

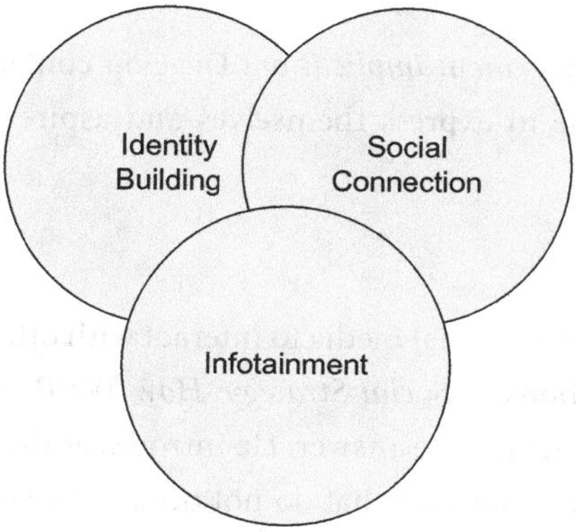

FIGURE 2.1 **Why Do People Use Social Media?**

Identity Building

There has been much debate in academia and the popular press as to whether social media is making people more narcissistic. Some studies say yes, and others suggest that self-promotion behavior is perfectly normal and that social media simply better enables this behavior.[19] The debate points to people's innate use of social media to build and showcase their identities.

Understanding why and how people build their identities via social media can be helpful to firms in designing social media strategy. In a prescient 1986 article, psychologists Hazel Markus and Paula Nurius introduced the concept of "possible selves," which "derive from representations of the self in the past and they include representations of the self in the future."[20] They go on to explain, "Possible future selves, for example, are not just any set of imagined roles or states of being. Instead they represent specific, individually significant hopes, fears, and fantasies."[21] Applied to modern-day social media, this means that some people express who they actually are on social media (their current self) and/or who they want to be (possible self). In fact, people represent both selves in numerous ways through their social media profiles and behavior.

People pursue these ongoing self-identity goals in a number of ways: what information they share on their social media profiles, who they connect with, the types of interests they pursue, what platforms and communities they join, and many other behaviors. The ubiquitous #selfie culture, in which millions of self-portraits are taken daily and posted on social media, is an important example of how people use social media to project their real or desired image. Social media is now an extension of one's identity and how friends, family, colleagues, and others come to know and understand one another.

- *Social media management implication*: Develop content and experiences that enable people to express themselves and aspire to something they want to be or do.

Social Connection

It's obvious that people use social media to interact with others. But what's driving this behavior? In his book *A Social Strategy: How We Profit from Social Media*, Mikolaj Jan Piskorski details the answer. He introduces the concept of social failures, which "are interactions that that do not occur, but would make two people better off if they did."[22] This concept is particularly relevant in social media, as social interactions that do not take place in the "offline" world may be possible in the online, social media space. According to Piskorski, there are two fundamental social failures: "meet," the "inability to meet new people," and "friend," the "inability to share private information or social support within the context of existing relationships."[23] His research shows that the platforms and firms that provide solutions to these failures will be the ones that are successful at social media strategy. Linkedin, for example, enabled employed people to "make themselves visible to recruiters" in ways that could not happen in the offline world.[24]

A key contribution of Piskorski's work is that he puts the audience's reasons for using social media at the core of effective social media strategy. Without helping the audience solve a fundamental social problem, firms will have difficulty finding success. Piskorski has found that "when a firm provides a valuable social solution, it can ask the beneficiaries to do something that benefits the firm in return."[25] Recall the Warby Home Try On program from the start of this chapter. Warby developed a social solution to buying eyeglasses online, an experience that not only drove sales but also encouraged customers to advocate on behalf of the brand. This value exchange, which is centered on the goals of the audience, is what helps organizations achieve success in social media management.

- *Social media management implication*: Firms should identify solutions that enhance and facilitate social interactions between people and their networks.

Infotainment

Finally, in addition to identity building and social connection, people increasingly use social media for information and entertainment.[26] The Pew Center found in 2015 that almost two-thirds of people use both Facebook and Twitter as a "source of news about events and issues outside the realm of friends and family."[27] This shift in behavior is why Facebook has developed new initiatives such as Instant Articles, which allow people to consume content from publishers more quickly and easily on the Facebook and Messenger platforms.

It's not just information and news that people are consuming on social media. These platforms have also become hubs for entertainment. Miranda Sings, a YouTube celebrity, has built a sizable following across a variety of channels. By 2016, she had 5.7 million YouTube subscribers, 1.6 million Facebook likes, 2.2 million Twitter followers, and 3.5 million Instagram followers. Largely because of her social media following and the fact that people watch her YouTube videos and musings on social media, Netflix signed her to a video series to be distributed across its global platform. It's indicative of the shift toward infotainment in social media. The increasing emphasis on video among many of the major social platforms is also a key contributor to the move toward infotainment.

- *Social media management implication*: To compete successfully in the social media space, your firm should carefully consider creating infotainment content.

How can an organization tap into all three social media goals? The marketing team behind the film *Straight Outta Compton* shows us one successful approach.

CASE STUDY: STRAIGHT OUTTA EVERYWHERE

To promote the film *Straight Outta Compton*, a biopic of the seminal rap group NWA, the Universal Movies Studio, Beats By Dre, and Apple jointly developed a social media experience that helped audiences express their identity, forge social connections, and enjoy infotainment. It was a "meme generator" website called StraightOuttaSomewhere.com. The user flow was simple: Upon visiting the site, people could create a meme in the same template as the *Straight Outta Compton* movie logo but customize the location to reflect their hometown and also add a photo of themselves, as in the screenshots shown here.

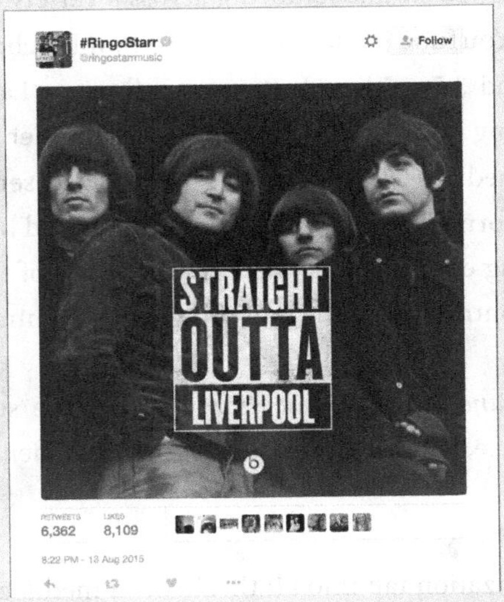

Not only was the experience simple to use, but it also tapped into fundamental reasons why people use social media. Representing your hometown or influential places in your life became the powerful hook in this initiative. As Omar Johnson, chief marketing officer of Beats By Dre, suggested, "It wasn't about Compton as a place anymore, it became about being proud of where you're from."[28] The memes enabled people to share that pride with their networks.

The results for this initiative were impressive. In just eight days, 7 million people visited the meme generator, and 6 million personalized memes were created. Interestingly, StraightOuttaSomewhere.com did not require a significant budget or even lead time. The website had fairly standard functionality (not significantly better or worse than other meme generators), and the domain name was claimed only days before it launched.[29]

In terms of business value, the reach, engagement, and advocacy the studio received from the meme generator, based on how little it cost, resulted in a far more favorable return on investment than a paid advertisement would. As a result, the brand marketed the film more efficiently

CONTINUED

CASE STUDY: STRAIGHT OUTTA EVERYWHERE *CONTINUED*

through this campaign. Ultimately, the film went on to make more than $100 million in ten days in the United States alone.[30] In retrospect, an experimental approach might be able to help determine the causal relationship between the meme generator and ticket revenue, but without it, it is fair to say that the minimal cost of this campaign alone—relative to other forms of advertising—impacted the bottom line of the film substantially.

Straight Outta Somewhere hit on all goals and engagement drivers of social media. The meme generator was grounded in identity building; people were able to represent their identity and where they're from (self-expression) and maybe choose an aspirational image for whom they perceive themselves to be (either current or possible). Social connection was also at play; it gave people a reason to connect with others in their network around commonalities or differences. Finally, from an infotainment standpoint, whether you participated in this event or not, the memes were a reliable source of entertainment at work, in the subway, at home (or maybe while reading this book).

In this section, we discussed the three main goals of social media audiences—identity building, social connection, and infotainment—and we examined one case of the Straight Outta Somewhere meme generator that leveraged each. As we'll see in the next chapter, people might use different platforms to achieve one, two, or all three goals. However, understanding the macro picture of social audiences at this point is an important context that should frame and inform your strategic decisions on platforms, brand, content, and distribution from here on out.

Social Audience Research

Social audience analysis should be an ongoing process for every organization. To facilitate it, having a robust research program in place is critical. If your organization is like most, you'll find yourself in one of two situations:

- Situation 1: You already know your audiences. Perhaps this is because you have a specific product in a niche market. Or maybe your audience has been the same for the life of your business. In cases like these, you could use social media to enhance your knowledge of your audience and serve them better across media platforms.
- Situation 2: You are still determining your audiences. Perhaps you are a business just starting out and looking to understand the market opportunity. Or maybe you're an established business that is exploring new audiences to drive growth. In cases like these, social media can serve as a tool to help find and quantify potential audiences to target.

Regardless of your situation, you can benefit from additional knowledge and information about your audiences. How? Through audience research and data collection. This means both knowing the different types of data you can use (data sources) and how to acquire it (research methodologies).

Data Sources

To begin your audience research and analysis efforts, you can collect data from a variety of sources:

- *First-party data*—data that you collect via proprietary or licensed tools. For example, if your organization maintains a customer relationship management (CRM) database of customer profiles and purchase history, that would be considered first-party data. First-party data are usually the most valuable data because they are yours. But sometimes they are difficult to collect and manage, and they may not have the scale that other sources might.

- *Second-party data*—first-party data of another company that you use to discover and target potential audiences. For example, if you have a Facebook page, the insights Facebook provides about your "likes" are second-party data. Second-party data are helpful because they are ostensibly of the same quality as your own first-party data. But procuring detailed second-party data can be difficult for many organizations.
- *Third-party data*—aggregated data from multiple sources. For example, research companies like Epsilon pull from a variety of datasets to provide broad-based information on a wide range of audiences. Third-party data are useful because they are usually representative of large populations, but because they are aggregated from many different sources, the reliability may be a liability.

To give you an example of how all three types of data might be used in a social media context, let's say an electronics company is introducing a new low-cost 3D printer. The company's first-party data would indicate existing customers who have bought or shown interest in their 3D printers. Meanwhile, the company could also consult second-party data from Twitter (which are Twitter's first-party data) to identify the people who have demonstrated interest in 3D printers in the past, perhaps by tweeting about them. To fortify its audience research, third-party data may also be useful, as a way to identify other audiences that may have bought 3D printers from competitors in the past and are in the market for a new one.

Social Research Methodologies

Over time, although second- and third-party data will be useful in many situations, it is ideal that your social media management efforts are informed largely by the first-party data your organization has. This means making an organizational commitment to social media audience research. That is, in addition to employing tried and true audience research methods, there are a number of quantitative and qualitative social media–focused approaches that can yield important insights on your audiences. These social media primary research methods include the following:

- *Surveys*: specific questions that yield self-reported answers across a representative sample of social audiences
- *Online focus groups*: in-depth questioning and discussions with a select group of potential audiences
- *Social ethnographies*: embedding researchers within a social community to understand their behavior
- *Behavioral tracking*: using tracking technologies to inventory and monitor audience behavior on your website and social platforms
- *Experiments*: facilitating experiments with A/B testing, a technique used to better understand cause and effect
- *Social monitoring*: listening and analyzing public social media conversations (see upcoming case)

As with most audience research, the best insights usually come from a multiple methodological approach over time. To the extent possible, build your audience research base from a variety of sources and methodologies. One approach that is increasingly of value to organizations is social monitoring.

CASE STUDY: SOCIAL MONITORING DRIVES BUSINESS RESULTS

The sheer amount of user-generated content on social media is staggering. For perspective, more than 3 billion images were are shared *per day* in 2015 on Snapchat, Facebook Messenger, Instagram, WhatsApp, and Facebook.[31] Because of vast amount of image, text, and video content on social platforms, a number of research organizations and methodological approaches have evolved to help businesses make sense of and act on what people are posting about brands and trends as well as individual needs and wants.

What makes this data particularly useful is that they are real-time data and usually unsolicited. Depending on an organization's goals, this "social data" can offer useful insights into brand reputation and what people are saying about you and your competitors and enable companies to operate more efficiently in customer service. Other potential use cases of social monitoring include the following:

- *Optimizing the supply chain*—the fashion industry can monitor what trends people are talking about in which locations and ensure that the right amount of product is shipped as quickly as possible.[32]
- *Uncovering growth opportunities*—Pizza Hut targeted Millennials with a new campaign to introduce its new products, but the Crimson Hexagon social listening platform also discovered that their parents were a viable market as well.[33]
- *Informing new product innovation*—companies can listen to feedback on new products via social media and integrate this input from employees or customers before launching it on a wide scale.[34]

Although social monitoring tools can increasingly deliver business value to organizations, there are limitations to keep in mind. One potential limitation is measuring sentiment, or how people feel about a brand or topic. Is a comment positive or negative? In some contexts, a post with a curse word can very much be a positive comment, whereas in other contexts, it's most certainly negative. Moreover, parsing real sentiment for or against a brand can be a challenge. To be sure, social monitoring companies are refining their natural language processing and machine learning capabilities to define consumer sentiment more effectively, and the progress is considerable. However, aspiring social media managers should continue to ask tough questions about sentiment methodologies. Another limitation is the representativeness of the sample size. Just because a certain number of Twitter users complain a product is lacking certain features may not be justification enough to make changes. Like other research methodologies, social monitoring has its limitations, and it is important to account for them in audience research.

Steve Jobs once famously said, "A lot of times, people don't know what they want until you show it to them." In today's era, where feedback and customer wants and needs are communicated daily on social media, Jobs's statement may be more the exception than the rule. Through social monitoring, we now have more information on audiences than ever before. In practicing sound social media management, it's important to capitalize on it.

The foundation of any social audience analysis is a strong research base. We discussed in this section two approaches to the data collection process, accessing first-, second-, and third-party data as well as conducting additional primary research via a variety of methodologies. No matter where you are in your audience research and analysis efforts, having more data about your audiences will result in more effective decisions.

Recap: It's Complicated

What is the relationship status between people and firms in social media? To use Facebook terminology, it's complicated. People are on social media to build their identity, connect with friends and family, and consume infotainment, not necessarily to be sold or marketed products and services. At the same time, firms can add significant value to these communities and are essential to keeping these platforms up and running (since so many social media companies are supported solely through advertising). Whether we like it or not, businesses and people must coexist on social media.

Within this context, connecting successfully with an audience in social media is a strategic process requiring research, analysis, and thoughtful prioritization. In this chapter, we presented a variety of questions and concepts to help you better analyze and select your target audiences. We discussed the importance of identifying primary, secondary, and tertiary audiences. We reviewed several key characteristics to help firms better understand and target their audience in social media. We flipped the perspective and examined why people use social media, laying the groundwork for engaging target audiences in social media. And we discussed options in social audience research, the foundation of your ongoing audience analysis efforts.

Now that you have a clearer idea of your target audiences, next up in the social media management framework is your decision on platforms. As you'll see, clearly defined goals and target audiences will help you make informed choices on which platforms to adopt for your social media strategy.

Your Turn: Analyze Your Class

The coal-fired pizza restaurant across the street from your building has identified your class as a potential audience for an upcoming social media campaign it is planning. Their goal is to increase customer volume.

Before they get to work on creating a concept, they are doing their research on possible audiences. Reward their sound social media management practices and give them advice on how to best target you.

The class should split into smaller groups. In each group, consider these elements of a social audience analysis:

1. Make decisions on which segments or groups of the class should be prioritized as primary, secondary, and/or tertiary audiences.
2. Analyze your class based on the characteristics discussed in this chapter: demographics, location, interests, behavior, and influence.
3. Identify and discuss your specific goals for using social media and the social media management implications for the pizza joint.

Once you've had a chance to address all three topics, come back as a class and debrief. The goal is to synthesize and prioritize the core audiences of the class that the restaurateurs should target. Who knows, there may or may not be free pizza involved? Good luck.

Notes

1. Columbia Business School, *Warby Parker's CEO on Disruption and Consumer Experience*, March 28, 2014, https://www.youtube.com/watch?v=7BFLO6RTr9o.
2. Douglas MacMillan, "Eyeglass Retailer Warby Parker Valued at $1.2 Billion," *WSJ Blogs—Digits*, April 30, 2015, http://blogs.wsj.com/digits/2015/04/30/eyeglass-retailer-warby-parker-valued-at-1-2-billion/?mod=mktw.
3. Jennifer Rooney, "In Advance of PTTOW!, Target, Coca-Cola, Warby Parker Execs Get Candid about Courting Next-Generation Consumers," *Forbes*, May 1, 2013, http://www.forbes.com/sites/jenniferrooney/2013/05/01/in-advance-of-pttow-summit-targets-jeff-jones-coca-colas-joe-tripodi-warby-parkers-neil-blumenthal-get-candid-about-courting-next-generation-consumers/.
4. WarbyParkerHelp, *Warby Parker | Home Try-On Frame Recommendations*, January 8, 2014, https://www.youtube.com/watch?v=-3uGSGjhk2A&feature=youtu.be&list=PL8FJn4Zr-lJYBFnrUJw53tCgkHuztmHmM.
5. "Warby Parker Marketing Tactics and Strategy: 8+ Examples," *Word-of-Mouth and Referral Marketing Blog*, accessed June 22, 2015, http://www.referralcandy.com/blog/warby-parker-marketing-story/.
6. Ibid.
7. Ibid.
8. John McDermott, "PlayStation 4 Ads Focus on Hardcore Gamers While Xbox Stresses the Living Room," *Ad Age*, June 12, 2013, http://adage.com/article/digital/playstation-4-marketing-focuses-gamers-unlike-xbox/242056/.
9. Ibid.
10. Charles Poladian, "PS4 Vs. Xbox One: Sony Has Sold over 35 Million PlayStation 4 Consoles Since 2013 Launch," *International Business Times*, January 5, 2016, http://www.ibtimes.com/ps4-vs-xbox-one-sony-has-sold-over-35-million-playstation-4-consoles-2013-launch-2250196.

11. Christopher Heine, "How IBM Got 1,000 Staffers to Become Brand Advocates on Social Media | Adweek," *Adweek*, July 1, 2015, http://www.adweek.com/news/technology/how-ibm-got-1000-staffers-become-brand-advocates-social-media-165664.
12. "IBM Viral Marketing | Stevie Awards," *Stevie Awards*, accessed April 18, 2016, http://stevieawards.com/aba/ibm-viral-marketing.
13. Dan Hecht, "A Beginner's Guide to Retargeting Ads," *Hubspot*, November 20, 2014, http://blog.hubspot.com/marketing/retargeting-campaigns-beginner-guide.
14. Yuliya Chernova, "ClassPass, Valued at More Than $200M, Taps Into Gym Craze," *The Wall Street Journal Venture Capital Dispatch*, March 12, 2015, http://blogs.wsj.com/venturecapital/2015/03/12/classpass-valued-at-more-than-200m-taps-into-gym-craze/.
15. Will Campbell, "Toronto, Montreal Named Some of World's 'best Cities for Millennials,'" *Global News*, March 8, 2016, http://globalnews.ca/news/2564436/toronto-montreal-named-some-of-worlds-best-cities-for-millennials/.
16. Sinan Aral, "What Would Ashton Do—and Does It Matter?," *Harvard Business Review*, May 2013, https://hbr.org/2013/05/what-would-ashton-do-and-does-it-matter.
17. Elihu Katz, Jay G. Blumler, and Michael Gurevitch, "Uses and Gratifications Research," *The Public Opinion Quarterly* 37, no. 4 (December 1, 1973): 509–523.
18. For a helpful overview of uses and gratifications research in social media, see Izzal Asnira Zolkepli and Yusniza Kamarulzaman, "Social Media Adoption: The Role of Media Needs and Innovation Characteristics," *Computers in Human Behavior* 43 (February 2015): 189–209.
19. Julie Beck, "How to Spot a Narcissist Online," *The Atlantic*, January 16, 2014, http://www.theatlantic.com/health/archive/2014/01/how-to-spot-a-narcissist-online/283099/.
20. Hazel Markus and Paula S. Nurius, "Possible Selves," *American Psychologist* 41 (September 1986): 954–969.
21. Ibid.
22. Mikolaj Jan Piskorski, *A Social Strategy: How We Profit from Social Media* (Princeton, N.J.: Princeton University Press, 2014), p. 9.
23. Piskorski, *A Social Strategy*, p. 2.
24. Piskorski, *A Social Strategy*, p. XII.
25. Piskorski, *A Social Strategy*, p. XII.
26. Monica Anderson and Andrea Caumont, "How Social Media Is Reshaping News," *Pew Research Center*, September 24, 2014, http://www.pewresearch.org/fact-tank/2014/09/24/how-social-media-is-reshaping-news/.
27. Michael Barthel et al., "The Evolving Role of News on Twitter and Facebook," *Pew Research Center's Journalism Project*, July 14, 2015, http://www.journalism.org/2015/07/14/the-evolving-role-of-news-on-twitter-and-facebook/.
28. Rebecca Ford, "How 'Straight Outta Compton' Viral Marketing Became a Sensation," *The Hollywood Reporter*, August 14, 2015, http://www.hollywoodreporter.com/news/how-straight-outta-compton-viral-815390.
29. "'Straight Outta' Viral Meme Launched on Days Old Domain By Apple / Beats By Dre," *TheDomains.com*, accessed August 22, 2015, https://thedomains.com/2015/08/20/straight-outta-viral-meme-launched-on-days-old-domain-by-apple-beats-by-dre/.
30. Devan Coggan, "'Straight Outta Compton' Tops the Box Office for the Second Weekend," *Fortune*, August 23, 2015, http://fortune.com/2015/08/23/straight-outta-compton-box-office/.
31. Mary Meeker, "2016 Internet Trends Report," *KPCB.com*, accessed July 21, 2016, http://www.kpcb.com/internet-trends.
32. Bob McKee, "Op-Ed: Future-Proofing the Fashion Value Chain with Social Media," *Sourcing Journal*, August 24, 2015, https://sourcingjournalonline.com/op-ed-future-proofing-the-fashion-value-chain-with-social-media/.
33. Crimson Hexagon, "The Surprising Audience That Responded to Pizza Hut's Rebranding," *Crimson Hexagon Blog*, February 6, 2015, http://www.crimsonhexagon.com/blog/opinion/surprising-audience-responded-pizza-huts-rebranding/.
34. Tero Peltola and Saku J. Mäkinen, "Influence of the Adoption and Use of Social Media Tools on Absorptive Capacity in New Product Development," *Engineering Management Journal* 26, no. 3 (September 2014): 45–51.

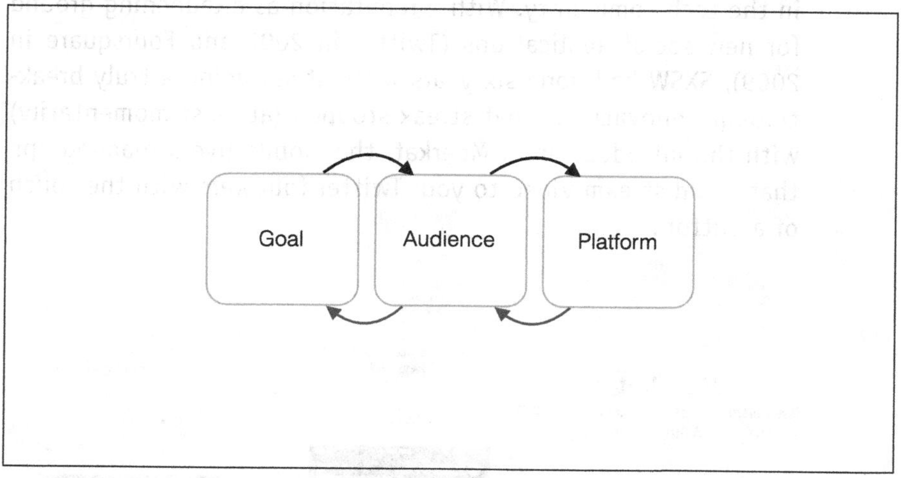

3 Adopting Social Platforms

March 1, 2015

"Meerkat is the live streaming app Twitter should have built"

—TechCrunch[1]

March 14, 2015 (13 days later)

"Meerkat basks in breakout glow, despite a Twitter snag"

—The New York Times Bits Blog[2]

April 1, 2015 (18 days later)

"Here's why Meerkat's popularity is suddenly plunging"

—The Verge[3]

Some may know the meerkat as a member of the South African mongoose family. But in the spring of 2015, it also became the social media star of the South By Southwest (SXSW) annual festival, which brings together key influencers and early adopters in the tech community. With a reputation as a launching ground for new social applications (Twitter in 2007 and Foursquare in 2009), SXSW had gone six years without surfacing a truly breakthrough innovation.[4] That streak stopped (at least momentarily) with the introduction of Meerkat, the mobile live streaming app that could stream video to your Twitter followers with the touch of a button.

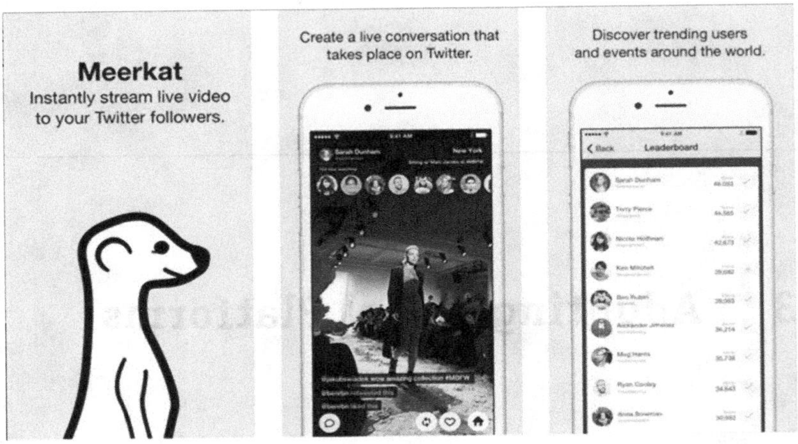

The "Technorati" that descends upon Austin, Texas, every year was abuzz about Meerkat. After CEO Ben Rubin and his team had tried and learned with similar apps, Yevvo and Air, they launched Meerkat with more knowledge and intuition about what users wanted in a mobile live streaming product. Literally overnight, conference goers downloaded and began using Meerkat. Brands and celebrities also started experimenting with the product. Actress Julia Louis Dreyfus, for example, used Meerkat while at SXSW to promote her HBO comedy, Veep.[5]

As quickly as Meerkat gained steam, it also met a challenge. Just a few days after its launch, Twitter introduced Periscope, an app Twitter had acquired that had largely the same functionality as Meerkat. Twitter also restricted Meerkat's access to their API, making it more difficult for Meerkat to thrive within the Twitter ecosystem. Meanwhile, Twitter's introduction of Periscope imbued Meerkat with even more cachet.[6] Because Twitter clamped down on Meerkat, SXSW conference goers and other early adopters found it even more desirable, perhaps in spite of Twitter.

But, again, change can be rapid in the social media space. Soon after SXSW, the "shiny new penny" that was Meerkat began to dull, as competition from the established players in the industry intensified. In the months that followed, Twitter's Periscope became a formidable threat and ran out to an early lead, claiming 10 million users and 21 million minutes watched per day.[7] Facebook also introduced its own live streaming product, Facebook Live, which at the start was only available to celebrities through Facebook's Mention app, but eventually became a key pillar of the platform's video strategy.[8]

• • •

In the span of one month, Meerkat burst onto the scene with transformational promise, faced a new and daunting competitor in Twitter's Periscope, and hype gave way to reality shortly after it arrived. It tried for the next year to compete in an increasingly crowded mobile social live streaming space, but ultimately shifted its strategic focus to become a "video social network."[9] The Meerkat experience is a cautionary tale of how social media platforms can rise and fall rapidly and unexpectedly.

How should you navigate the complicated and hype-filled waters of the social media landscape? The key for social media managers is to stay goal oriented and audience centered amid the change, chaos, and exaggeration. Admittedly, this is not easy. The fear of missing out (FOMO) is not only relevant in personal social media use but also for businesses looking to capitalize on the next game-changing platform. In addition, the barrier of entry to launching a social platform is fairly low; in many cases, all you need is an email address to create a brand page. For too long, organizations have been able to "check the box" on social media strategy by saying they have a Facebook page or Twitter feed.

Above all else, avoid Platform FOMO. Just because a platform exists does not mean you have to use it. In truth, some organizations have no business managing certain social presences. Being on a platform without a purpose is an easy trap for many organizations. Effective social media managers are adept at making tough choices. To realize business value from social media, select platforms with intention and ensure that they align with your corporate strategy, goals, and audience, as discussed in the "Social Media Management Framework" section in chapter 1.

This chapter will explore the details of the platform selection process to help you find platforms that fit. We will examine this challenge in a variety of ways. First, we'll take a look at the classic question of "renting or buying" within the context of social media platforms. Next, we'll equip you with a tool to perform ongoing audits of the social media platforms of the moment. Then, we'll introduce the Platform Fit Test, which can help you make strategic decisions about which platforms to adopt. Everything we do in this chapter is intended to help you make strategic platform selections that align with your goals and audience. As will become evident, "platforms with a purpose" is our mantra.

Renting or Buying in Social Media

One of the first platform decisions is whether to "rent" or "buy" a social media platform. In this context, renting means creating a presence on a third-party social media platform like Instagram or Pinterest. Buying refers to establishing your own proprietary social media platform like IBM did to facilitate its employee advocacy program as we discussed in the last chapter. For the vast majority of organizations, this decision may be a simple one: you'll "rent" and extend your brand onto a third-party social platform. However, some organizations might find an owned and operated social network is the most appropriate direction. It is also possible to have a mix of both. Let's take a look at each possibility.

Why Would You Rent?

There are at least three reasons why an organization might capitalize on a third-party social network to achieve its business goals.

1. *Go where your audience is.* Since many social networks have large audience bases, your target audiences may be on the platform as well. Why ask them to go elsewhere if you can reach them where they are spending time?
2. *Low technical costs.* In many cases, the technical costs of operating a business presence on a social media platform are low. Successfully maximizing social networks is more about strategy, content, and marketing and less about technical maintenance, since the social platform is responsible for making sure it functions well.
3. *Leave with little consequence.* If your business goals change or your audience shifts, closing down a social media presence is usually not an onerous challenge. Delete the account and move on.

Why Would You Buy?

The question here is whether you would create your own social platform, rather than renting a brand-name third-party platform. This could mean white-labeling a "software as a service" platform provided by players like Salesforce or Socialcast. Or, if your organization is inclined, you might build a social platform from scratch. Buying may be the appropriate choice in the following circumstances:

- *Data ownership and security are critical to your organization.* You may be in a business that requires the utmost security over your users' data and/or the content that is discussed on a social network. Let's say a B2B pharmaceutical company is looking for a better way to interact with its customers. Because it may not be advisable for data from this industry to be in the full view of others (or entrusted to a third party), building a proprietary social network may be the best (and only) possibility.
- *You have a closed network.* Building your own social network may also make sense if your audience is part of a closed network. This can apply to enterprise social networks, in which employees are the target audience (a subject we will discuss in depth in chapter 9). However, brands can also seek to bring customers and other partners into the fold. EMC not only has the EMC One internal social networking audience, but it has also launched the ECN, EMC Community Network, which connects its employees with its myriad business partners.[10]
- *Rented platforms cannot accommodate desired functionality.* Your brand could have a vision for its social media strategy that existing platforms do not have the technology to support. For example, after its Dell Hell fiasco in 2005, when a well-known blogger, Jeff Jarvis, chronicled his disastrous customer service experience with the company, Dell moved aggressively to become a more customer-focused company, and social media became a major part of that vision. One innovation was the Dell IdeaStorm, a social platform where customers could sign up, suggest new product ideas and innovations, and vote on which ones would be produced. This online social community helped Dell foster stronger relationships with its customers in a way that a Facebook page or Twitter feed could not.[11]

Today, "buying" will likely be appropriate only in specific contexts such as the aforementioned instances. Indeed, because many decisions in the social media management space will be about using third-party social platforms and extending brands into community-controlled spaces, we'll spend the rest of this chapter focusing on rented social media platforms. To begin this work, we'll further examine the possible social media platforms from which to choose.

Conducting a Platform Audit

Amid the uncertainty in the social media space, there are three things we can count on. *First, not all social media platforms are the same.* Let's return to our social media definition from chapter 1: "Social media are computer-mediated tools that allow people to create, share, or exchange information, ideas, and pictures/videos in virtual communities and networks."[12] This necessarily broad, all-encompassing definition is where the similarities end. Facebook is different from YouTube, and YouTube is different from Twitter, and Twitter is different from Pinterest. To gain traction in the marketplace, new social platforms must offer different features and functionality. Instagram could not "out-Facebook" Facebook. Indeed, because Instagram had built a unique platform and grew it to promising levels, Facebook bought it for $1 billion.[13]

Second, as if to keep social media managers on their toes, *platform change is a constant.* In its short history, Facebook has changed its NewsFeed algorithm multiple times, emphasizing likes, comments, shares, time spent reading, and time spent watching all at various points. Alterations or restrictions in the organic reach of posts from brand pages have also been part of the constant evolution of NewsFeed.[14] Even if you already have a presence on Facebook, the frequent changes seemingly turn it into a new platform with new rules on a consistent basis. And Facebook is not alone. Every social media platform evolves over time to include new functionality and features based on its users' preferences, resulting in a fresh set of challenges for social media managers.

Finally, in the context of all this change—and somewhat paradoxically—*the lines between some social platforms are blurring.* As French intellectual Jean-Baptiste Alphonse Karr said, "The more things change, the more they stay the same." For example, with its increasing emphasis on video, Facebook has become more like YouTube in its quest for additional advertising dollars.[15] Meanwhile, Twitter has become more like Facebook, and vice versa, as both now include hashtags, trending topics, and support for rich multimedia within posts. Certainly, Facebook, YouTube, and Twitter still have different propositions and use cases, but social media is proving to be a copycat industry (like others) where successful features on one platform are replicated on others.

In light of the differences between platforms, how quickly things can change, and the blurring lines between some platforms, selecting and adopting the appropriate channels for a social media strategy is an increasingly complex task. To help monitor the prevailing platform trends of the day, a useful social media management routine is the Platform Audit. Whether your organization is just starting out in social media or fairly advanced in using a variety of tools to accomplish your goals, conduct the Platform Audit with a comprehensive list of platforms on a regular basis.

How can you approach a Platform Audit? Despite the dizzying array of platform possibilities, there are theoretical constructs that can help guide and organize this information in a digestible and actionable way. For example, MIT Sloan Distinguished Professor JoAnne Yates and her colleagues developed the Genre Model, a method to help organizations make decisions to implement a particular technology. Importantly, the Genre Model does not suggest that there is a "right" or "wrong" way to use a technology. The challenge is to determine why a technology works within the context of your organization.[16] To do so, the Genre Model identifies the key dimensions to understanding media and the risks, benefits, and complexities of adopting a new technology (especially alongside current technologies an organization might use). The dimensions include questions of why, how, and by whom a technology is used.[17]

Guided by the Genre Model, the Platform Audit approach outlined here is tailored to the unique dynamics of the social media space. It inventories a platform according to the following dimensions, which are also outlined in figure 3.1:

	Platform
Type	What type of social platform is it?
Audience	Who uses the platform and why?
Content	What content do people create?
Engagement	How do people engage on the platform?
Brand Integration	How can brands fit in and add value?

FIGURE 3.1 **Elements of the Platform Audit**

type, audience, content, engagement, and brand integration. Let's look at each in more detail.

Type—What Type of Social Platform Is It?

The Platform Audit should begin with defining the type of social media platform. Classifying the platform into a particular category can inform how an organization programs to it. There are many classification systems that organize in one place the complex and growing world of social media platforms. The Conversation Prism, which is a "visual map" of twenty-six different types of social media, is a particularly thorough representation of the space.[18] For the purposes of simplicity, let's synthesize platforms into five different categories. It's important to note that these categories are fluid and can change as platforms change.

- *Macro networks*—platforms that enable people to connect and communicate many-to-many in a variety of ways, often through their real identity. Examples include Facebook and LinkedIn.
- *Micro networks*—platforms that serve primarily as messaging services, connecting people within smaller networks. Examples include Whatsapp, WeChat, Line, and Facebook Messenger.
- *Content communities*—platforms that are based on the sharing of specific content types. Examples include YouTube, Twitch, Vine, and Instagram.
- *Social broadcasters*—platforms that enable "one-to-many" broadcasting but also have the built-in sharing capabilities of social networks. Examples include Tumblr, Medium, and Twitter.
- *Collaborative networks*—platforms that are created and maintained by and for the community. Examples include Reddit, Digg, and Wikipedia.

Audience—Who Uses the Platform and Why?

For the audience dimension, apply the social audience analysis techniques and questions from the previous chapter to define who uses the platform and why. For instance, you might analyze the demographics and usage of the audience base. Moreover, you could also examine audience characteristics such as audience location, interests, and behaviors. Underlying your audience analysis of the platform should also be a clear explanation for why people use it, whether it's to accomplish identity building, social connection, and/or infotainment goals.

Content—What Content Do Users Create?

In analyzing the content of the platform, inventory both the content formats and varieties. For content formats, do people communicate via text only, or does the platform support multimedia content as well? If so, what format of content is used most frequently? Photos, videos, animated gifs? For the content varieties, think about the different subjects of content people create and share on the platform. Is it pertaining to personal relationships, news or entertainment oriented, creative arts, or gaming? Knowing the content formats and varieties will inform what content you create for the platform, if you choose to adopt it.

Engagement—How Do Users Engage on the Platform?

Each platform has its own rules of engagement. Ask yourself, "How do users participate in this community?" This includes both actions and norms. Actions refer to methods of endorsing (liking or favoriting content) and sharing (retweeting or reblogging). Norms refer to the rules governing behavior on the platform. For example, does a social community "self-police" rude comments and actions toward other community members? Or is a platform known for bullying and trolling? Understanding how people interact and coexist will give you a better sense of how to engage as a firm, if you do.

Brand Integration—How Do Brands Fit In and Add Value?

Last, but not least, since you are likely auditing platforms to define the opportunities for your business, gauge how other brands have approached the platform. Areas of exploration could include the number of brands and categories of industries involved. You might also look at the brands that are gaining the most traction on the platform and seek to understand their reasons for success. Inevitably, there will be brands that misstep here and there, so learning what pitfalls to avoid can also be helpful.

To give you a sense of how a Platform Audit can work in practice, let's apply it to a sample social platform, Snapchat, and examine its type, audience, content, engagement, and brand integration. Disclaimer: given the pace of change mentioned previously, the specifics of this analysis will likely be different when you read it. I encourage you to see this simply as an exercise applying the Platform Audit template (and maybe have a laugh at how much and quickly things have changed.).

PLATFORM AUDIT CASE STUDY: SNAPCHAT CIRCA 2016

Type—Snapchat is a micro-network that was founded in 2011 on the concept of ephemeral messaging, also known as "snaps," messages that disappear after a defined period of time. It has since rolled out a feature called "Memories" that enables users to save and re-use snaps.[19]

Audience—The Snapchat user base comprises more than 100 million daily active users.[20] Users skew young. According to the company, "On any given day, Snapchat reaches 41 percent of all 18 to 34-year-olds in the United States."[21] It also has a growing international footprint.[22] Snapchat usage is only through mobile devices.

People use Snapchat to come to know and express their identities (either current or possible), and they also foster social connections either by strengthening existing relationships or meeting new people. Infotainment is also an important hook. Snapchat founder Evan Spiegel once noted that "entertainment" was a core driver of the platform.[23]

Content—People create two different content formats on the platform. The first is snaps, photos or videos that last 10 seconds or fewer. Once a user sees the snap in its entirety, it disappears, ostensibly forever. Snaps are sent as direct messages to audiences of your choosing. They can also be included in Live Stories, a user-generated content feature curated by Snapchat editors, usually centered on major events. For example, during New York Fashion week, Snapchat staffers edit together snaps in a continuous stream of live coverage from both users and brands. The second content format is *stories*, which enable users to string together multiple snaps into a "story" for their followers to see. They expire after 24 hours, but can be re-watched during that time period. Whereas snaps are a single message, stories take on the characteristics of a social broadcast (like a status update) to a user's friends.

Additional content format features include Snapchat *doodles*, which are a dominant form of art on the platform. Users take a photo or video and, using the doodle tools provided by Snapchat, mark up their snaps accordingly. *Captions* are also added to snaps to further personalize the communication, as the snap from Snapchat luminary DJ Khaled illustrates.

Users can also apply *lenses* to their snaps to add special effects. For example, it is possible to turn your face into a puppy dog. *Stickers*, Snapchat's version of emoji, are available as well. *Filters* such as time and outside temperature can also be overlaid on top of snaps. *Geofilters* can only be accessed if you are within a designated geographical location. For example, weddings can create their own on-demand geofilters for a fee, so that all snaps taken from the event have a graphical overlay celebrating the couple and your attendance.

CONTINUED

PLATFORM AUDIT CASE STUDY: SNAPCHAT CIRCA 2016 *CONTINUED*

Finally, *vertical videos* have become the primary mode of video on Snapchat. This is in contrast to widescreen horizontal videos, which people have to rotate their phones to shoot or view. Vertical videos have long been an Internet faux pas, but because of their popularity on Snapchat, this change in user behavior has forced content creators to adjust their approach to creating videos for the platform.[24]

Engagement—Users engage on Snapchat according to several norms. All content on Snapchat is "tap to view"; users opt-in to see a particular message from friends or brands. In previous versions of Snapchat, users had to hold down on their phones for the duration of the snap. Now, it's just one tap. In addition, all Snapchat Stories and Discover content (more on this feature later) must be viewed within 24 hours. Users also have the ability to share Discover content with their friends. Finally, because of the immediacy of the platform, users are frequently opening the app. For example, video views on Snapchat across the platform were 10 billion daily in 2016.[25]

Brand Integration—Brand integration on Snapchat is accelerating. Companies from various industries, most of which already have strong social media content operations, are participating. Brands can integrate into Snapchat in a few ways. The first is through Snapchat accounts. Any organization or brand can have its own Snapchat account. This entails acquiring followers and creating snaps or Snapchat stories to share directly with them. The second integration possibility is through Live Stories. As mentioned earlier, Snapchat offers this feature around major shared experiences, such as concerts, sporting events, big cities, and political campaigns. Brands have the opportunity to sponsor and/or have their content included in these curated stories. The third integration opportunity is more exclusive. It's through Snapchat's Discover product, in which brands create premium Snapchat content every 24 hours, which can be found within the Discover section of the app and alongside other Discover partners. National Geographic, CNN, and ESPN were among the initial Snapchat Discover content creators. Discover is an early attempt by Snapchat to not only enhance the quality of content on the platform but also generate advertising revenue, which is the final way brands can integrate. Brands can create ads in the form of snaps, which are integrated into both Live Stories and Discover content. Importantly, the ad effectiveness metrics can tell brands who watched, for how long, and when they swiped the snap away. Brands can also buy sponsored geofilters and sponsored lenses.

By auditing Snapchat according to its type, audience, content, engagement, and brand integrations, we now have a more detailed understanding of the platform (see figure 3.2). Snapchat is a novel social media network that has a young, highly engaged user base creating and engaging in various forms of content on a daily basis. The platform has also developed various entryways for brands to contribute to the community and connect with this notoriously difficult-to-reach demographic.

Type	Micro Network
Audience	DAUs > 100MM Reaches 41% of 18-34 year-olds in the U.S. daily
Content	Snaps (photo and video) Snap tools (doodles, captions, lenses, stickers, filters) Stories
Engagement	Create Tap to play
Brand Integration	Accounts Live Stories Discover Ads

FIGURE 3.2 **Snapchat: Ephemeral Messaging Service Expanding into Content**

How can the Platform Audit process be useful? For starters, it encourages you to ask and answer more detailed questions about a social technology. It can also be a helpful social media management routine. Whether your organization has a large or small social media operation, doing ongoing platform audits on the various platforms is a smart—and indeed, invaluable—way to stay abreast of the changes in the social media space. Finally, and most important, the Platform Audit serves as the foundation of understanding whether a certain platform fits your business. After any Platform Audit, the next question becomes: is this platform aligned with my social media strategy? In the next section, we'll introduce a test to help answer this question.

Platform Fit Test

More platforms, more problems. With so many platforms in the marketplace today, and the pace of change continuing to increase, it is understandable if social media managers feel on the defensive at times. Another day, another platform and with it comes pressure to adopt it. Although experimentation is important, proceeding strategically with these platforms, rather than trying to do everything, is an approach most organizations should take.

In the previous section, we explored a template that will help you audit social media platforms. The next step is to evaluate whether these platforms can be a fit for your organization's goals and audience. This tool is called the Platform Fit Test (PFT). It has the following three components (see figure 3.3):

- *Audience connection*—Can we reach and engage our target audience on the platform?
- *Brand association*—How does my brand align with the platform's brand and its users' behavior?
- *Goal alignment*—How can we achieve our goals via this platform?

The answers to each of these questions depend on the organization and the platform. No organization will have the same answers. If the fit between audience, brand, and goal is not strong, you should consider passing on the opportunity. To explore the Platform Fit Test in action, here are three organizations that have achieved a strong platform fit. Calling back to the Snapchat audit, let's start with how fast-food brand Taco Bell embraced and helped shape that platform.

	Platform 1	Platform 2	Platform 3
Audience Connection			
Brand Association			
Goal Alignment			

FIGURE 3.3 **Platform Fit Test**

PFT CASE 1: TACO BELL AND SNAPCHAT

When Snapchat achieved critical mass in 2013, brands faced a couple of barriers to adopting the platform. For starters, the platform did not yet offer brand pages like Facebook, Twitter, or Instagram, so any brand would have to operate a standard user account. That meant it was more difficult to accumulate followers at a large scale. Brands had to be added by individual users one by one, which was a change for many brands with millions of fans and followers on other platforms. The other barrier was Snapchat's reputation for rampant sexting between its teenage and young adult users. And since the app was so popular among this audience, brands that were interested in using Snapchat were in a precarious situation. As a result, many brands shied away from Snapchat so as to avoid the association.[26]

Any brand seeking to use Snapchat would have to reconcile these two challenges. After careful consideration of the brand fit and their business options, Taco Bell decided to move forward with a Snapchat experiment in 2013, and because of discoverability challenges on Snapchat at the time, used its Twitter account to create awareness and interest in the tweet here. The next day the brand revealed on Snapchat the return of the Beefy Crunch Burrito, a fan favorite that had gone on hiatus.[27] As we'll discuss in detail in chapter 5, the brand understood how to tailor content to the

CONTINUED

PFT CASE 1: TACO BELL AND SNAPCHAT *CONTINUED*

platform, leveraging the language cues and other norms from Snapchatters to create the snap shown here.

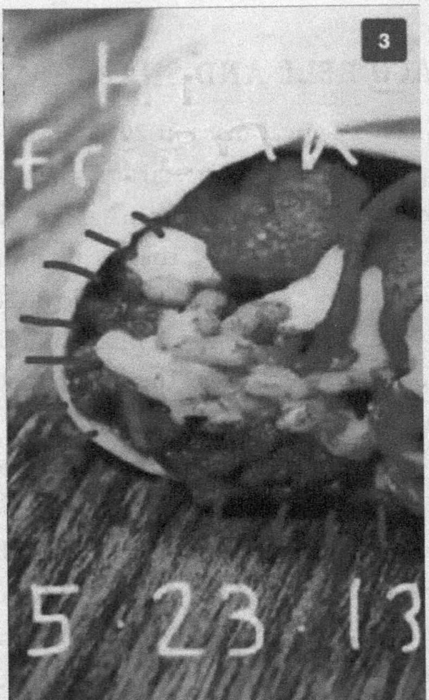

Why did Taco Bell adopt Snapchat? There are several reasons. For starters, the teenage and young adult audience on Snapchat fit with the target audience for Taco Bell. Connecting with young people and building relationships early in the customer life cycle was critical to Taco Bell as a business. They also realized that people at the time used the Snapchat platform for direct, one-to-one communication, almost as a text messaging service. They saw this as an opportunity to come across more as a friend and less as a corporate brand trying to market a product, which is usually a social media sin among their target audience. Moreover, because the medium was largely visual, it was a natural fit for a food brand that had already built up a robust presence on the Instagram platform using strong visual communication tactics. In the end, because of the strong audience, brand, and goal alignment, Taco Bell was willing to take the risk in the initial days to overcome the barriers.

The experiment turned into a more permanent Snapchat strategy for Taco Bell. Taco Bell built on the initial announcement of the Beefy Crunch Burrito and expanded its content offering on Snapchat, including other product announcements. For example, it created a short movie on Snapchat (yes, a movie) announcing the debut of the Spicy Chicken Cool Ranch Doritos Locos Tacos.[28] The risk to being on Snapchat was well worth it because the platform aligned well with Taco Bell's goals, brand, and audience. Taco Bell's first mover status on Snapchat has helped pave the way for the ways in which other brands now connect with people on the platform.

Platform Fit Test Summary—Taco Bell and Snapchat

- *Audience connection.* Taco Bell could reach its teenage and young adult target audience on the Snapchat platform.
- *Brand association.* Both the Taco Bell and Snapchat brands aligned. As a younger-skewing brand, Taco Bell positioned itself as edgier than competitors like McDonalds. Despite and maybe because of its risqué reputation, the Snapchat brand helped Taco Bell attract attention to its innovative campaign ideas. Moreover, the platform lent itself well to visually showcase Taco Bell's core product: food.
- *Goal alignment.* Taco Bell used Snapchat primarily to achieve brand value, building awareness for new products and inspiring advocacy with its core market.

PFT CASE 2: HEFTER, LESHEM, AND MARGOLIS CAPITAL MANAGEMENT OF WELLS FARGO AND LINKEDIN

For the financial services sector, acquiring and retaining customers—and their assets—is the number-one priority. Increasingly these firms are turning to social media to build their businesses and clientele. One example is the Wells Fargo firm of Hefter, Leshem, and Margolis Capital Management in Illinois.

The firm has a number of options when considering which social platforms to adopt and use. They could launch a Twitter feed to publish company updates or a Facebook page to keep current and prospective customers in the know as well. But given their goals and priorities, they have been more focused about channel choice and emphasized LinkedIn as a key social media outreach vehicle.

LinkedIn was a strong fit for the firm for two main reasons. First, the firm's target audience is on the platform. LinkedIn users are professionals, who detail their current job status, previous career stops, and connections, all of which can indicate potential net worth. In this context, it is not a stretch to think that financial planning would be an appropriate connection point. Second, LinkedIn was a place where the firm could more easily prospect new clients. As Charles Margolis said, "If we're going to meet a prospect or there's somebody that we're going to try to cold contact, we will look on LinkedIn to learn about the individual and try to establish commonalities."[29] LinkedIn served as a digital tool to prospect, generate leads, and convert new customers.

The results have been positive for the Hefter, Leshem, and Margolis Capital Management team. After adopting LinkedIn, the firm acquired 15–20 new clients via the platform in 24 months, which contributed new assets between $30 million and $40 million (overall assets were $2.3 billion).[30] Facebook and Twitter are the popular possibilities and have significant name recognition, but for this firm's goals and audience, LinkedIn was the best fit.

Platform Fit Test Summary—Hefter, Leshem, and Margolis Capital Management and LinkedIn

- *Audience connection.* Strong fit, as LinkedIn is a network of professionals, many of whom may be prospects for financial management.
- *Brand association.* Clear brand associations between LinkedIn and Hefter, Leshem, and Margolis Capital Management, as both are in the business of personal and professional services (for different needs, of course).
- *Goal alignment.* Hefter, Leshem, and Margolis Capital Management was able to directly link their LinkedIn efforts to revenue goals, acquiring and retaining new customers that contributed to their overall assets.

PFT CASE 3: CASPER AND TWITTER

Casper, the sleep startup, set out to disrupt the mattress industry. They developed a medium-firm mattress that would come shipped directly to customers in a box, priced it simply and fairly, and would accept returns (no questions asked) if customers didn't like it. They targeted Millennial professionals who lived in cities, but took a decidedly different approach to marketing than incumbent mattress sellers did. CEO Philip Kim observed, "Most people in their 20s and 30s don't have problems with sleep, don't have back issues. And yet the industry got caught up with marketing that's like, 'Solve your back pain with this product.' We wanted to get away from that kind of product solution-type marketing."[31]

As part of their marketing strategy, Casper turned to Twitter as a key social platform, a decision that paid dividends for a startup getting off the ground. For starters, Twitter at the time was especially popular among users who skewed younger, lived in cities, had college degrees, and made $50,000 or more in household income. This segment of Twitter's base aligned with the audiences Casper was seeking to engage.[32]

In light of their effort to market to its customers differently from its competitors, Casper capitalized on the public, real-time, one-to-one

CONTINUED

PFT CASE 3: CASPER AND TWITTER *CONTINUED*

communication capabilities of Twitter to not only deliver superior service but also get attention for it. @Casper not only answered routine queries about the product and shipping status, but it also occasionally delivered random acts of kindness, including sending champagne to one of its most avid customers as part of a Valentine's Day promotion. These acts helped the brand attract the attention of consumers as well as the media, which, in turn, wrote positively about the company.

Twitter also became a channel for new customers to advocate for the brand, generating awareness as a result. The mattress in a box was tailor-made for social media advocacy and sharing, as satisfied customers would share the awe-inspiring moment of unwrapping a mattress in a box—a behavior that Casper would positively reinforce.

@Casper's Twitter activity enabled the company to achieve a range of business value. From the brand standpoint, it created awareness and customer advocacy. Operationally, the cost efficiencies were significant. For a company that did not have much of a marketing budget, the Twitter platform was a relatively low cost way to attract attention, which also translated into free media coverage. Also, the customer service the company was able to offer through Twitter was far less expensive than operating a full-time outsourced call center. All told, the scrappy and smart startup both surprised and delighted customers and achieved value through Twitter along the way.

Platform Fit Test Summary—Casper and Twitter

- *Audience connection.* The key targets for Casper were young, college-educated, urban-dwelling customers, which also tended to be Twitter users.
- *Brand association.* Compared to the traditional mattress companies, Casper's brand was relatable, likeable, accessible, and customer-centric. They could emphasize these brand traits through the public, real-time, and interactive Twitter platform. Moreover, since other brands had been using Twitter as a customer service tool, Casper's efforts responded to and exceeded customer expectations in the space.
- *Goal alignment.* Without a significant budget for marketing or customer service, Casper made the best use of the Twitter platform to drive brand advocacy and customer satisfaction at an affordable operational cost.[33]

With both the Platform Audit and the Platform Fit Test, you now have tools to help inventory and evaluate social platforms. Both are flexible and intended to be starting points. If necessary, modify these templates according to your organization's specific challenges. The bottom line is this: if a social platform does not help you further your audience connection, build a positive brand association, and achieve your business goals, you should think twice about using it.

Adopting Multiple Platforms

For most of this chapter, we have focused on adopting single platforms, one at a time, to achieve various business goals. The reality is you will probably be adopting and managing multiple platforms throughout your time in social media. This is true for at least a couple reasons. For starters, people are now using more than one social media platform on a daily basis. Depending on who your audiences are, you may need to reach them in multiple places and in different ways based on how they use a particular platform. Second, although social media platforms blur at times, there are some fundamental differences between the players, as we discussed in the typology section of this chapter. LinkedIn, for example, has an audience with different purposes and needs than Pinterest does. The key is ensuring that each platform you choose is grounded in goal- and audience-centered thinking.

As you build out and seek to arrange a platform portfolio, consider these guiding principles:

- Each platform should go routinely through the Platform Audit and Platform Fit Test. If your target audience and the user base are not aligned, then you should reconsider your approach. Of course, if you are not achieving your goal, that will make the decision to move on even easier.

- Understand the differences between each platform and create content for them accordingly (a topic we'll discuss in chapter 5 on content).
- Each platform should complement and extend one another. Think about how all your platforms are going to coexist in a coherent brand portfolio, which we'll discuss in the next chapter, and work together to maximize the distribution of your social media initiatives, which is a key subject in chapter 6 on distribution.

GoPro is a good example of a brand that has adopted multiple platforms but ensured that each fits within its overall social media strategy. Their core product is a portable, durable video camera that encourages its customers to "be a hero" and "capture + share your world." It leverages the content its customers create with its cameras to power their social media presences on Facebook, Instagram, YouTube, and Twitter. Because all four are designed for people to share their lives easily, GoPro makes it a regular practice to curate the best of what their customers share. For example, see these Instagram and Twitter posts.

GoPro also launched and managed a Pinterest page, which has achieved less than the other four in terms of audience scale. Given the user-generated content focus of the GoPro social strategy, a valid question from the social media manager's perspective is whether the Pinterest page is a strong fit. Are people sharing their GoPro-captured adventures via Pinterest? If not, what other strategic purpose would a GoPro Pinterest page serve? Perhaps as a planning tool for GoPro users to plot out their next adventures? Over time, GoPro will continually evaluate goal and audience considerations, especially when new platforms become available that people use to share their GoPro adventures. The key is ensuring that all platforms complement one another and fit under the GoPro social media strategic umbrella.

Building and managing a social media portfolio is core to successful social media management. In the ensuing chapters, we'll discuss at length the key considerations and decision points in developing a portfolio approach. But for now, the most critical component is platform selection and on a case-by-case, platform-by-platform basis, ensuring that the strategic fit is strong.

Recap: Platform Analysis Never Stops

Remember Tom? He was everybody's friend. For every new user signing on to the MySpace platform, the cofounder Tom Anderson would be there to greet you and be your first friend. It was a fitting gesture for a new social network with the slogan "a place for friends." By 2005, Tom soon had a lot of friends—5 million, in fact. He also made friends with the highest ranks of NewsCorp, which bought the company in a deal that valued MySpace at $580 million.[34] In the ensuing years, MySpace grew to represent over 80% of the traffic to social networks and also was the number-one visited site on the Internet, even eclipsing Google.[35]

By 2007, the business started to falter. The site had so much pressure on it to generate revenue that the ads were cluttering the experience. There were also security concerns about teenagers using the platform, which set off numerous reports by the mainstream media and an investigation into the platform by the Connecticut Attorney General. Meanwhile, other providers like Facebook were offering a cleaner, less ad-polluted, and ostensibly safer environment for MySpace members to use. And as it turned out, the merging of two different cultures, MySpace and News Corp, proved to be too difficult to manage.[36] Tom and his cofounder Chris DeWolfe ended up leaving. By 2011, NewsCorp decided to sell Myspace for a paltry $35 million, a small sum compared to what they paid for it.[37] It's yet another cautionary tale of how quickly platforms can rise and fall in the social media space.

Ongoing social platform analysis should be an essential routine for any firm. In this chapter, we've shared a variety of tools to help in this process. It's important to evaluate constantly your options to rent and/or buy social media, monitor and audit all available and trending platforms, and assess platform fit according to your audience, brand, and goals.

The platforms you choose to manage are just open vessels. As we'll find out in the next two chapters, how you brand the platforms and infuse them with content will bring to life your social media strategy.

Your Turn: Strategic Platform Choice

Form small groups. Each group will be charged with developing a social platform recommendation for one of the following local organizations:

- Public transportation authority
- Museum
- Hospital
- Library
- Bank
- Sports team

Considering the business's goal(s) and audience(s), you must make a recommendation on which social platforms the organization should adopt. Assumptions and recommendations on business goals and audiences are allowed and encouraged. You should also not assume that any social platforms the organization is using are the right fit. Question the status quo and bring your own knowledge, expertise, and strategic thinking to the question.

You can select up to three platforms. You must have a strong business rationale for each of your choices. Leverage the Platform Fit Test to help in your deliberations.

In the debrief, one person from each team will report out, explaining the group's choices and rationale. Good luck.

Notes

1. Josh Constine, "Meerkat Is the Live Streaming App Twitter Should Have Built," *TechCrunch*, March 1, 2015, http://social.techcrunch.com/2015/03/01/meerkat/.
2. "Meerkat Basks in Breakout Glow, Despite a Twitter Snag," *The New York Times Bits Blog*, March 14, 2015, http://bits.blogs.nytimes.com/2015/03/14/meerkat-basks-in-south-by-southwest-glow-despite-a-twitter-snag/.
3. Ben Popper, "Here's Why Meerkat's Popularity Is Suddenly Plunging," *The Verge*, April 1, 2015, http://www.theverge.com/2015/4/1/8319043/why-is-meerkats-popularity-suddenly-plunging.

4. "Meerkat Basks in Breakout Glow, Despite a Twitter Snag."
5. Dale J. Roe, "Julia Louis Dreyfus Talks HBO's 'Veep' (and Meerkat) at SXSW | Austin Movie Blog," *Austin 360 Movies Blog*, March 16, 2015, http://movies.blog.austin360.com/2015/03/16/julia-louis-dreyfus-talks-hbos-veep-and-meerkat-at-sxsw/.
6. "Meerkat Basks in Breakout Glow, Despite a Twitter Snag."
7. Christopher Heine, "Periscope Now Has 10 Million Users Who Watch 21 Million Minutes a Day," *AdWeek*, August 12, 2015, http://www.adweek.com/news/technology/periscope-now-has-10-million-users-who-watch-21-million-minutes-day-166361.
8. Maya Kosoff, "Mark Zuckerberg Is Turning Facebook into a Live-Streaming Empire," *Vanity Fair*, April 6, 2016, http://www.vanityfair.com/news/2016/04/mark-zuckerberg-is-turning-facebook-into-a-live-streaming-empire.
9. Kurt Wagner, "Meerkat Is Ditching the Livestream," *Re/code*, March 4, 2016, http://recode.net/2016/03/04/meerkat-is-ditching-the-livestream-and-chasing-a-video-social-network-instead/.
10. EMC, *EMC Social Media Caveman EXTERNAL 5-4*, June 27, 2011, https://www.youtube.com/watch?v=ah8aHIsAJfc.
11. Shel Israel, "Dell Modernizes Ideastorm," *Forbes*, March 27, 2012, http://www.forbes.com/sites/shelisrael/2012/03/27/dell-modernizes-ideastorm/.
12. "Social Media," *Wikipedia, the Free Encyclopedia*, May 22, 2015, http://en.wikipedia.org/w/index.php?title=Social_media&oldid=663553791.
13. Evelyn M. Rusli, "Facebook Buys Instagram for $1 Billion," *The New York Times*, April 9, 2012, http://dealbook.nytimes.com/2012/04/09/facebook-buys-instagram-for-1-billion/.
14. Jayson DeMers, "Why Your Organic Facebook Reach Is Still Falling—And What to Do about It," *Forbes*, May 13, 2015, http://www.forbes.com/sites/jaysondemers/2015/05/13/why-your-organic-facebook-reach-is-still-falling-and-what-to-do-about-it/.
15. Arjun Kharpal, "Facebook's New Video Ad Feature Could Worry Google," *CNBC*, July 2, 2015, http://www.cnbc.com/2015/07/02/facebooks-new-video-ad-feature-could-worry-google.html.
16. JoAnne Yates, Wanda J. Orlikowski, and Anne Jackson, "The Six Key Dimensions of Understanding Media," *MIT Sloan Management Review* 49, no. 2 (January 1, 2008): 63–69.
17. Ibid.
18. "The Conversation Prism (Brian Solis + JESS3)," accessed April 19, 2016, https://conversationprism.com/.
19. Sarah Frier, "Snapchat Adds 'Memories' Section to Let Users Save Stories," *Bloomberg.com*, July 6, 2016, http://www.bloomberg.com/news/articles/2016-07-06/snapchat-adds-memories-section-to-save-snap-stories-for-later.
20. "Ads • Snapchat," accessed April 19, 2016, https://www.snapchat.com/ads.
21. Ibid.
22. Dylan Tweney, "Engagement to Die for: Snapchat Has 100M Daily Users, 65% of Whom Upload Photos," *Venture Beat*, May 26, 2015, http://venturebeat.com/2015/05/26/snapchat-has-100m-daily-users-65-of-whom-upload-photos/.
23. Ibid.
24. Farhad Manjoo, "Vertical Video on the Small Screen? Not a Crime," *The New York Times*, August 12, 2015, http://www.nytimes.com/2015/08/13/technology/personaltech/vertical-video-on-the-small-screen-not-a-crime.html?ref=topics.
25. Mary Meeker, "2016 Internet Trends Report," *KPCB.com*, accessed July 21, 2016, http://www.kpcb.com/internet-trends.
26. John McDermott, "Brands Experiment with Photo-Messaging Service Snapchat, Facebook Poke," *Ad Age*, January 4, 2013, http://adage.com/article/digital/brands-experiment-photo-messaging-service-snapchat-facebook-poke/238979/.
27. Todd Wasserman, "Taco Bell Joins Snapchat to Reintroduce the Beefy Crunch Burrito," *Mashable*, May 1, 2013, http://mashable.com/2013/05/01/taco-bell-joins-snapchat/#13JfLDs495k3.
28. Maureen Morrison, "Snapchat 'Live Film' Introduces Taco Bell's Next Locos Taco," *Ad Age*, April 13, 2014, http://adage.com/article/news/snapchat-live-film-introduces-taco-bell-s-locos-taco/292629/.
29. Clare Trapasso, "Financial Advisers Turning to Social Media," *Financial Times*, March 25, 2015, http://www.ft.com/intl/cms/s/0/2851d51a-ad62-11e4-a5c1-00144feab7de.html#axzz3efirgj2f.

30. Ibid.
31. Lily Hay Newman, "Casper: A Friendly Mattress Startup Worth Millions," *Slate*, August 7, 2014, http://www.slate.com/blogs/moneybox/2014/08/07/foam_mattress_startup_casper_has_one_density_option_and_delivers_in_a_box.html.
32. Maeve Duggan et al., "Demographics of Key Social Networking Platforms," *Pew Research Center: Internet, Science & Tech*, January 9, 2015, http://www.pewinternet.org/2015/01/09/demographics-of-key-social-networking-platforms-2/.
33. Caitlin Huston, "How a Mattress Startup Made $20 Million in Its First 10 Months through Word-of-Mouth," *MarketWatch*, February 23, 2015, http://www.marketwatch.com/story/mattress-startup-casper-relies-on-social-media-word-of-mouth-2015-02-18.
34. Dominic Rushe, "Myspace Sold for $35m in Spectacular Fall from $12bn Heyday," *The Guardian*, June 30, 2011, http://www.theguardian.com/technology/2011/jun/30/myspace-sold-35-million-news.
35. "MySpace Is Now Officially Huger Than Everyone | WIRED," *Wired*, July 14, 2006, http://www.wired.com/2006/07/myspace_is_now_officially_huger_than_everyone.
36. Felix Gillette, "The Rise and Inglorious Fall of Myspace," *Bloomberg Business Week*, June 22, 2011, http://www.bloomberg.com/bw/magazine/content/11_27/b4235053917570.htm.
37. Rushe, "Myspace Sold for $35m in Spectacular Fall from $12bn Heyday."

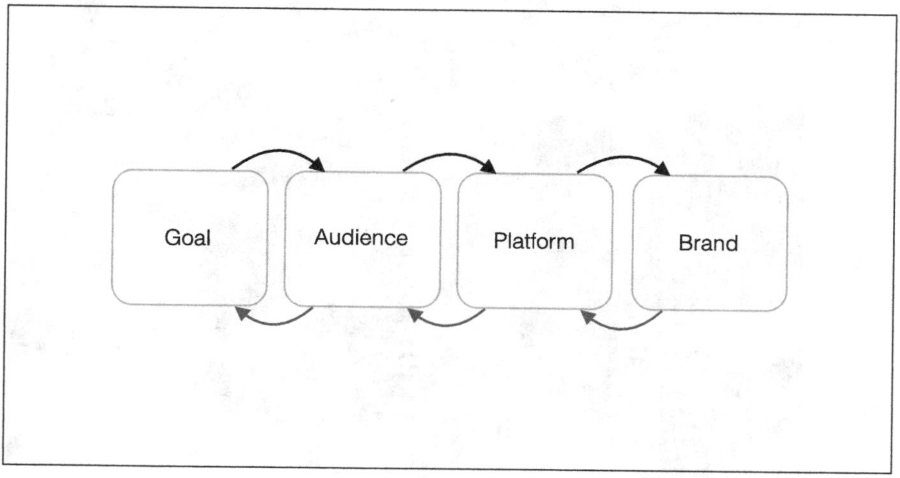

4 Developing Social Brand Strategy

Whole Foods Market is an upscale grocery chain that emphasizes local, healthy, sustainable, and high-quality foods. Although it offers a range of products at comparably affordable price points, it has also become widely known as "Whole Paycheck" because of what it seemingly costs to shop there. In part to justify their prices and increase customers' willingness to pay, Whole Foods has historically focused on the in-store experience (complete with elaborate olive bars, prepared food options, free samples, and other accoutrements) to communicate its value, differentiate itself from its competitors, and build ties to local communities.

With the advent of social media, Whole Foods saw a new opportunity—outside the store—to grow their brand and strengthen customer relationships. In doing so, they narrowed in on their core targets—health-conscious, educated customers—and selected both the Facebook and Twitter platforms to reach and engage them. For a company that historically had not spent much on traditional advertising and relied

more on word of mouth, social media was a cost-effective and logical outreach vehicle.

Although embracing social media made strategic sense, the pragmatic question remained: how would they go about launching a Whole Foods presence on Facebook and Twitter? In many ways, the answer came down to brand strategy. With hundreds of stores all over the country and sights on a growing international presence as well, Whole Foods had several branding options:

- *Option 1*: Whole Foods could use just one master or "flagship" account: the Whole Foods global brand presence. The benefit of this branding approach is that the organization would control the messaging and ensure that it aligned closely with its overall strategy. The downside of a single master account is that it would not allow the company to connect as closely to its customers. For example, if a customer in Michigan had feedback on a local product, it might be inefficient for the corporate management team to route that comment to the appropriate store.
- *Option 2*: Whole Foods could allow each individual store to have its own Facebook page and Twitter feed. The advantage of this strategy is that it would bring Whole Foods

stores closer to their customers. The downside is that the corporate management team would not be able to control strategy and messaging as tightly and thus the brand could be more vulnerable to mistakes or crises.

- *Option 3*: Whole Foods could implement a combination of the two—a global master brand account as well as local accounts on both Facebook and Twitter. The advantage of this strategy is both the corporate brand team and local stores would be involved in extending the Whole Foods brand onto Facebook and Twitter. The downside is logistical; with so many stakeholders, ensuring the brand is implemented with consistency and efficiency would be a challenge.

In the end, Whole Foods chose option 3. Because the customer relationship was a key strategic priority, a single global account was not the best fit; neither was a completely decentralized brand portfolio with only local stores, which would fall short on measures such as brand consistency and quality control. The hybrid approach was the best of both worlds. The master accounts give them the latitude and reach to shape brand messaging, while the local presences, according to Whole Foods, "enable us to build deeper community ties and connect more directly to the tastes and needs of the local customers we serve."[1] To be sure, this broad and deep option required a significant amount of coordination, training, and trust, but it has been a successful branding decision for the brand's social media presences over time. Whole Foods is a leader in the supermarket industry, amassing 4 million Facebook likes and 4.5 million Twitter followers in the span of six years, dwarfing its competitors.[2]

Beyond the fan counts, the Whole Foods hybrid branding approach is also an effective reflection (and reinforcement) of its overall brand strategy. Every store within the Whole Foods ecosystem is given freedom to customize and tailor their products and experience to the local market. This way, individual stores are empowered to best serve their customers, which in turn receive a more personal, customized touch from a chain grocer—less of a big box, more of a local market. The Whole Foods team decided to mirror and extend this brand strategy in social media.[3] With guidance and support from the corporate social media team, each individual store has developed its own content approach, campaigns, and events, while maintaining some level of brand consistency, as the profile pictures indicate in the Facebook search shown here.

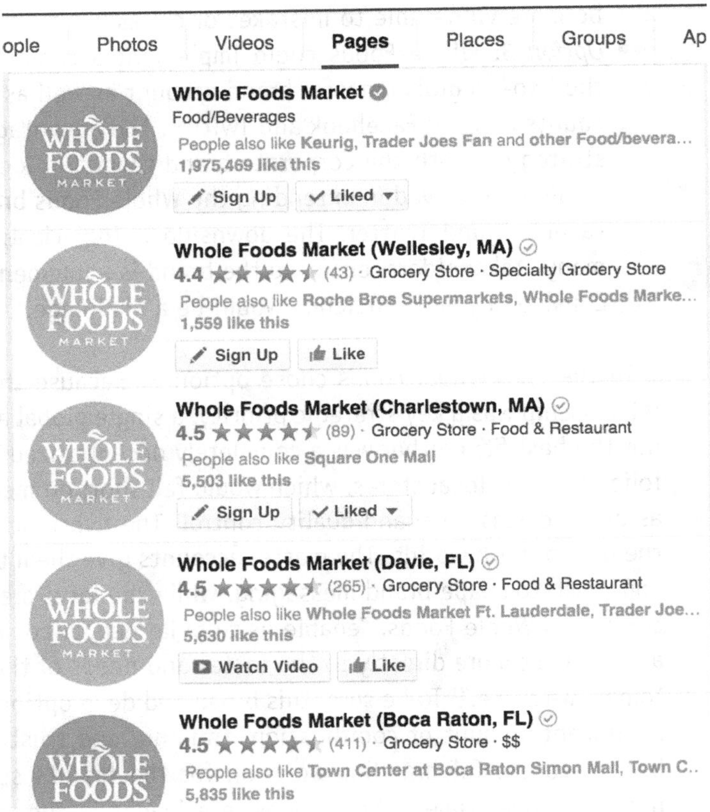

• • •

Whole Foods orchestrated their hybrid brand strategy through a central social media team that helped set strategy, provide best practices, and share brand assets for the local stores to use. It's an approach that has worked so well for Whole Foods that the company has since replicated a similar brand model on Instagram, with a master brand and individual store accounts. Such an approach may not be for every company, but for Whole Foods and its specific brand strategy, it has proven to be the best, most audience-centered way to maximize its brand in social media.

In light of your goals, audience, and platforms, this chapter focuses on social brand strategy, which is the development, extension, and management of your brand on social media platforms. To inform your social brand strategy, we will cover a few areas within this topic: (1) branding social media presences, (2) extending a brand personality into social media, and (3) creating and managing a social brand portfolio. But before we move forward with these strategic branding considerations, let's first take a look at the importance of social brand strategy.

Why Brand Strategy in Social Media Matters

For starters, let's align on the definition of the term "brand." Although many definitions exist, there is considerable consensus around Kotler and Keller's. They define brand as "a name, term, sign, symbol, or design, or combination of them, intended to identify the goods or services of one seller or group of sellers and to differentiate them from those of competitors."[4] Usually the best brands are a combination of all the elements Kotler and Keller cite. In addition, these brands make clear to all their stakeholders (customers, employees, shareholders, and others) *who they are* and *what they stand for*. For instance, Cisco, which was fifteenth on the annual Forbes list of most valuable brands in 2015, has developed an all-encompassing brand strategy that integrates all these key elements to communicate, "Cisco is the leader in world-changing technology that improves our everyday experience."[5]

Just as in the Whole Foods example, the overall brand strategy should shape and inform how you build your brand in social media. Cisco's Facebook pages, Twitter feeds, Instagram feeds, and other social platforms should all support its overall brand vision to enhance our daily lives through innovative technology. Of course, the ways in which Cisco's social media presence delivers on its brand strategy can be varied and different, and, in fact, multiple expressions of the brand can be a necessary best practice to reach certain audiences. But in general, brand strategy and social media management should be inextricably linked. Here's why:

First, brand promises must be kept in social media. At its core, brand is a promise of a distinct product, service, or experience. Wherever an audience encounters your brand, whether it is on television, at a retail store, on a website, or in social media, it is important that the interaction is consistent with what you want your brand to be. The expectations set for your organization in other channels will inevitably carry over to the social media space, and it is your job to meet or, better yet, exceed them.

Second, brands can command attention in the social media marketplace. In a sea of endless amounts of information, building a strong brand in social media can help organizations separate the signal from the noise, so to speak, and connect with their audiences. As Rishad Tobaccowala of Publicis once observed, "Brand is the ultimate navigator."[6] If an organization has a brand with strong loyalty, when it says something in social media, the message will stand a better chance to break through.

Finally, relationship building, a core function of brands, is a priority in the public, two-way, immediate, and networked social media space. The fundamental premise—and promise—of social media platforms is to enhance communication between people. Brands are invited, but only on your audience's terms. As a result, organizations must think about how their brand's personality can come to life in social media and thus contribute to the communities they are joining. Brands that communicate with audiences in corporate-speak (think terms like "synergy") may have a more difficult time connecting with their audiences in social media (or any channel for that matter).

Strategic brand thinking in social media cannot be emphasized enough. In a world where brand promises matter, brands command attention, and brands must build relationships, the brand decisions you make for your social media platforms are instrumental to effective social media management. The first of those decisions is what to brand the social platforms you've chosen to adopt.

Branding Social Media Presences

Branding in social media is easy, right? When you launch an Instagram feed, all you need to do is input the name of your company, add a logo, start posting, and you're good to go. Not quite. Although this setup is technically possible (e.g., a brand Instagram feed can be started in a matter of minutes), organizations seeking to maximize the business value of social media might consider a more deliberate approach to social branding.

For any organization in social media, the reality is your brand will be appearing alongside your audience's parents, friends, and significant others in most social media feeds. Within this context, where firms are effectively outsiders and information overload is on high, the brand name you select for your social media presences becomes increasingly important. This brand must have the flexibility to serve these four purposes:

1. Attract attention.
2. Communicate your brand positioning quickly and clearly.

3. Engage with your audience in direct, two-way communication, when appropriate.
4. Navigate your audience to another experience (e.g., connect, engage, buy) within your brand portfolio.

Fortunately for most organizations, there are naming options from which to choose. These include master brands, subbrands, people, and new brands. Let's look at each in more detail and discuss when to choose which option and the risks involved. Please note: none of these is mutually exclusive. Depending on the organization's goals, you may construct a social media portfolio with all four brand types.

Master Brands

The master brand refers to the flagship name of the organization or initiative. In some cases, choosing the master brand is the most logical decision. Indeed, for a few organizations, it may be the only decision.

When to Choose

- The brand is already "audience facing." It is the same brand your target audience will encounter in other places (e.g., on your products and services, website, TV advertisements).
- The brand has a distinct personality (or has the potential to develop one). It can be a challenge to establish a brand presence on social media without a meaningful narrative.
- Awareness among target audiences is a key business goal. If this is the case, you'll need visibility in a wide variety of channels, not the least of which your social media presences.

Risks to Consider

- Can the master brand be all things to all people? If your brand portfolio is more comprehensive (and complex), then it could be too difficult to accomplish multiple goals and reach multiple audiences via one brand. Conversely, if your goal and audience are narrow, then you may not face this challenge and should proceed with the master brand approach.
- Compared to other branding possibilities, the master brand may not have a compelling reason for audiences to connect with and follow it on social media.

- Maintaining a consistent, high-quality brand experience across channels and platforms. You may position your master brand in a TV commercial one way, but your social media presence does not reinforce or build on that same positioning.

Example: Ford Motor Company

Ford Motor Company is a strong brand with a long history. Its product offerings may change over time, but the Ford name remains front and center as a key customer, shareholder, dealer, and employee connection point. With its flagship Facebook page, Ford serves as the central hub of the company on the platform, highlighting and sharing what makes its brand unique and different compared to others.

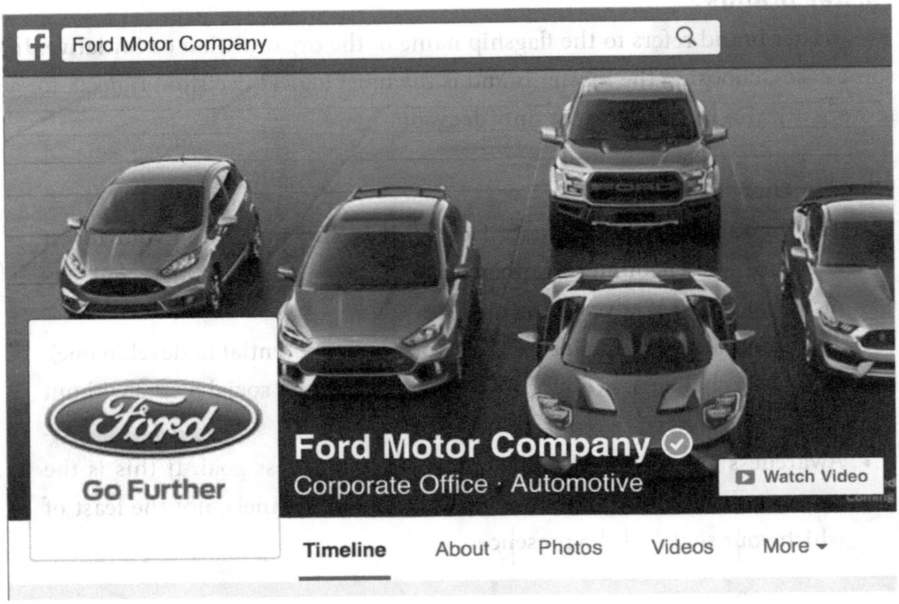

Subbrands

A subbrand is associated with the master brand, but it has a different proposition and set of characteristics.

When to Choose

- Your organization is promoting a niche offering and targeting a unique audience.

- It is possible to achieve audience scale and engagement with the subbrand, without cannibalizing the other brands and subbrands in your ecosystem.
- The subbrand can complement existing brands within the portfolio in social media and other channels.

Risks to Consider

- Subbrands may dilute other brands within your portfolio. There could be overlap in audience and content, which could lead to inefficiencies.
- By dividing off into subbrands, you also run the risk of decreasing the potential audience scale. In total, you might reach fewer people than if you concentrated efforts on building around the master brand on social media.

Example: Ford's Subbrands. Ford has also implemented a subbrand strategy effectively. In addition to its master brand presences, it has also launched subbrands for popular cars like the Ford Mustang and Ford Fusion.[7] Because Mustang fans in particular are numerous, Ford could not adequately serve this segment through its flagship social accounts. Moreover, the passion and avidity of Mustang supporters gave the company enough justification to dedicate resources to specially branded Mustang social communities. Ford's subbrand pages also become a source of content for the master brand pages. The example here illustrates Ford sharing the Mustang post for the broader Ford community on Facebook.

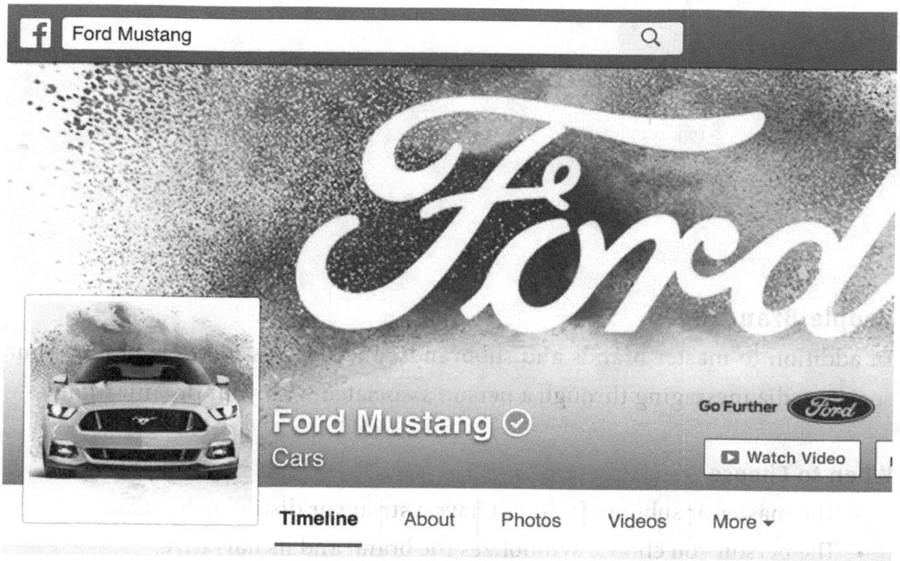

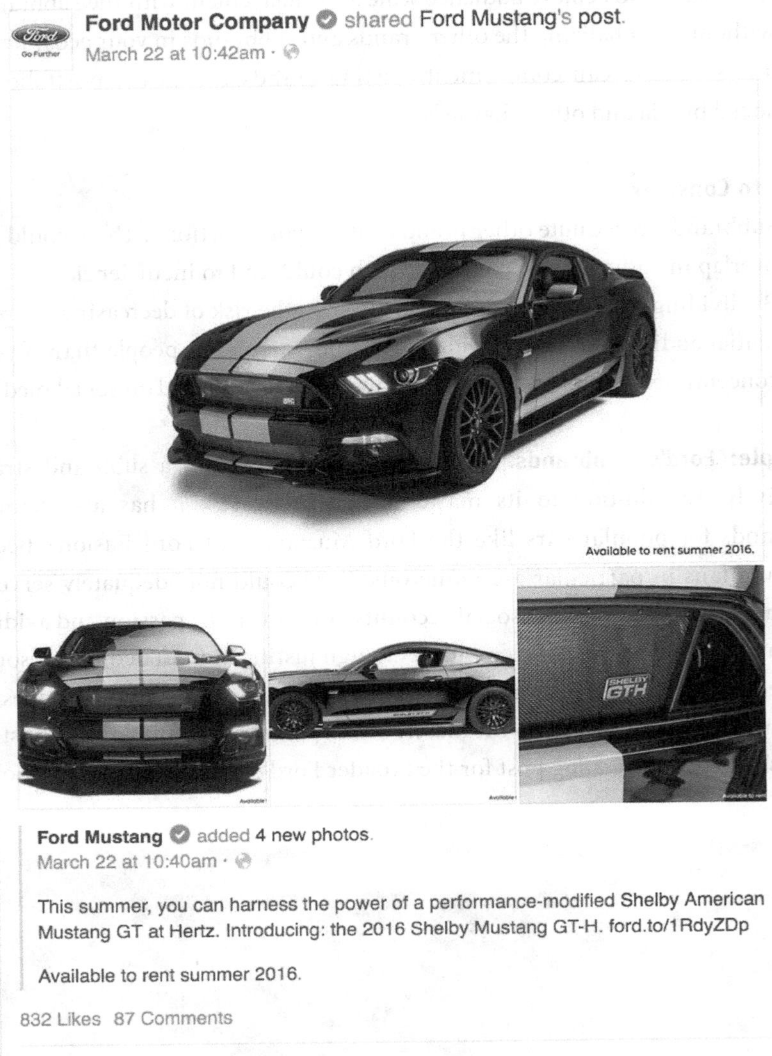

Ford Motor Company shared Ford Mustang's post.
March 22 at 10:42am ·
Available to rent summer 2016.
SHELBY GTH
Ford Mustang added 4 new photos.
March 22 at 10:40am ·
This summer, you can harness the power of a performance-modified Shelby American Mustang GT at Hertz. Introducing: the 2016 Shelby Mustang GT-H. ford.to/1RdyZDp
Available to rent summer 2016.
832 Likes 87 Comments

People Branding

In addition to master brands and subbrands, another possibility is to flow your social media messaging through a person associated with your organization.

When to Choose

- The master or subbrands do not have a strong or distinct personality.
- The person you choose symbolizes the brand and its narrative.

- The industry is a commoditized business in which people are key differentiators.

Risks to Consider

- Placing emphasis on a single person for your social media strategy could put an organization in peril if the person leaves or misbehaves.
- Building around a person could overshadow or reduce the equity of the master and subbrands.

Example: Brian Wong of Kiip. Following are two Twitter feeds. One belongs to Brian Wong, the founder and CEO of Kiip, a mobile advertising startup. The second is Kiip's master brand account, @Kiip. Brian has more than 20,000 followers, whereas his company has almost 9,000. For this early-stage company, messaging from Brian's handle will more often than not generate more engagement and reach, simply because of the difference in scale, not to mention Brian's ability to easily communicate in a relatable tone as a human being. As Kiip continues to grow its social media strategy, building around Brian's presence will be an important component to creating awareness, driving investment, and acquiring and retaining customers.

Creating a New Brand

As a final possibility, create a new brand if your goals, audiences, and platforms dictate it.

When to Choose

- You have a goal and an audience that you cannot reasonably reach through your other brands.

- The new brand could be a long-term asset for the company and thus is worth the investment.
- You have the resources to manage this new brand in social media, and it can be integrated into other aspects of the business as well.

Risks to Consider

- No matter how big or small the organization, it takes resources to launch and manage a brand. These resources could come at the expense of your other branding and social media efforts.
- The short-term efforts to build this brand and grow the audience may not result in long-term benefits.

Example: Customer Service Twitter Handles. The customer service genre within social media is a good example of organizations creating new brands specifically for social media. Many companies have taken the approach of handling complaints and issues through customer service handles like @UPSHelp and @MicrosoftHelps[8] These handles are differentiated from the other branded platforms within their

UPS Customer Support
@UPSHelp
Hello Twitter! This is the official UPS customer support account. We are here to help 24/7. Please choose DM when providing a tr# or other private info. Thanks!
UPS
ups.com
Joined March 2011

portfolio. It also is a clear proposition to customers; they know exactly what they are getting when they follow or reach out to one. In times of crisis (which we'll discuss at length in chapter 8), the customer service brand can often make statements that the master brand may not be in a position to say. Moreover, because more people are turning to Twitter for customer service, the resources dedicated to these types of handles are usually justified.[9]

As you decide what to brand your social presence, there are multiple naming conventions: master brands, subbrands, people brands, and new brands. Again, depending on how many presences your strategy calls for, all four branding possibilities are relevant and can coexist within the same portfolio. In any event, once you decide on your brand name, the next question is how to bring that name to life in social media.

Extending a Brand Personality

The brand strategy discipline covers a number of different concepts that go beyond the scope of this text.[10] Within the context of social media management, however, one brand strategy concept that is particularly relevant is brand personality. Brand personality is "the human characteristics or traits that can be attributed to a brand."[11] The characteristics or traits that a brand can possess are wide ranging. Millward Brown, a research company, has tested twenty-four different characteristics of brands worldwide, including "trustworthy," "in control," "brave," "arrogant," and "idealistic." In their work, brand personality traits correlate to brands bonding successfully with their target audiences across cultures.[12]

Functional and Emotional Benefits

Why should a brand develop a personality? Most brands offer functional and emotional benefits. Functional benefits refer to the utility of the product, service, or experience that an audience receives from a brand. Emotional benefits are the psychological needs that a brand satisfies when an audience engages with it.

Both functional and emotional benefits can be differentiators. If a product's functional benefits are its key differentiator, then emotional benefits may not be as important and vice versa. For example, Tesla is a market leader in electric cars because the functional benefits are considered the best among luxury cars. However, if a competitor (say a Mercedes-Benz) were to offer a comparable version, emotional benefits (such as the sleek design features or the association with Tesla founder Elon Musk's reputation for trailblazing innovation) could be important in attracting and retaining customers. In the end, successful brands (like Tesla) usually provide both functional as well as emotional benefits. The point is that one can be a more effective differentiator than the other, depending on the market and competition.

Why is the distinction between functional and emotional benefits relevant in social media? Through social media platforms, which are built primarily for people to interact with one another, brands have an opportunity to develop and communicate their personality through their social presences. This is not to say that touting functional benefits is irrelevant in social media. However, brands are uniquely positioned, because of the interactive, personal way people use social platforms, to foster emotional connections through social media.

The Brand Personality Exercise

How can you extend your brand personality in social media? As you launch or refine your social media presence, consider these three elements of brand personality:

- *Voice*—What the brand says
- *Behavior*—How the brand acts and interacts
- *Design*—How the brand looks

If you are in the early stages of brand personality development or are looking to uncover additional insights, a useful brainstorming tool can be the brand personality exercise. It encourages you and your team to imagine your brand as a person. Ask yourself: If your brand walked through the door, what would it look like? How old is it? What would be its hobbies? What type of food would it eat? What type of family did it come from and from what hometown? On the surface, these questions may seem a bit abstract (and perhaps a bit ridiculous), but once you begin to unpack the answers, they can be helpful in rounding out the type of personality characteristics and traits that you desire for your brand. Let's look at a couple of examples of brands and what they say (voice), how they act and interact (behavior), and how they look (design).

Example: The Sharpie Marker

On the surface, the Sharpie marker may seem like a difficult branding challenge. How can you give a marker personality? A quick glance at the Sharpie Facebook page and its intended personality comes through rather clearly. With its authentic

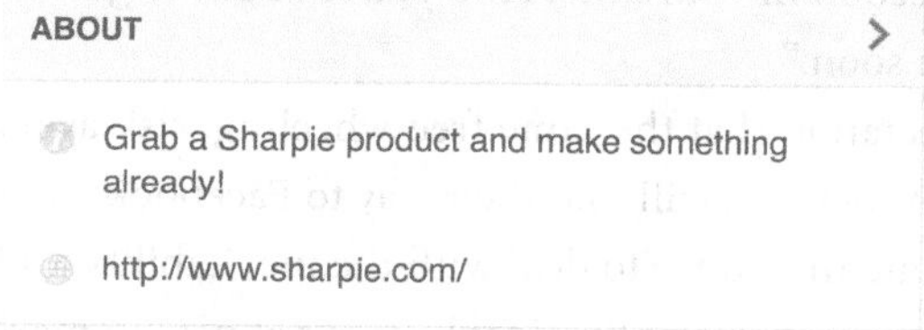

"do-it-yourself" inspired cover photo (rather than something overly produced) and an "about" statement that urges people to "grab a Sharpie product and make something already!", the Sharpie personality comes across as creative, spunky, fun, supportive, and productive.[13] If Sharpie were a person, perhaps it is someone living in Brooklyn or San Francisco that has a day job, but spends free time creating art, collaborating with other artists, and also raising a family. Of course, there could be other dimensions and interpretations of this brand personality. The important point is that even simple brand features, such as a cover photo or an "about" statement, can communicate your desired personality.

Example: Allstate Mayhem

You might think brand personality applies only to organizations that have an inherently fun brand proposition. What about insurance? To stand out in a commoditized market, Allstate Insurance created a persona called Mayhem, played by actor Dean Winters. He was the principal in a series of commercials touting the needs and benefits of Allstate (to protect against, well, mayhem). He also became a social media personality, posting musings to his 1.8 million Facebook fans and 90,000 Twitter followers (as a point of reference, Allstate had 450,000 fans on Facebook and 75,000 followers on Twitter). Introducing himself to his Facebook audience, he delivered a promise: "Call me Mayhem. I'm anything from your

blind spot to a raccoon in your attic. And you're about to get to know me a whole lot better. See you soon."

It sets the expectation that the same free-wheeling, risk-averse shenanigans in Mayhem's TV commercials will find their way to Facebook, all of which reinforce the need for Allstate Insurance to deal with the inevitability and unpredictability of mayhem. Creating a persona like Mayhem is not new in marketing communications (best wishes to the Kool Aid Man and the Hamburglar), but social media platforms give brands the structures and tools to develop and dimensionalize their personalities.

Example: Spotify Profile Picture

Sometimes organizations can use design to reflect their personalities and values in real time. When the Supreme Court ruled in favor of gay marriage in the United States, many social media users changed their profile pictures to celebrate the moment. Along with a number of other brands,[14] Spotify showed their support by modifying their logo. Changing profile pictures can be a quick and easy way to make a statement that reflects your brand's personality and values.

Brand personality is a key differentiator for any social media presence. It manifests in the voice (what you say), behavior (how you act and interact), and design (how you look). Even if your brand is highly functional, identifying the characteristics and traits that you represent and deciding how they manifest can help you further define what your social media presence should (and should not) be.

Most social platforms give brands many of the same features and functionality they offer people—post content and interact with others. In this two-way environment, brands that focus on personality development, thinking about how they speak, act, and look in social media, will put themselves in a better position to foster emotional connections with their audiences. A social brand personality is simply an extension of your broader brand strategy and should be consistent with what the brand represents in other channels. The same is true for all the brands within your social media portfolio.

Structuring a Social Media Portfolio

Because a growing number of people use several social media platforms on a daily basis, it is likely that you will manage multiple brand presences on multiple social media platforms, regardless of how large or small your organization. This is a resource issue as well as a branding challenge. If you have many different brands that your audiences can interact with, how should you arrange and organize those brands in a manner that is clear?

Answering this question draws on the considerable contributions of David Aaker on brand portfolio strategy. He and others have articulated an approach for companies that are looking to accelerate growth and position themselves for clear and strong offerings to each of its target audiences. To this end, Aaker writes:

> *The brand portfolio strategy specifies the structure of the brand portfolio and the scope, roles, and interrelationships of the portfolio brands. The goals are to create synergy, leverage, and clarity within the portfolio and relevant, differentiated, and energized brands. The portfolio brands, both owned brands and brands linked through alliances, should be considered a team of brands working together, each with assigned roles to enable and support business strategies.*[15]

Aaker advanced a brand relationship spectrum with two extremes. On the one end is the *branded house*, whereby all the brands within a portfolio are derivatives of the master brand. A well-known example is Virgin, which has launched a wide range of businesses branded as Virgin, such as Virgin Mobile, Virgin Money, and, well, Virgin Balloon Flights. The other end of the spectrum is the *house of brands*, which includes a wider variety of different brand names that all fall under an umbrella brand. Proctor and Gamble is one of the most well-known global examples of a house of brands, as brands in its portfolio like Tide and Pantene stand on their own, with the name Proctor & Gamble playing little role in driving awareness or credibility for its portfolio.[16] The *house blend* is a third term that has been used to refer to portfolios resting in the middle of these two extremes, with a main difference being the master brand plays a key audience-facing role. Alphabet, the parent company of Google, is an example of a portfolio with elements of both a branded house and a house of brands. It has a series of Google-branded products such as Google, Google Maps, and Google Fiber as well as distinct brand names such as Android, YouTube, and Calico. In fact, Aaker identified the two extremes of the branded house and house of brands, recognizing that many organizations would fall somewhere in between.

Because the barrier of entry of launching a brand in social media is so low, the idea of a brand portfolio strategy is especially relevant in social media management. Even a small, growing startup with a single brand will have to think about its social brand portfolio strategy and how it organizes and differentiates each of its brands: its master brand or subbrands, its people, its social media–created brands, and others.

With brand portfolio strategy as a backdrop, how can we apply this idea to the social media space? For starters, organizations can arrange and organize a social portfolio along two dimensions:

- *Within platform*—within each platform, create a brand portfolio system so as to avoid overlap and/or dilution of efforts and inefficiencies.
- *Across platforms*—create a brand portfolio across social platforms and focus on how each of the platforms can support one another.

Let's look at a couple of examples that vary along these dimensions: branded house and house of brands and by platform and across platforms. The first is Disney's Facebook portfolio.

CASE STUDY: DISNEY—A HOUSE OF BRANDS WITHIN FACEBOOK

The Disney brand was an avatar for social media brand portfolios. Spearheaded by their in-house social media agency DigiSynd, Disney reached 100 million Facebook likes in less than two years.[17] It did so with a sophisticated brand portfolio strategy of more than 200 different pages organized into three categories: brands, franchises, and characters.

- Brands: Disney, Disney Pixar, Walt Disney Animation Studios, Disneyland
- Franchises: Beauty and the Beast, Toy Story, Pirates of the Caribbean, Tron
- Characters: Mickey Mouse, Dory, Winnie the Pooh, Captain Jack Sparrow

With this social portfolio, the brand communicated clear offerings to its wide variety of audiences—brand pages served as the hubs for Disney-related content. Of course, the Disney page was for all things Disney, but

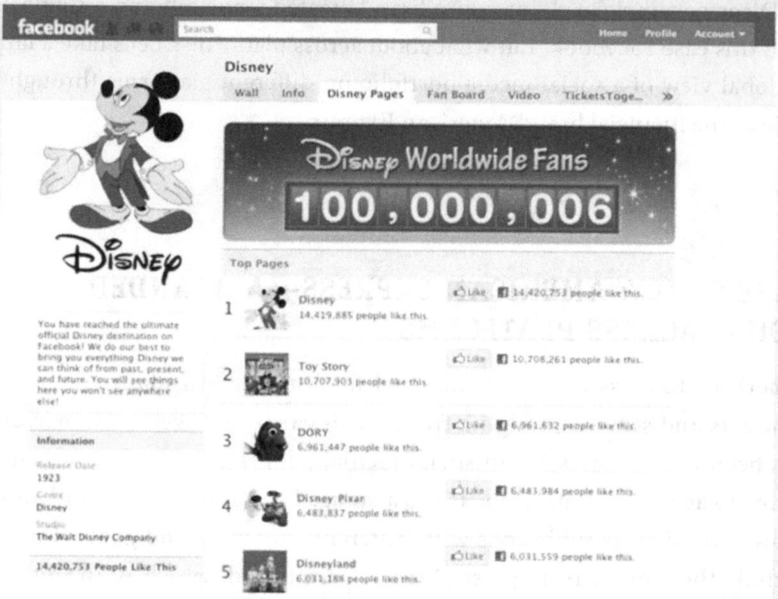

pages like Disney Pixar featured content specific to its films. Franchises like *Pirates of the Caribbean* revisited beloved memories from its multiple sequels, and characters such as Dory were a compilation of the greatest moments in that fish's life.

The portfolio was also able to facilitate connections and sharing among its various pages. So, for example, the Facebook page of the film *Finding*

CONTINUED

CASE STUDY: DISNEY—A HOUSE OF BRANDS WITHIN FACEBOOK *CONTINUED*

Nemo might share content from one of its character pages (e.g., Dory) to make fans aware that Dory also has a page (or vice versa). Or, in coordination with the Disney Parks team, the Disney Facebook page might share recent announcements and content from the Disneyland page. In these and other examples, all of the pages worked together to present a coherent and organized content experience to Disney fans all over the world.

The Disney example explains how a brand created a portfolio on a single platform, in this case Facebook. But what about across platforms? Let's take a larger, more global view of a social media portfolio on different platforms through the example of the financial brand American Express.

CASE STUDY: AMERICAN EXPRESS—A BRANDED HOUSE ACROSS PLATFORMS

American Express is a large financial institution with many different products and services, ranging from credit cards to travel assistance. It has been fairly aggressive in social media, adopting a number of platforms to accomplish its goals. It has also used social media to build and grow several of its subbrands with different audiences and goals. These include the American Express Open Forum brand, which is an initiative targeted to small business owners, and the American Express Serve brand, which is a prepaid card targeted to people who may not be likely credit card users. There's also been a trend toward individual countries launching their own country-specific social media accounts, especially on Twitter.

Figure 4.1 provides a snapshot of the company's social media portfolio. It is intended to be comprehensive, though not 100% exhaustive.

	Facebook	Twitter	YouTube	Instagram	Tumblr	Pinterest
Master Brand	AMERICAN EXPRESS	@AmericanExpress	American Express	American Express	American Express	American Express
Sub-brands	OPEN forum AMERICAN EXPRESS serve	@AmexOpen @AmexServe	American Express OPEN Forum		American Express Open Forum American Express Serve	
Country-specific sub-brands		@AmexUK @AmexIndia @AmexAU @AmexCanada @AmexJP				
New brands		@AskAmex @AskAmexUK @AskAmexCanada @AskAmexAU @AmexOffers				

FIGURE 4.1 **American Express's Social Media Portfolio**

What can we observe from American Express's social media brand portfolio? For starters, the master brand has a logical presence on each of the platforms. However, American Express also has a business case for its separate subbrands of Open and Serve, since both have different goals and audiences from the master brand. Interestingly, Serve does not have a presence on YouTube, but Open does; perhaps this is simply because the video content in support of the Open campaign is more significant. In addition, American Express created a new brand, @AskAmex, to serve in a customer service capacity. Finally, you'll notice that there is only one master brand account on Instagram and Pinterest. If those accounts grow, then there could be the option to expand to others. But American Express is limiting its presence on these platforms for now.

A helpful best practice with social brand portfolios is to monitor them closely and make changes over time. To give you a sense of the types of questions American Express could ask as part of its normal routines, consider the following:

- Is there potential audience overlap between American Express, American Express Open Forum, and American Express Serve? It'll be critical to

CONTINUED

CASE STUDY: AMERICAN EXPRESS—A BRANDED HOUSE ACROSS PLATFORMS *CONTINUED*

see whether those pages and feeds can stay differentiated over the long term.

- Does Tumblr warrant three different blogs? What is the justification?
- What unique role can the American Express Pinterest page play within the broader portfolio? How can the financial services category thrive on that platform?
- If the country-specific accounts from the United Kingdom, India, Canada, Japan, and Australia on Twitter are serving a unique and valuable purpose, what other countries might warrant a country-specific account? Under what circumstances are country-specific accounts appropriate for other platforms?
- What other questions would you have of American Express's social media portfolio?

The examples of Disney and American Express should offer ideas on how you might structure your own social media portfolio. Although each is different, both Disney and American Express have launched social presences that are distinct and complementary to their overall brand portfolio. However, if there's one thing we know about social media, it's that it's always changing, so you should also be strategic in how you manage (expand or contract) your social media portfolio.

Managing a Social Brand Portfolio

As with any portfolio, it's important to constantly check in and evaluate its performance. Should you redistribute resources? Add more? Subtract? The same thinking should be applied to social media portfolios. Following are a few situational factors to consider, which can serve as a checklist in your deliberations.

Expansion—When Should You Expand?

- *Unique purpose*—a new social media presence will have a unique offering that is different from (and perhaps better than) the offerings within the existing portfolio

- *Complements existing portfolio*—a new social media presence will not duplicate the other social media presences in the brand portfolio
- *Resources to manage*—a new social media presence will be supported with sufficient resources for content, marketing, measurement, and other functions
- *Potential upside*—there is a business case for what the new presence can add to the overall portfolio

Contraction—When Should You Contract?

- *Overlap*—duplication in audience, content strategy, marketing, or other ways that dilute the offerings rather than make them stronger
- *Platform fatigue*—the platform itself is no longer growing as strongly as it might be. For example, Foursquare was once popular and fast growing and many brands jumped on the bandwagon, but ultimately it lost favor with users and many brands moved on.
- *Inefficiencies*—if there are inefficiencies or the platform is not helping you achieve your goals, strongly consider contraction.

There could be additional reasons or circumstances as to why you might expand or contract. But being rigorous in your evaluation (based on some of the tools discussed in chapter 3 as well as the forthcoming chapter 7 on measurement) will be essential to effective social media management.

Recap: The Cocktail Party

Social media has frequently been described as a cocktail party. It is a wide mix of people who interact and discuss the issues of the day, share a few laughs, and maybe talk a little business from time to time. The insurance salesperson who walks up to a group of people, doesn't even say hello, and proceeds to hand out business cards while simultaneously pitching his services is typically unwelcome at the party. Similarly, brands that operate in the social media space without sensitivity to how people use the platforms and consistently sell, sell, sell will find themselves shut out of the conversation.

Organizations must operate in this context, and to do so effectively, they should think strategically about the role of brand in social media management. Indeed, organizations large and small have difficult branding decisions like the ones we discussed in this chapter. Those include brand selection, brand personality development and extension, and brand portfolio organization and management. You now have a set of tools and concepts to evaluate what brand strategies make sense for your organization.

Looking ahead, brand will help inform content and distribution decisions that you will make in your social media management strategy. In the next chapter, we first look at social content approaches that are appropriate to your brand, platform, audience, and goals.

Your Turn: Trader Joe's Social Brand Strategy

We started this chapter with Whole Foods. We'll end it with an exercise on its fierce competitor, Trader Joe's. Trader Joe's is a private company owned by German food chain Aldi. Its core customers tend to be singles, couples, and small families that are well educated but have diverse incomes. A vast majority of the products it sells are branded Trader Joe's. Some of these products are megastars in their own right, like cookie butter and the wine formerly known as "two buck chuck." Employees serve in the role as brand ambassadors, asking sincerely how you are doing and commenting on the items you're buying that resonate most with them. TJ's, as it is also known, fundamentally believes that grocery shopping should be fun.

Different from Whole Foods, Trader Joe's has historically had no official brand presences on social media whatsoever. Searching for the brand on a variety of platforms turns up either Trader Joe's pages and feeds run by fans or dormant store-specific pages that have no content. For a brand with an estimated $11 billion in revenue in 2013,[18] which is up from $8.5 billion in revenue in 2011,[19] and with 400+ stores around the country,[20] you could make a convincing argument that this grocer really does not need social media.

However, for the purposes of this exercise, things are changing for Trader Joe's. The brand is opening 30–35 new stores per year going forward, a growth goal that is aggressive to say the least. To attract, engage, and retain customers in new markets, it is finally turning to social media as an important tool in its marketing mix.

Your challenge is to help them think about how they can extend their brand onto Instagram. Provide Trader Joe's recommendations on the following brand strategy questions:

- How many Instagram accounts should Trader Joe's launch?
- What should the Instagram accounts be branded?

- How should the Trader Joe's brand personality come to life in social media? What should its voice, behavior, and design be?
- Construct a social media portfolio for Trader Joe's. How is it organized?

You should present not only a short-term brand strategy but also a compelling long-term vision for what Trader Joe's on Instagram could look like. Good luck.

Notes

1. "2014 Whole Foods Market Annual Report," 2014, http://assets.wholefoodsmarket.com/www/company-info/investor-relations/annual-reports/2014-WFM_Annual_Report.pdf.
2. The numbers cited are from its 2014 Annual Report. Whole Foods launched its global brand accounts on Facebook and Twitter in 2008.
3. Jay Baer and Adam Brown, *How Whole Foods Focuses on Customer Needs to Succeed in Social Media, Social Pros*, accessed September 2, 2015, http://www.convinceandconvert.com/podcasts/episodes/whole-foods-focuses-on-customer-needs-in-social-media/.
4. Philip Kotler and Kevin Lane Keller, *Marketing Management* (Upper Saddle River, N.J.: Pearson Prentice Hall, 2009).
5. "Cisco Brand Overview," accessed September 4, 2015, http://www.cisco.com/assets/swa/flash/partners/brand/.
6. George Bodenheimer and Donald T. Phillips, *Every Town Is a Sports Town: Business Leadership at ESPN, from the Mailroom to the Boardroom* (New York: Grand Central Publishing, 2015).
7. "Ford Mustang," accessed September 13, 2015, https://www.facebook.com/fordmustang?fref=ts; "Ford Fusion + Hybrid," accessed September 13, 2015, https://www.facebook.com/fordfusion.
8. "UPS Customer Support (@UPSHelp) | Twitter," accessed September 13, 2015, https://twitter.com/UPSHelp; "Microsoft Support (@MicrosoftHelps) | Twitter," accessed September 13, 2015, https://twitter.com/MicrosoftHelps.
9. Katie Lobosco, "Comcast to Take More Complaints via Facebook and Twitter," *CNNMoney*, March 23, 2015, http://money.cnn.com/2015/03/23/news/companies/comcast-social-customer-service/index.html.
10. For more information on brand strategy and how to apply it to your organization, several #goodreads include the following: Al Ries and Jack Trout, *Positioning: The Battle for Your Mind*, 1st ed. (New York: McGraw-Hill, 1986); David A. Aaker, *Building Strong Brands* (New York: Free Press, 1996); Tim Calkins and Alice Tybout, *Kellogg on Branding: The Marketing Faculty of The Kellogg School of Management*, 1st ed. (Hoboken, NJ: Wiley, 2005).
11. Kevin Lane Keller and Keith Richey, "The Importance of Corporate Brand Personality Traits to a Successful 21st Century Business," *Journal of Brand Management* 14, no. 1 (2006): 74–81.
12. Graham Staplehurst and Suthapa Charoenwongse, "Why Brand Personality Matters: Aligning Your Brand to Cultural Drivers of Success," 2012, http://www.millwardbrown.com/docs/default-source/insight-documents/points-of-view/Millward_Brown_POV_Brand_Personality.pdf.
13. "Sharpie," accessed September 13, 2015, https://www.facebook.com/Sharpie.
14. Patrick Kulp, "The Best Brand Reactions to the Historic Gay Marriage Decision," *Mashable*, June 26, 2015, http://mashable.com/2015/06/26/brands-gay-marriage-legalized/.
15. David A. Aaker, *Brand Portfolio Strategy: Creating Relevance, Differentiation, Energy, Leverage, and Clarity* (New York: Free Press, 2004), 13–14.
16. Aaker, Brand Portfolio Strategy, 46–64.
17. Lauren Indvik, "Disney Celebrates 100 Million Facebook Fans," *Mashable*, December 5, 2010, http://mashable.com/2010/12/05/disney-100-million-facebook-fans/.

18. Packaged Facts, "Trader Joe's and the Natural Food Channel: Market Research Report," *Packaged Facts*, February 14, 2014, http://www.packagedfacts.com/Trader-Joe-Natural-8031891/.
19. "Trader Joe's Market," *Supermarket News*, accessed July 22, 2016, http://supermarketnews.com/trader-joes-market-0.
20. Facts, "Trader Joe's and the Natural Food Channel: Market Research Report."

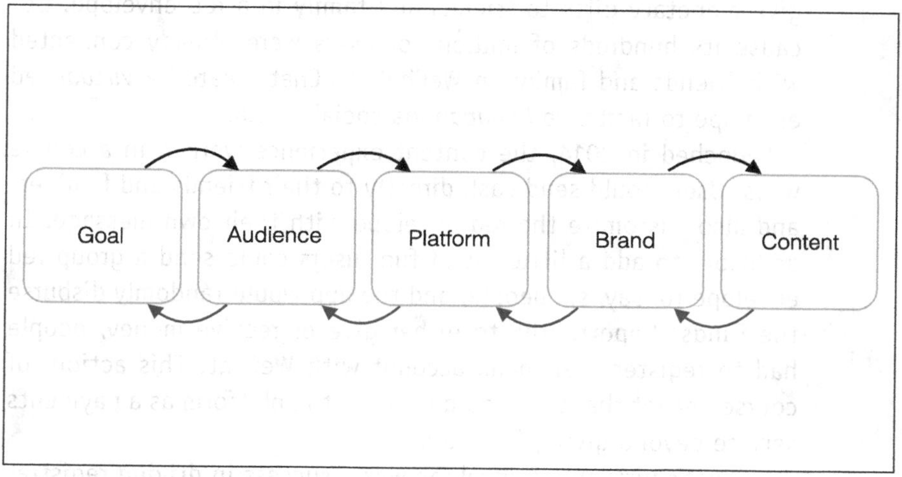

5 Designing Social Content

WeChat, the popular social messaging mobile application in China owned by Tencent, was at an inflection point. Its fiercest competitor, e-commerce giant Alibaba, had already made significant inroads into the mobile payments business, the next frontier in China's technology sector, with its Alipay app. Given WeChat's own ambitions to become a one-stop Internet shop, ceding share of this growing mobile payments market to Alibaba could be a long-term strategic misstep. In practice, WeChat faced an uphill battle to convince users to pay for goods and services through a social messaging service rather than use an incumbent e-commerce provider.

To spur adoption of its mobile WeChat Payments service, WeChat looked no further than its own platform. In doing so, they designed a social content experience that was driven by a key cultural insight about its audience. Every Lunar New Year, the Chinese practice the long-standing tradition of *hongbao*, in which they give monetary gifts to friends and family in a red envelope. Because its hundreds of millions of users were already connected with friends and family on WeChat, WeChat created a *virtual* red envelope to facilitate *hongbao* via social media.

Launched in 2014, the content experience worked in a couple ways. Users could send cash directly to their friends and families, and also customize the red envelope with their own message. In addition, to add a little bit of fun, users could send a group red envelope to, say, six people, and the app would randomly disburse the funds. Importantly, to either give or receive money, people had to register their bank account with WeChat. This action, of course, meant that they could now use the platform as a payments service beyond giving *hongbao*.

WeChat's virtual red envelope was a success in driving registrations for its mobile payments service. In the first year, more than 40 million red envelopes were sent by 8 million users.[1] At the time, Jack Ma, founder and executive chairman of Alibaba, called WeChat's move around the Spring Festival and Lunar New Year a "Pearl Harbor moment," a sound bite that ricocheted across the media.[2] A year later, Alibaba ramped up its own virtual red envelope promotion, but WeChat still won the day, with 1 billion virtual red envelopes gifted on Lunar New Year's eve via WeChat versus 240 million on Alipay. This time, WeChat also partnered with CCTV,

the dominant television network in China, for a live New Year's Eve gala broadcast, during which WeChat users could win money by shaking their phones while using the WeChat application. Most important, as a result of the *hongbao* promotion via WeChat and CCTV, WeChat was estimated to have registered at least 100 million users for its payment service.[3]

Within the context of their original goal—attracting registered users of WeChat Payments—the virtual red envelope promotion was effective. They benefited from a clearly defined business goal, an expert understanding of their audience, an intimate knowledge of their platform, and a clearly defined and logical brand—WeChat Payments. Informed by all these components, they developed a social content experience in the virtual red envelope that effectively engaged its audience, putting WeChat in a position to become a dominant mobile payment services provider. Although WeChat Payment attracted millions of new registrants, their next challenge is to encourage repeat visits and usage of their payment system, which will require another set of platform-appropriate content strategies.

• • •

In analyzing social media success stories, it is often easy to jump to the oft-cited conclusion that "content is king." To be sure, this axiom is true to a degree; brands need strong content—whether it's text, video, image, animated gif, an interactive experience, or any other format—to attract and engage an audience. And in the unpredictable social media space, content can go "viral" for seemingly random and head-spinning reasons, leading to the belief that strategy has little to do with content creation. But these situations are the exception, not the rule. Practicing effective social media management means grounding your content development approach in the underlying goals, audience, platform, and brand decisions driving your social strategy.

In this chapter, we'll discuss the strategies and best practices of social content creation. (1) First, we'll review the building blocks of social content. (2) Then, we'll address the importance of tailoring your social content to the platform. (3) Finally, we'll examine the numerous ways to source and develop content. By the end of this chapter, you will have a variety of tools and perspectives to create remarkable, shareable, and strategically sound social content.

Building Blocks of Social Content

In a social media environment with endless choices, instantaneous feedback, and seamless network effects, content creators face new challenges to an age-old question: how to attract and engage an audience. However, while the question may remain the same, applying the content development formula from a television network (or another traditional medium) to a social platform would be like trying to fit a square peg in a round hole. Successful content in social media requires a unique and different approach.

This approach centers on social content, which is defined as *platform-appropriate content designed for audience engagement and sharing.* It can take a number of different forms, from textual content like status updates, tweets, and captions to the vast and growing library of visual content, including but not limited to video, images, photos, and animated gifs.

Underlying effective social content are three key building blocks. As you begin to create your own, you can use the building blocks as a strategic roadmap to help you develop engaging and shareable content. The purpose of these building blocks is to bring strategic rigor to the social content development process, rather than relying on a haphazard approach.

The building blocks of social content are as follows:

1. *Message*—Distill the key message to communicate.
2. *Voice*—Adapt and express your message consistent with your brand personality.
3. *Share proposition*—Include why your audience benefits from sharing.

Let's look at each of these building blocks in more detail, along with examples for each.

Message

The first building block of social content is your message. What exactly are you trying to communicate to your audience? If you could summarize your message in one sentence—one takeaway—what would it be? The reason message development is so critical in the social media space is simply a matter of time. Whether it is a 140-character tweet, 15-second video, or one photo in a barrage of many, the window to communicate in social media is very short. As a result, your message must be focused and discernible (either explicitly or implicitly).

Mashable, the social media news service, is expert in cutting to the core of its message and communicating it explicitly and clearly. Here are a few of its headlines:[4]

Mashable
Royal family shares photo of Princess Charlotte with Prince George, Internet loses it

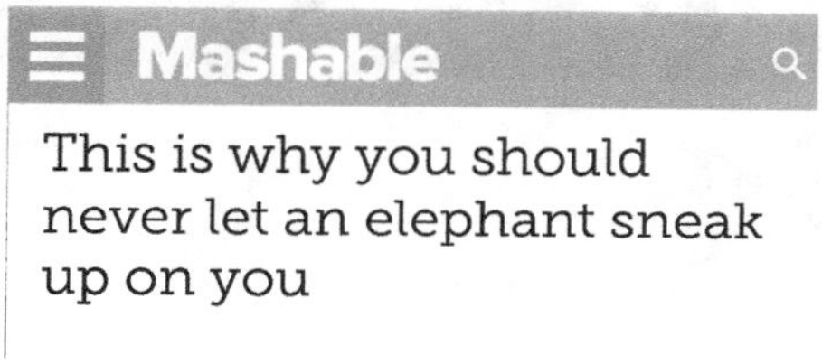
Mashable
This is why you should never let an elephant sneak up on you

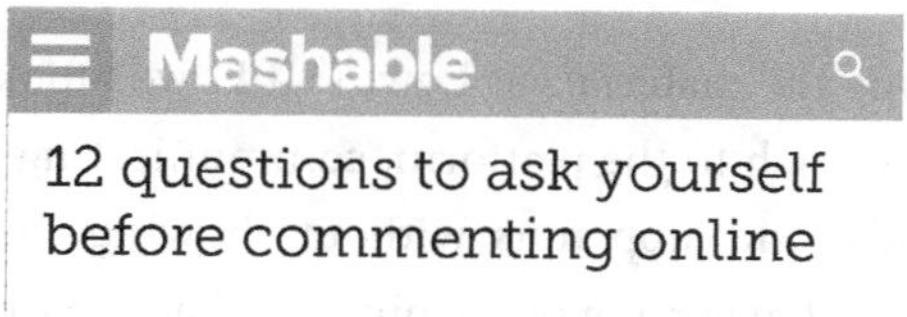
Mashable
12 questions to ask yourself before commenting online

With each headline, the user can get a sense of what the article is about without clicking through, passing the TL:DR (too long, didn't read) test. At the same time, just enough information is withheld so as to encourage a click to read (or see) more if you are so inclined. These headlines are upfront with the key message and news item and communicate it clearly and succinctly to prospective readers.

In social media (and all of communication, in fact), some brand messaging can be more effective if it does not "hard sell" the audience. Lowe's Home Improvement is one particular brand that has taken such an approach, embedding its core message to drive product sales into its social content in user-friendly ways. On its robust Pinterest page, which has attracted more than 3 million followers, Lowe's posts a wide variety of do-it-yourself (DIY) home improvement ideas. One of its most successful pins was the DIY welcome doormat, which has been saved more than 200,000 times.[5] That pin, pictured here, combines an eye-catching product with a thoughtful idea for Pinners to create themselves, many of whom use the platform for DIY ideas. The underlying message is that should you decide to make

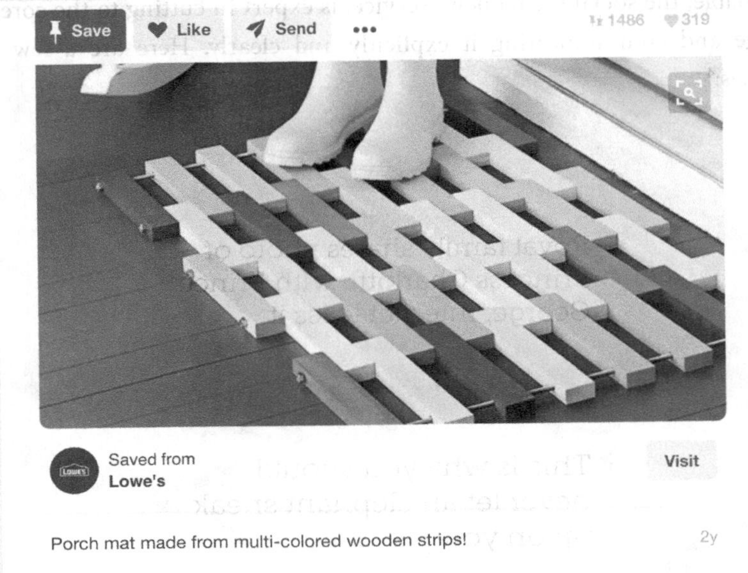

a similar doormat, buy the materials at Lowe's. If Lowe's took a more traditional direct advertising approach to the platform, communicating the pricing for pine boards, threaded rods, and stop nuts without showing the beautiful finished product, it is safe to say that version of the pin would not be shared nearly as many times.

Regardless of the type of social content you create (text-only, animated gif, video, etc.), every social communication should have a message: the key idea you want your audience to understand, feel, and act on. The message can be as literal as an informational headline like the Mashable example, or it can be as nuanced to include subtler calls to action like the Lowe's case. Regardless, the message is the foundational building block for social content. Voice and the share proposition are the layers on top that differentiate the content and make it shareworthy.

Voice

In the last chapter, we discussed the overall brand personality for your social media presences and how it includes three elements: voice, behavior, and design. Because voice is a critical component of social content, let's examine it even more closely. Voice is the expression of your brand's personality through content. Think of it this way: Personality is who you are; voice is what you say. Usually the two should be inextricably linked, as personality informs and shapes your voice. If there are inconsistencies between the two, your audience will see through them and your brand's credibility may suffer as a result.

Voice is important in social content for a number of reasons. As with the broader idea of personality, it can serve as a differentiator, especially if you are operating in a market with plenty of competitors selling similar products or services. It can also help you become more relatable to your audience. If you speak and act the way they do (or the way they wish they did), you can position yourself to forge strong connections. And last, but not least, it helps you attract attention, engage and encourage sharing.

Red Bull has consistently been a preeminent brand in social media. In addition to expertly tailoring content to the platform (a concept we'll address shortly), Red Bull's voice has evolved into a distinct and identifiable driver of its social content strategy. To align with its high-caffeine energy drink products, they have developed a risk-taking, active, and aspirational voice that informs all their social content. The tweet shown here is a good illustration of the voice, as it reflects the live-life-to-the-fullest ethos of the brand. Importantly, the caption is written in a way to inspire sharing by those who hold the same philosophy. Moreover, the

photo is not of a celebrity, but seemingly an everyday Joe, making the Red Bull lifestyle (and product) attainable for everyone.

Another brand, with a decidedly different voice from Red Bull, is Innocent Drinks, a juice and smoothie company out of the United Kingdom. Their slogan is "innocent by nature" and they come across as a group comprised of people in their twenties and thirties, many with young families that just like to have fun, in a kid-like (read: innocent) fashion. Their wry, at times clever, and at other times corny sense of humor imbues the Innocent brand with a clear and differentiated voice, to help it stand out against competitors in the commoditized juice market. Here is an example of one creative, decidedly outlandish, and self-aware persuasive attempt. The message is to buy more smoothies, but the way in which it is framed and communicated illustrates the role and importance of voice.

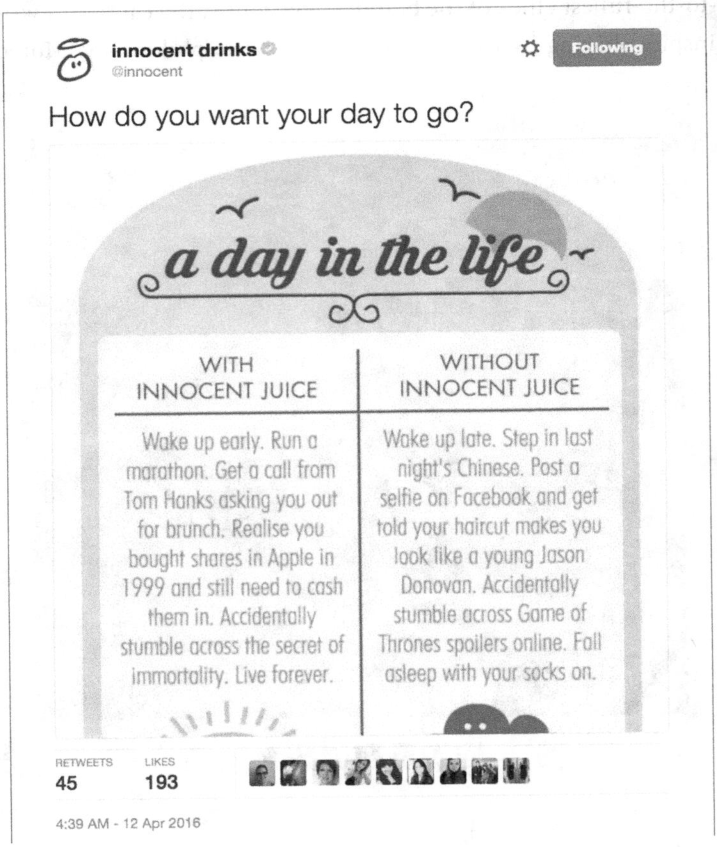

If you have clearly defined your brand personality, your brand voice will be easier to discern, as it is simply the expression of your personality through content. As you explore the opportunities and boundaries of your voice, consider asking this question with every potential social content idea: would our personality say something like this? This can be a quick and helpful benchmark for evaluating whether your content is relevant and appropriate.

Share Proposition

The final building block of social content is the share proposition, which is the reason why your audience should share your content. Because social media is a two-way communication platform, the gold standard for social media content is for someone to share (or share in) your message. To be clear, we consider the term "sharing" to have multiple meanings in social media. It can mean to share with your friends and followers in social media. It can mean to tell your friends offline. It can mean a simple like, favorite, or endorsement of the content. It can also mean sharing in the movement by creating your own content in support of it. In the end, if your content does not elicit sharing, it effectively becomes a one-way broadcast message, which is not taking advantage of the full capabilities of social media platforms.

In the study of persuasion, the concept of what's in it for them (WIIFT) is an oft-cited audience analysis principle for designing effective communications. In social media, we can extend this concept to ask, "Why should your audience share?" In order for it to be effective, your social content must give your audience a reason to share. To help you think through the possibilities, consider some of the STEPPS from Jonah Berger's book *Contagious*.[6] In that book, he identified the six key elements of why content is shared or talked about. They are as follows:

- *Social currency*—"We share things that make us look good."
- *Triggers*—"Stimuli that prompt people to think about related things."
- *Emotions*—"When we care, we share."
- *Public*—"If other people are doing something, it must be a good idea."
- *Practical value*—"People like to pass along practical, useful information."
- *Stories*—"Information travels under the guise of idle chatter."

As you develop social content, ask yourself questions about the share proposition along the way. How might this video give my audience social currency? Does this tweet play to a specific emotion? How can I use public strategies (i.e., social proof) to demonstrate the campaign's growing popularity? These are the types of filters you can apply as you evaluate various content ideas for social media.

It is important to note that, like the "message" building block, the share proposition can be either implicit or explicit. The implicit approach is akin to the soft sell; people may be more receptive to your message, but the danger is they may not understand what action you would like them to take as a result of consuming your content. Conversely, the explicit approach ensures the call to action is clear to your audience, but you might turn them away with direct language and content. Deciding when to use implicit versus explicit should be based on past performance of both approaches as well as the value exchange you are offering your audience. That is, if an audience receives high value in return for sharing your message, an explicit share proposition may be warranted.

Let's examine the share proposition through a couple of different examples. First, Fractl and BuzzStream, two social media analytics companies, studied the most shared content in social media. Over a six-month period, they found that lists, otherwise known as listicles, were consistently among the most shared.[7] Lists have been made (in)famous by Buzzfeed and are widely used around the social web. The list format is catered to an Internet readership with little time and short attention spans, but importantly, it is also conducive to sharing. In the Fractl and Buzzstream study, the list format worked particularly well in the travel vertical. Here's one from Buzzfeed: "19 Surreal Places to Visit in Australia before You Die."[8] I encourage you to view the list; the photos are stunning. However, for the purposes of this analysis, all we need is the headline. (Indeed, it is not unlikely that people will share content without reading any more than the headline.) So, what is the share proposition? According to Berger's STEPPS, practical value would certainly be a factor; if you are planning a trip to Australia at some point, knowledge of great places to visit in the country would come in handy. How about social currency? Where you travel (or want to travel) tells your friends and followers something about you; if you identified Australia as a travel destination—and some of the locations included within the list—certainly you would look good to your network. Finally, there is an element of public, or social proof, operating. Given the dramatic headline, which suggests Australia should be on everyone's bucket list, nothing should be stopping you from going to Australia either, or at the very least, sharing the link on your Facebook page.

We can also see the share proposition at play in the category of the "viral" YouTube video, which came to define a whole new category of social content. One of those videos was from the Dollar Shave Club, the startup razor company seeking to take on the established brands. In the video screenshotted here, the founder of the company spends almost 90 seconds extolling the virtues of his product (they're . . . great), dismantling his competitors' offerings (who needs so many blades?), and promoting the low cost of his offering (one dollar per month). The video was shareable for a variety of reasons: it relied significantly on humor to play to the audience's emotions, it communicated the practical value of the products versus others in the market, and it told the story of the product clearly and succinctly. As a result, the video accumulated more than 22 million views and counting and was critical in launching this new brand, which Unilever eventually acquired for $1 billion.[9]

Although all of the STEPPS Berger offers are critical factors in shareability, emotions can be an especially effective lever in social content creation. Karen Nelson from the Ehrenberg-Bass Institute has studied which emotions lead to more sharing. A common finding is that positive emotions stimulate more sharing than negative emotions. However, the key is striking high-arousal emotions such as hilarity and exhilaration as opposed to amusement and happiness.[10] There is also evidence that negative emotions can drive sharing, but the same principle about high-arousal emotions still applies. For example, anger will lead to sharing more than sadness.[11] There is no surefire formula that will work every time, but designing social content for high-arousal emotions will position you for success.

The share proposition is the third and final building block of social content creation. Without a reason to share, your social content may not be able to fully capitalize on the unique network effects that social media offers. "Why would my audience share this content?" should be a routine question for any social media management initiative.

How do the three building blocks of social content work together? Let's look at an Instagram post from Nike, one of the most successful brands on the platform, to see how a shareable post can be built from the ground up.

CASE STUDY: A NIKE INSTAGRAM POST

Let's break down a post together piece by piece. For starters, we have this photo of an athlete jumping over a bench. It fits the Instagram platform well, as the camera angle is unique and eye-catching.

Now, let's add on the layers. When we include the Nike brand, what does that do to the post immediately? Because of its brand personality, Nike communicates that everyone's an athlete and encourages people to try their best and never give up. These are important brand attributes that the brand alone communicates.

With the brand in place, how should Nike express its personality through its voice? In this case, it tells the story of Liza Maman, pictured, and her quest to become a better athlete. The voice in the post carries with it the same message of hope, aspiration, and hard work that has come to personify Nike, which subtly encourages Nike fans to buy gear to help fulfill their own goals.

CONTINUED

CASE STUDY: A NIKE INSTAGRAM POST *CONTINUED*

Finally, there's a share proposition. Implicitly, this post inspires and encourages Nike's millions of followers to "just do it" as well. Explicitly, Nike also adds a call to action of "show us how you #justdoit" to share in the movement.

nike
Follow
1 week ago
Set the benchmark. #justdoit
Where others take a seat, @lizamaman takes it up a notch. Show us how you #justdoit

The results of this post are staggering. There were more than 300,000 likes soon after it was posted and 421,000 at the time of publication. Moreover, because they frequently included #justdoit in their Instagram posts, the number of hashtag mentions at the time of the post was in the 5 million range.

To summarize, this Nike Instagram post exhibits the three main building blocks of social content in the following ways:

- *Message*—Nike products can help anyone fulfill her or his personal goals.
- *Voice*—Nike communicates self-improvement, aspiration, fearlessness, and competitiveness through the story of Liza Maman, who embodies the Nike brand personality.
- *Share proposition*—Nike invokes social proof to encourage participation and opens the door to social currency, inviting people to use the #justdoit hashtag to show them how they are like Liza (or better).

The building blocks of social content should provide a solid foundation from which to develop your own social content approach. Although social content shares certain universal characteristics, like message, voice, and share propositions, it is not necessarily one-size-fits-all across social platforms. Indeed, as you move forward with your strategy, another key component is tailoring to the platform.

Tailoring Social Content to the Platform

As we discussed in chapter 3 on platform choice, each social media platform differs on dimensions like type, audience, content, engagement, and brand integration. From a social content creation standpoint, this means a video you have created for your organization's Facebook page may not be appropriate for your Tumblr account. Or perhaps you developed a series of images that are ideal for Pinterest but will not work as well on Twitter.

This brings us to a key principle of social content creation: *Social content should be tailored to the platform.* Throughout modern media history, content creators have taken different programming approaches to television, radio, film, and print media. You rarely hear the term "traditional media content strategy," as each of these platforms has unique characteristics and audience expectations and thus requires a custom approach. The same general principle applies in social media. Tailoring your content to the platform will signal an understanding and respect for the space, which can help you build the audience connections you need to advance your goals.

In tailoring your social content to each platform, some of the areas you can consider include content formats, language norms, and design tools. Let's look at each possibility in more detail.

Content Formats

What formats does the platform support? For example, if you are developing video as part of a campaign and have chosen Facebook, YouTube, Instagram, and Vine as distribution outlets, you will need to consider carefully the format differences within each. Although Facebook and YouTube have no time limits, Instagram and Vine do—60 seconds and 6 seconds, respectively. Moreover, both Instagram and Vine videos "loop," meaning they never stop playing in a user's feed until a user moves on to something else, while YouTube's videos stop after one play (and usually transition to another, somewhat related video). Facebook's videos also do not loop automatically, but they do start playing automatically with the sound off once they are in your News Feed, which has led some content creators to use subtitles for Facebook (users must click on the video for sound).[12] For example, as part of the Captain Obvious campaign, Hotels.com created a satirical Facebook video calling attention to the autoplay. It is most pleasing to the ear if watched on silent because, as the Captain mentions here, he has no idea what to do with those ivories. Setting up the joke, the two frames leading up to the one shown here are: "Ads autoplay silently on Facebook . . . which is good for you . . . "

"...because I don't know how to play piano..."

These specific content formats have implications for how you can create and then distribute your social video content. Other examples of content format types include vertical versus horizontal visuals (video or image) and support for animated gifs.

Language Norms

How do people communicate on a social media platform? For example, Line, the social messaging service popular in Japan, is perhaps best known for its stickers and emojis, leading CEO Jeanie Han to claim, "We've created a whole new language."[13] For example, rather than praise a friend for a job well done in text, why not send a cartoon-like image with musical icon Paul McCartney flashing a big thumbs up with a "good job" quote? That's right, as part of the 46,000 stickers and emojis available on the platform, brands like Coca-Cola, KFC, and Sir McCartney now also have their own themed stickers.[14]

Other language norms include hashtags, which not only help organize topics of conversation on platforms such as Twitter, Instagram, Facebook, and Tumblr but also serve as another form of expression (#sorrynotsorry). Another example is

captions, which usually accompany and enhance the storyline of a video or photo on content-sharing social networks.

Design Tools

What design tools are available through the platform? For example, Tumblr gives its users considerable latitude to develop their own "theme" for their blog. The platform offers standard themes, but other themes can be downloaded for free or for purchase through various third-party providers. As a result, Tumblr users have considerable flexibility in how they present their brand and content, based on the tools the platform provides. For the more creative and technically inclined, Tumblr also allows its users to build their own designs on top of their platform. Other examples of design tools include Instagram filters, which can enhance the static photos users upload to the platform, and Snapchat doodles, which, as mentioned, allow users to draw on their snaps.

Mastering the content formats, studying the language norms, and taking advantage of the design tools in ways that are authentic to the platform can go a long way in establishing a credible, interesting, and engaging brand presence on social media. General Electric has repeatedly practiced this principle of tailoring to the platform. One example is their Emoji Science campaign.

CASE STUDY: GENERAL ELECTRIC'S EMOJI SCIENCE EXPERIMENT

General Electric, the 122-year-old primarily B2B brand, has aggressively used social media to enhance their brand's relevance with the Millennial generation. As a covering law, the brand is trying to make science cool. The Emoji Science campaign was one effort in this overall initiative. Working with Bill Nye the Science Guy, a well-known science evangelist, the brand opened up a "pop-up" lab at New York University and hosted a day full of science experiments.[15] The resulting experiments were then shared across social media on Snapchat, Tumblr, YouTube, and other social platforms. Let's look at a few of the examples. Note that in all of them, General Electric tailors to the platform.

Snapchat

Snapchat served as center of the campaign's interactive components. If Snapchat users sent @GeneralElectric a snap with an emoji, then GE would send a snap back with a science experiment bringing to life that emoji. In the example shown here, Emoji scientists combined baking soda and vinegar to fill a heart-shaped balloon as an homage to the broken heart emoji, while also using Snapchat doodles to explain the details.

Tumblr

Tumblr was the home of the campaign's microsite. In contrast to Snapchat, more and different types of content were available on Tumblr, which can support these various formats. The brand took advantage of the flexible design platforms offered by Tumblr and created an interactive Emoji Science periodic table. Clicking on one of the "elements" would bring users to another section of the site for additional information and content in the form of gifs, videos, and photos. If users were looking for a broader and more detailed content experience than Snapchat, Tumblr served that need.[16]

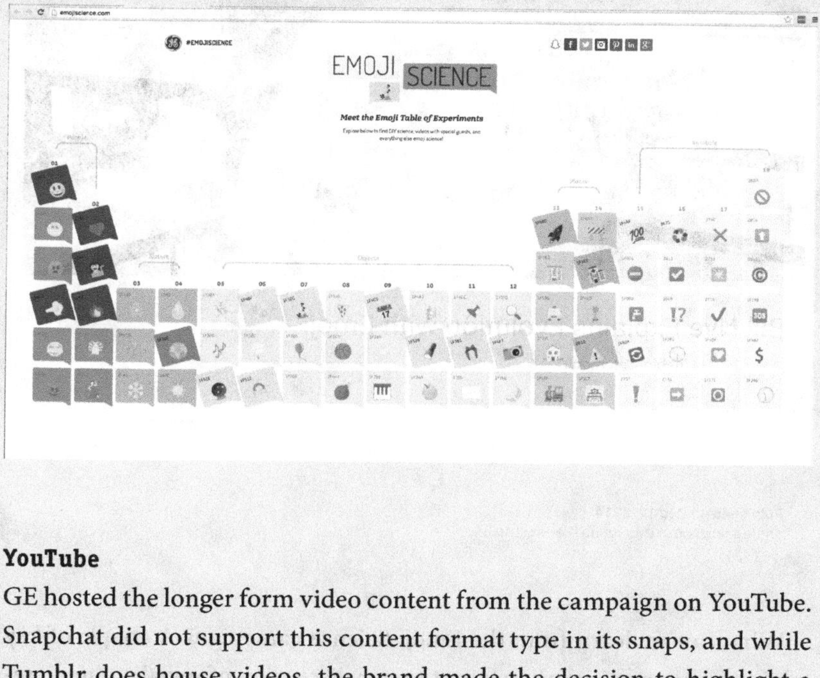

YouTube

GE hosted the longer form video content from the campaign on YouTube. Snapchat did not support this content format type in its snaps, and while Tumblr does house videos, the brand made the decision to highlight a different content experience on that platform. This introductory video with Bill Nye was viewed more than 1 million times on YouTube.[17] GE also linked to it on its Facebook page and Twitter feed to help drive awareness of the campaign and encourage people who may not follow General Electric on Snapchat to add them and start sharing in the initiative.

CONTINUED

CASE STUDY: GENERAL ELECTRIC'S EMOJI SCIENCE EXPERIMENT *CONTINUED*

Undoubtedly, this YouTube video was also a way to reach GE's secondary and tertiary audiences, which could range from potential customers outside their target Millennial demographic to employees to the news and trade media.

What can we learn from the Emoji Science campaign? A couple of key takeaways are particularly relevant to our discussion of social content creation. First, GE created a common content theme across platforms. It was clear that all social content in support of the campaign was operating from the same foundation. Second, GE tailored content to different platforms. GE used the language and style of Snapchat to communicate Emoji Science. On Tumblr, the brand created a rich-media microsite, which that platform can support. And finally, YouTube hosted the longer form versions of the content. An overall content theme that is adapted according to the characteristics of each platform was a winning social content approach for GE.

Social Content Development

Some of the best content ideas will always be created seemingly out of thin air from brilliant minds. Creative directors Don Draper and Peggy Olsen in the fictional AMC series *Mad Men* each happened upon their breakthrough advertising concepts with a mix of intuition, experience, and torment. Creative thinking can sometimes just occur, which can be a magnificent outcome of the human experience.

At the same time, social media has opened up a host of new social content creation possibilities and approaches. The reasons? First, we now have more information (often in real time) about what our audience likes, dislikes, and wants to share. This data can serve as an additional input in the creative process. Depending on your organization, you can calibrate how influential social data should be in content development, balancing it against other factors such as brand personality and values, gut instinct, and prior experience. A second reason is that people are now content creators themselves. The era of three television networks gave way to 100 cable networks. Today, every person is effectively her own media network. For social content creators, this means there are new types of creative collaborations available from any number of content creators.

In light of these data- and user-generated content trends, there are three social content development approaches that can be integrated into your own creation process: data driven, cocreated, and curated. None of these approaches is mutually exclusive. An organization can use all of them at any given time. In fact, because of the extreme demand for constant new content, a multifaceted approach to development is likely necessary for a wide variety of brands. Let's look at each in more detail.

Data-Driven Content

This form of content development leverages audience, platform, and brand insights to develop new creative content. This idea is not unique to the social media space, as it has been applied to other forms of content as well. Netflix famously developed its breakthrough global series *House of Cards* by analyzing the data of what its users watched to inform its initial $100 million investment in two seasons of the drama.[18]

Although insights can be used more longitudinally, data-driven content can also inform the development of original content in real time. For example, Oreo set up a social listening center for the 2014 Super Bowl that just about redefined marketing, at least for a short while. After the lights unexpectedly went out in the New Orleans Superdome, Oreo quickly created the graphic shown here and posted it on Twitter. It was real-time marketing arguably at its finest point. Because they were prepared to produce content that was contextual and in real time, Oreo capitalized on what people were talking about and reaped millions of impressions from the Super Bowl.[19]

Another example of data-driven original content is from Nissan Luxury Restored. A car owner posted on Craigslist that he was selling his 1996 Nissan Maxima. Accompanying the post was a humorous and ironic YouTube video he created entitled "Luxury Defined," positioning the "land-ship-yacht" as an elegant and classy product. Because of the uniqueness of his sales pitch, it started gaining traction. Through Nissan's social media listening tools, the brand picked up on the listing and decided to buy the car and remodel it, based on input from Nissan customers. They also donated $1,000 to the owner's charity of choice. By monitoring its brand mentions, Nissan sourced a creative and relevant new content idea via social media. In turn, Nissan's customers gave the brand positive feedback for its actions.[20]

Memes are an additional data-driven opportunity for content creators. Depending on what topics are trending, brands have the opportunity to capitalize on an existing conversation. This approach, also known as "meme jacking," has been successful for smaller organizations seeking to gain more exposure. Hipchat, a local startup in San Francisco, leveraged the Y U No meme and created the offline billboard shown here to drive brand awareness. In part because of the online pickup of the story, Hipchat's meme garnered free media coverage in key outlets like TechCrunch, an increase in online searches for the company, and new customers. Based on the comparatively low cost of the billboard, the company achieved a healthy return on investment.[21]

Of course, there are risks with data-driven content. If your organization is tonally off when trying to capitalize on these trends, the ramifications can be significant. As we'll discuss in chapter 8 on crisis, there have been many instances of tweets gone awry. One in particular was DiGiorno's insensitive tweet about #WhyIStayed. At the time, the hashtag was trending as part of a platform-wide conversation about domestic violence, spurred by the domestic violence scandal involving former NFL player Ray Rice. DiGiorno's claimed that it did not understand the broader context of the trending hashtag before tweeting (victims of domestic violence were discussing the reasons #WhyIStayed or #WhyILeft), but in the end the damage was done. The tweet was seen as tone deaf and roundly criticized.[22]

Consulting the data on what your audiences are thinking and saying can be a helpful way to create new, contextually relevant content. At the same time, it does have some risks. Most notably, being too data-driven can potentially stymie other creative thought and activity. Striking the right balance between gut creative instinct and audience insights will be an ongoing dilemma in social content development.

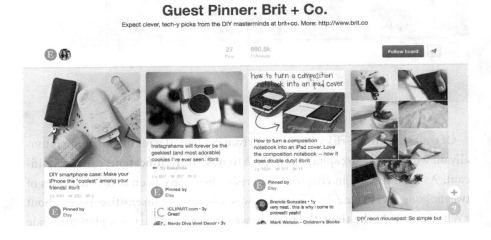

Cocreated Content

Cocreation, working with others to create content together, is the second content development approach. This approach has a number of advantages. It can give you more content and sources of creativity than you can create yourself. It can cut down on operational expenses. And it includes your audience (or representatives of your audience) in the final product, which can help inspire advocacy and strengthen loyalty to your brand.

Etsy is an online marketplace for independent designers, artists, and other small businesses to sell their products. The company must not only attract customers but also suppliers. Without suppliers, of course, it has nothing to sell, so to make sure its suppliers have a platform to be successful, Etsy has implemented a

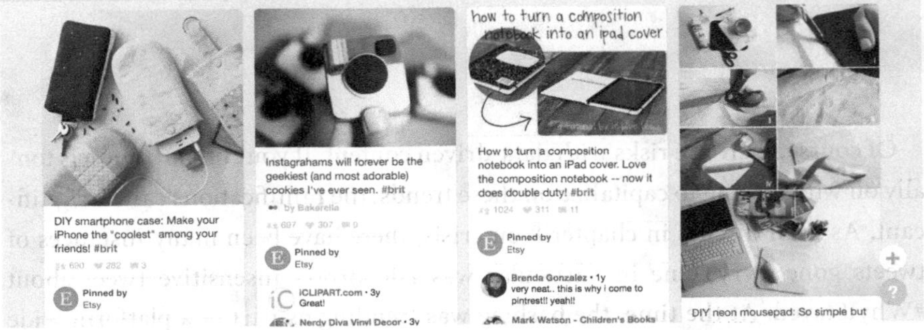

cocreated content strategy for social media. For starters, they use the goods and services of their providers/business partners as a consistent source of content. They also often bring in guest pinners on their Pinterest page to help run the page for a day, which the example here from Etsy supplier Brit + Co illustrates.[23] This gives the Etsy brand another authentic voice in the form of its business owners. This cocreation strategy is not only on brand, but it serves a functional purpose: to highlight the platform's wide range of creative and innovative products.

Another example is in the television industry, with Jimmy Fallon's regular *Tonight Show* hashtags segment. He and his team create a hashtag and then challenge their viewers to craft a funny tweet in response to it. The best tweets are shared on air and via Fallon's social media platforms. Following are a couple of tweets from the #myworstcar hashtag. Fallon is involving audience members in the show, while still maintaining the relatively high standards of humor his viewers have come to expect.

#MYWORSTCAR
BuddySaanGuy
The horn would honk on its own sometimes. So when it did I would just wave my hand out the window like I had seen a friend. #MyWorstCar
PirateKnits
My air vents didn't work because they were blocked up by a squirrel nest. #MyWorstCar

Of course, there are risks with cocreation as well. The quality of user content may not meet the standards of your brand or fit with the creative theme you are exploring. There may also be legal restrictions with intellectual property that organizations will have to navigate. In addition, you should be thoughtful about what you ask customers to create for you. Ideally, the content is inherently social and includes a share proposition. However, if you can overcome these barriers, the cocreated content development approach can result in on-brand, low-cost, and effective social content.

Curated Content

Curated content is the practice of selecting, surfacing, and framing the content of others. Of course, this does not mean that the content is not credited. The h/t (hat tip) is a universal norm in social media. However, with the proper crediting, curating can be a useful source of content, especially if you do not have a budget for original content or if you are just starting out in the social media space.

Upworthy is one example of an organization that has built its social content strategy—and its brand—through curation. Celebrating positive moments in society on a daily basis, Upworthy shares ("passes along") inspiring stories its staff members find from all over the web.[24] Upworthy, of course, gives credit to the original source, and the quid pro quo of clicks and traffic to the home platform is in effect.

There are also downsides to the curatorial approach. If you devote your content strategy solely to curation, you will lack original content that you solely own, which is usually more profitable and sustainable. Although it grew initially through a curation approach, Upworthy eventually made the shift to investing in and creating original video content, a move that positioned the company for continued growth.[25] In the end, strong, original content is what will help your brand and social media strategy stand out in the marketplace. Curation can be an important starting point or complementary content approach, but for the vast majority of organizations, the big hits may not be achievable without an original and/or cocreated content development strategy.

Recap: Creating and Evolving

When Jim Henson, the creative visionary behind the Muppets, first developed the internationally known Kermit the Frog, Kermit barely resembled the green friend many of us now know and love. Kermit's color was blue, and he wasn't even a frog; he was more like a lizard. Yet, over time, as Henson worked on Kermit and refined the concept, he eventually landed on the version famous today.[26] Henson's experience is a reminder that great creative content is not developed overnight; rather, it is the result of hard work and discipline. The same can be said for creating social content as part of your social media management efforts.

In this chapter, we explored strategies and best practices of creating social content, platform-appropriate content designed to be shared. First, we identified the building blocks of social content—a clear message shaped by a distinct voice and a strong share proposition. We also discussed the importance of tailoring to the platform, an acknowledgment that each social platform is different and requires a customized approach. Finally, we discussed several content development approaches that take advantage of newfound audience data and content creators in social media.

By applying the principles from this chapter, you will be in a position to create remarkable and shareworthy content that is aligned with your platforms, brand, audience, and goals. However, if you do not distribute it effectively, then you may not maximize the potential for audience engagement. Not to worry. The next chapter on social distribution will equip you with a set of distribution strategies to ensure that your content breaks through and engages your audiences.

Your Turn: Represent Your Culture

It's time for you to apply some of the social content principles we just discussed. Think broadly about your culture, which can refer to your school, your family, your company, or any other collective group of people that has influenced who you are.

Your challenge is to create a piece of social content that represents your culture. Here are the ground rules:

- It can be any content type: image, meme, gif, video, Vine, and so on.
- It can be for any platform, as long as you tailor the content to it accordingly.

Create it and then present it to your colleagues. You might show it to them first and then see if they can discern (1) your key message, (2) your voice, and (3) your share proposition. (Note: this is also a reminder to leverage the building blocks of social content to create your own.) Good luck.

Notes

1. "Technology Giants in Flap over Gift Envelopes," *Beijing International*, accessed September 6, 2015, http://www.ebeijing.gov.cn/BeijingInformation/BeijingNewsUpdate/t1380646.htm.
2. Qu Yunxu and Wang Qionghui, "Not in Holiday Spirit: Alibaba and Tencent Spar over Virtual Hongbao," *Caixin*, February 4, 2015, http://english.caixin.com/2015-02-04/100781582.html.
3. Gabriel Wildau, "Tencent Beats Alibaba in 'Red Envelope' App War," *Financial Times*, February 27, 2015, http://www.ft.com/cms/s/0/c39c96c6-be2a-11e4-8cf3-00144feab7de.html#axzz3eSvD6omh.
4. Brian Koerber, "Royal Family Shares Photo of Princess Charlotte with Prince George, Internet Loses It," *Mashable*, June 6, 2015, http://mashable.com/2015/06/06/princess-charlotte-prince-george-photo/#mIkgl64s9mkI; Sam Haysom, "This Is Why You Should Never Let an Elephant Sneak Up on You," *Mashable*, September 7, 2015, http://mashable.com/2015/09/07/grumpy-elephant-headbutts-tourists/#8hSPWUHZFkk5; Chloe Bryan, "12 Questions to Ask Yourself before Commenting Online," *Mashable*, September 6, 2015, http://mashable.com/2015/09/06/questions-before-comments/#uVgkrFb59ikW.
5. "Lowe's: Inspiring Home Improvement on Pinterest," *Pinterest for Business*, accessed September 13, 2015, https://business.pinterest.com/en/success-stories/lowe%E2%80%99s.
6. Jonah Berger, *Contagious: Why Things Catch On* (New York: Simon & Schuster, 2013).
7. Andrea Lehr, "New Data: What Types of Content Perform Best on Social Media?" *Hubspot*, February 2, 2015, http://blog.hubspot.com/marketing/content-social-media-popularity.
8. Simon Crerar, "19 Surreal Places in Australia to Visit before You Die," *BuzzFeed*, September 4, 2015, http://www.buzzfeed.com/simoncrerar/surreal-places-in-oz-to-visit-before-you-die.
9. Saabira Chaudhuri, "Unilever Gets More Than a Name in Dollar Shave Club," *Wall Street Journal*, July 20, 2016, http://www.wsj.com/articles/unilever-gets-more-than-a-name-in-dollar-shave-club-1469013915.
10. Marguerite McNeal, "The Secret to Viral Success," *Marketing Research* 24, no. 4 (Winter 2012): 10–15; Karen Nelson-Field, *Viral Marketing: The Science of Sharing* (South Melbourne, Vic.: Oxford University Press, 2013).
11. Berger, *Contagious*, 108-112.
12. David Griner, "Hotels.com Created a Facebook Autoplay Ad That's Infinitely Better without Sound," *AdWeek*, June 2, 2015, http://www.adweek.com/adfreak/hotelscom-created-facebook-autoplay-ad-thats-infinitely-better-without-sound-165133.
13. Christopher Heine, "With 1.7 Million New Users a Day, Will This App Be the Next to Take America by Storm?" *AdWeek*, accessed September 6, 2015, http://www.adweek.com/news/technology/17-million-new-users-day-will-app-be-next-take-america-storm-163262.
14. Ibid.
15. General Electric, *Meet the Emoji Table of Experiments - #EmojiScience*, YouTube, December 16, 2014, https://www.youtube.com/watch?v=Vyc8eMXas5E.
16. "GE Emoji Science," accessed September 13, 2015, http://emojiscience.com/.
17. The Watercooler, *Bill Nye Explains Evolution with Emoji*, December 12, 2014, https://www.youtube.com/watch?v=PGRRXKek8Go.
18. Brian Stelter, "'House of Cards' Arrives as a Netflix Series," *The New York Times*, January 18, 2013, http://www.nytimes.com/2013/01/20/arts/television/house-of-cards-arrives-as-a-netflix-series.html.
19. Jennifer Rooney, "Behind the Scenes of Oreo's Real-Time Super Bowl Slam Dunk," *Forbes*, February 4, 2013, http://www.forbes.com/sites/jenniferrooney/2013/02/04/behind-the-scenes-of-oreos-real-time-super-bowl-slam-dunk/.
20. "Sold! Nissan Purchases 1996 Maxima from Brilliant Craigslist Ad Is up for a Shorty Award!" accessed July 9, 2015, http://industry.shortyawards.com/nominee/7th_annual/oZr/nissan-and-a-1996-maxima; Nissan, *Nissan 1996 Maxima—Luxury Restored—Luke Aker's Story*, November 18, 2014, https://www.youtube.com/watch?v=oYN_gTuobrk.
21. Pete Curley, "A Tale of a Ridiculous Billboard," *HipChat Blog*, June 23, 2011, https://blog.hipchat.com/2011/06/23/a-tale-of-a-ridiculous-billboard/.
22. Laura Stampler, "DiGiorno Used a Hashtag about Domestic Violence to Sell Pizza," *Time*, September 9, 2014, http://time.com/3308861/digiorno-social-media-pizza/.

23. "Guest Pinner: Brit + Co," *Pinterest*, accessed September 14, 2015, https://www.pinterest.com/etsy/guest-pinner-brit-co/..
24. Derek Thompson, "Upworthy: I Thought This Website Was Crazy, but What Happened Next Changed Everything," *The Atlantic*, November 14, 2013, http://www.theatlantic.com/business/archive/2013/11/upworthy-i-thought-this-website-was-crazy-but-what-happened-next-changed-everything/281472/.
25. Ricardo Bilton, "A Year into Its New Original Content Strategy, Upworthy Is Focusing on Do-Good Videos Instead of Clickbait," *Nieman Lab*, April 13, 2016, http://www.niemanlab.org/2016/04/a-year-into-its-new-original-content-strategy-upworthy-is-focusing-on-do-good-videos-instead-of-clickbait/.
26. Brian Jay Jones, *Jim Henson: The Biography* (New York: Ballantine Books, 2013).

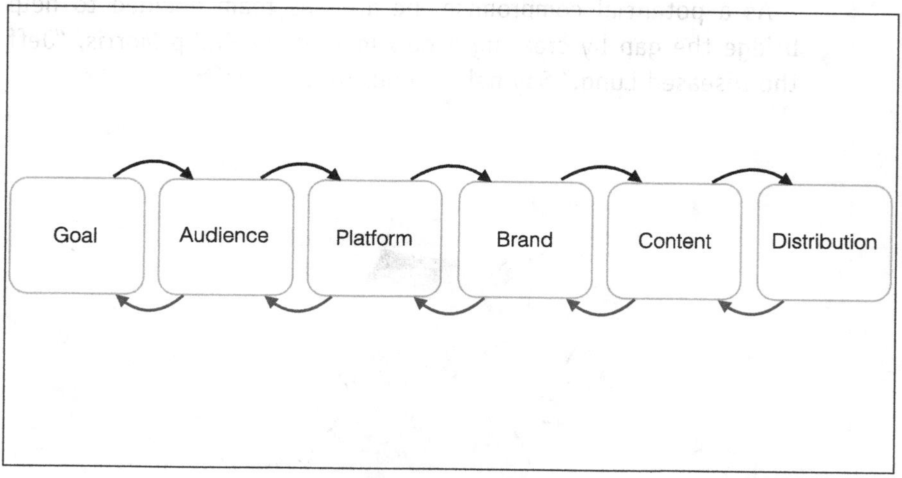

6 Distributing Social Content

Comedian John Oliver is nothing if not controversial. The host of the HBO show *Last Week Tonight* often uses his weekly pulpit to advance causes in the public interest. One week he selected the tobacco industry as his target. Although smoking rates have decreased significantly in the United States, due in part to stringent regulations on advertising, Oliver reported that Philip Morris Inc. has focused on parts of the world with less oversight in order to grow market share.[1]

Oliver and his team had a problem with that strategy—and thought their audience should as well. But as both an entertainer and pragmatist, Oliver wasn't about to identify a problem without proposing a solution. Seeking to demonstrate his understanding of the issues, he noted that governments are looking to communicate the health hazards of smoking, whereas the tobacco industry is seeking ways to market their products.

As a potential compromise, he and his team decided to help bridge the gap by creating a new mascot for Philip Morris, "Jeff the Diseased Lung." Say hello to our readers, Jeff:

A cross between the Marlboro Man and, indeed, a diseased lung, Jeff served both as a television element and, just as importantly, as valuable social content. This image would become the centerpiece of a cross-platform initiative that rallied support across the globe and brought the still-new show millions of impressions in free exposure across a variety of media platforms, including Twitter, Facebook, and the news media.[2]

Although Jeff the Diseased Lung was a compelling (and startling) mascot, the image alone would not be enough to attract the attention its creators intended. Behind the Jeff movement was a coordinated cross-platform distribution strategy that maximized its potential impact. For starters, in near real time, as soon as the mention of Jeff and the corresponding #JeffWeCan hashtag occurred on the show, this tweet from the *Last Week Tonight* Twitter account complemented the on-air messaging.[3]

LAST WEEK TONIGHT
Last Week Tonight
@LastWeekTonight
Following
Let's make Jeff the Diseased Lung the new face of #Marlboro by getting #JeffWeCan to trend worldwide!
RETWEETS
10,525
LIKES
4,108
11:30 PM - 15 Feb 2015

In part because of the real-time TV mention and the strong and clear call to action to get #JeffWeCan trending worldwide, audiences began supporting the cause in a number of ways. Retweets of the launch tweet reached the thousands. One user, David Palomino, was so inspired by the movement's message that he decided to send his first tweet. Meanwhile, other people reappropriated the Jeff mascot and created additional content as part of this movement. In this sense, Jeff was an asset that the community could mold and shape into something of its own. In addition, to close the loop on the interaction, the *Last Week Tonight* Twitter feed retweeted its supporters, recognizing them for their contributions to the cause.

What were the results? The initial goal of #JeffWeCan trending worldwide was achieved within 24 hours. Over the course of four days, the YouTube video of the segment on the *Last Week Tonight with John Oliver* YouTube channel had more than 2.7 million views, which is significant given its running time of more than 15 minutes. There were also 65,000 mentions of #JeffWeCan on Twitter alone during this short time period.[4] Meanwhile, the

David Palomino
@thefriendlydave
Follow
First tweet! Totally worth it. #JeffWeCan @LastWeekTonight
RETWEETS
67
LIKES
108
11:47 AM - 16 Feb 2015

Derek Montilla
@Cap_Kaveman
Follow
Marlboro can have this one for free too. #JeffWeCan @LastWeekTonight
Come to where the flavor is.
Come to Marlboro Country.
Marlboro
You get a lot to like with a Marlboro.
RETWEETS
138
LIKES
75
9:43 AM - 16 Feb 2015

articles written in the mainstream media about this campaign ranged from *The Wall Street Journal* to *USA Today*.[5] All told, the Jeff We Can initiative was more than just a funny image. It was a low-cost, cross-platform marketing campaign that drove awareness and sampling of the show in ways that traditional advertising could not.

• • •

This chapter is about distributing your social media initiatives and how content and distribution must work together for effective social media management. The mantra "If you build it, they will come" does not always apply in social media. If you release content in social media and expect it to go viral, you will be disappointed more often than not. To ensure your content reaches and engages your target audiences, it's important to also devise distribution strategies to help it break through like the Jeff We Can example demonstrated here. To equip you with core marketing and distribution strategies for social media, we will be addressing three key steps: (1) inventorying social media marketing assets, (2) deciding on social media marketing campaigns, and (3) implementing and executing these campaigns from start to finish. By the end of this chapter, you will have a set of social media–specific marketing strategies to apply to your initiatives. Let's begin our work with a discussion of inventorying your marketing assets.

Inventorying Social Media Marketing Assets

Where can you reach your audience? This fundamental challenge has influenced the work of marketers for decades. In the social media era, this question is as relevant as ever. What's different is the sheer number of media devices and platforms where people spend their time. This means that firms must make choices on which vehicles to use to reach their audiences.

To help in this decision-making process, an important first step in most social media marketing plans is to inventory the media assets you have at your disposal. You can group your assets into four main categories—organic, sponsored, shared, and influencer media. Some of you may be familiar with the model of owned, paid, and earned media, which have helped countless marketers develop and execute effective campaigns.[6] The terms "organic," "sponsored," "shared," and "influencer" evolve and tailor this model specifically to the social media space. Let's define each in more detail:

- *Organic media*—distribute your message through your official social media platforms.
- *Shared media*—distribute your message through your audiences.
- *Sponsored media*—distribute your message through paid advertising products and services.
- *Influencer media*—distribute your message through a well-known or influential person.

Let's examine each of these media assets in more detail and the differences between them.

Organic Media

Organic media refers to the distribution of messages through a firm's branded presences on third-party social media platforms. Examples include posts to a brand page on Facebook or videos uploaded on a company's YouTube channel.

The primary advantage of organic media is the cost. Save for the resources to create the content in the first place, the cost of distributing it is zero. A brand, for instance, does not have to pay Twitter for each tweet it sends. Another advantage is the relative control a brand has over its messaging. Everything from the text to visual content is within the brand's control; Twitter does not tell a brand what it can or cannot tweet. (How the audience will react is another matter.)

Organic media also has limitations. For one, if your organization does not have the quantity or quality of audience on your social presence to drive business impact, then this media asset will have less value. Additionally, although most social platforms give brands the opportunity to reach their followers organically, social networks tend to have in place barriers (either through deliberate strategic choices or inherent platform characteristics) that restrict the possibilities of organic reach. For example, in its effort to increase usage and monetize its platform, Facebook modified its News Feed algorithm to prioritize content from friends and family versus content from publishers and brands, presenting more difficult challenges for firms to reach their audiences organically.[7] Brands face similar organic reach challenges on Twitter, because of the often overwhelming amount of content on the platform and the historical lack of filtering and surfacing of the most relevant tweets to its users. If a brand has 500,000 likes on Facebook and

50,000 followers on Twitter, it is virtually guaranteed that each post or tweet it sends will reach only a fraction of that audience. As a result, brands have to rely on other factors to spread their message for them. This is where shared media comes into play.

Shared Media

Shared media refers to the distribution of your message through your audiences. Examples include a customer liking, commenting, or sharing a post from your social media presence or reappropriating your content and creating something new (as in the Jeff We Can example).

Of all the media assets, shared is the most valuable. For starters, people are more likely to trust recommendations from friends or people they know than formal brand communications.[8] It is also a form of free media. When a brand posts on its Instagram feed and its followers like or repost the photo, the network effect begins—those followers are spreading your message to their followers without you having to pay for that exposure. A free, highly credible message? Yes, please.

Unfortunately, shared media is not that easy. Compared to organic and sponsored media, brands have little control over if—and how—its audiences will respond to and share their messaging, making it difficult to plan for in social media marketing. Thus, relying solely on shared media to distribute your message is a high-risk, high-reward proposition. If your content does not evoke the desired response at the outset, it may never.

Shared media can come from a variety of audience types. Of course, customers tend to be a primary source. Users of Spotify, the music subscription service, can easily share the songs and playlists they're listening to with their friends in Facebook Messenger's threads. An example is on the next page. This process of sharing turns Spotify customers into distribution drivers for the service.[9]

Employees are another potential audience for shared media. According to the Edelman Trust Barometer, customers trust everyday employees more than a CEO.[10] Finally, the media, which can include television, radio, print, and digital news outlets, is an important type of shared media. Increasingly, these organizations have social media news beats that track "what's trending" and then report on social stories through their "mainstream" channels. Interestingly, mainstream media still has a critical role to play in generating visibility and attention for certain social media content and initiatives.

In short, shared media is when your audiences distribute your message for you. Whether it's your customers, employees, or the media, all can play a role in

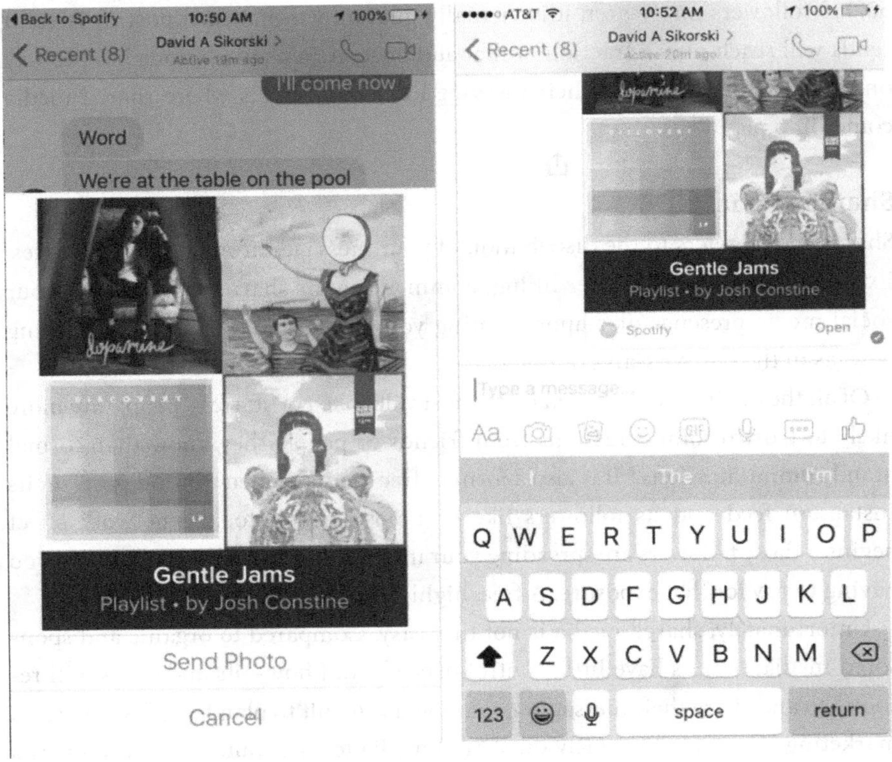

communicating a more credible message than an organic brand post and certainly a more cost-effective message than sponsored media.

Sponsored Media

Sponsored media refers to the distribution of your message through paid advertising products and services. Several types are available in the marketplace, including acquisition, amplification, and native advertising.

The first type of sponsored media is acquisition advertising. These ads help brands increase the following of their presence on third-party social platforms. Think number of Twitter followers. They can be helpful in growing the scale of your audience and potentially acquiring your specific target, which you can then message organically through your brand page/feed. However, because of the organic reach issues we just discussed, the challenge with this approach is that acquiring fans does not necessarily mean they will always see your message.

A second type of sponsored media is amplification advertising. These include the growing number of advertising products that social networks offer, including, but not limited to, sponsored posts, promoted tweets, and promoted pins. Essentially, these products help brands overcome the challenges in organic reach. Based on the sophisticated targeting techniques and tools that social

platforms now offer, brands can pay for their intended target audiences to see their message. The amplified post often begins as an organic post on the brand page/feed and then the social platform "boosts" the post. This feature is useful, especially for organic posts that are not gaining the traction on their own and need some assistance.

The third type of sponsored media is native advertising. Although social platforms have been monetizing through both acquisition and amplification types of paid media assets, media companies and other content creators have been leading the movement toward native advertising, also known as sponsored content, in the social media space. This is the practice of presenting advertising as content. Aetna, the insurance company, worked with Buzzfeed's sponsored media group to create a video in support of its Mindfulness campaign. Aetna was not only tapping into Buzzfeed's creative content expertise but also the distribution network it has developed, which helped this video receive more than 1 million views, which is likely more than Aetna could have achieved on its own.

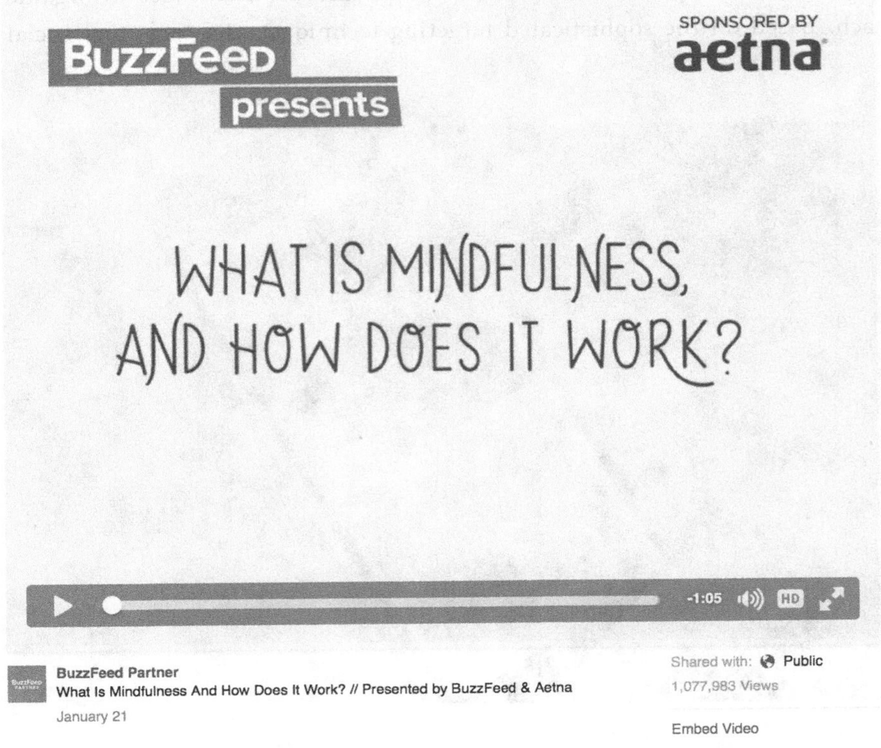

The advantage of the native advertising format is it can be engaging and interesting content, which can increase the chances an audience will actually consume it rather than skip it. Moreover, because native advertising typically appears in users' "feeds" alongside content from family and friends, it can be immune to new ad blocking technology, which is threatening the economics of other forms of digital advertising such as display ads.[11] The challenge with native advertising is the blurred line between editorial and advertising, a complex dynamic that the FTC is monitoring.[12] Notice on the Buzzfeed post shown here that it is posted not on Buzzfeed's master brand page, but on its Buzzfeed Partner page, the home for all its sponsored content. This is an attempt to clarify the line between content and advertising. Despite the blurred lines, native advertising has emerged as an increasingly relevant sponsored media product and is a key consideration in any social media asset inventory.

Sponsored media assets such as acquisition, amplification, and native advertising will only increase in use, as media spending continues to shift to social media. However, brands will have to contend with an undeniable fact of marketing—some audiences are repelled by ads, particularly in the social media space. This means that social media marketing campaigns will need to carefully balance the amount of sponsored media they use versus other media assets, like influencer media.

Influencer Media

Influencer media refers to the distribution of your message through a well-known person. Different from targeting influential customers to stimulate shared media, influencer media is a paid media asset, in which brands pay social media celebrities to create content that promotes their messaging and distribute it to their social media following.

Influencers are akin to the celebrity endorsement industry that has been in operation for decades. These are social media users that are creating unique or unexpected content and gaining rapid widespread attention and respect from the specific communities. For example, the Vine platform has spawned a number of new celebrities that create 6-second videos for brands.[13] The advantage is that someone other than the brand is communicating your message but at a scale that is likely greater than what you can achieve through shared media alone. It also has the potential to be more credible and actionable than if the brand communicated their message themselves. One challenge brands face with influencers is no different from other marketing techniques: is the investment worth it? For example, celebrity entertainer Selena Gomez reportedly can charge an estimated $550,000 for one post across her Facebook, Instagram, and Twitter feeds.[14] In the next chapter, we'll explore ways to answer this question.

Shonduras is an influencer who has built a strong following on Snapchat. Because he is an adventure seeker and showcases his unpredictable daily activities, he partners with brands that fit his content and style. One brand was Marriott, which sent him on a trip to Bangkok based on an informal poll of his followers.[15] He then chronicled his travels via Snapchat and Twitter with his fans following along, perhaps living vicariously through him, as the exchange here with his follower about the favorite part of the day's trip illustrates. Finally, he is up front with his fans about any brand partnership, as he does in the post here, so as not to mislead his fans as to why he is promoting Marriott. This transparency has become critical for his brand and business.[16]

Marriott Hotels
@Marriott
Follow
We challenge you, @shonduras, to the ultimate @Snapchat trip! Let your followers choose whether you to go Bangkok, London or Berlin. Accept?
RETWEETS 28
LIKES 88
9:04 AM - 17 Dec 2014

Shonduras @Shonduras · 21 Dec 2014
What was your favorite part about today's snapchat adventure with @Marriott I'm curious!? GO!
Patri T.
@patrixtirado
Follow
@Shonduras @Marriott i fell in love with this little tiger
RETWEET 1
LIKES 3

Shonduras
@Shonduras
Following
Huge thanks to @Marriott for hooking it up!! This place is bomb!
#Bangkok
RETWEETS
23
LIKES
103
3:16 AM - 20 Dec 2014

There are many other examples beyond Shonduras. Outlets like CAA and theAudience have developed businesses around brokering deals with influencers to sponsor various brands.[17] This is celebrity endorsement updated for the digital age. But similar to native advertising, the FTC is keeping a close eye on the influencer marketing industry. Department store Lord & Taylor ran an Instagram campaign promoting a new line of clothes through Instagram influencers who were paid for their services. The FTC took issue with this approach and brought charges against Lord & Taylor because it did not clearly communicate to its customers that the influencers were paid to advertise the product. Per the FTC, all posts from this campaign and others like it should disclose that it is an advertisement. Lord & Taylor eventually settled with the FTC, but it served as a warning for other companies looking to leverage influencer media.[18]

Social media marketing campaigns can include a mix of all four assets—organic, shared, sponsored, and influencer—but it is not essential. Depending on the goal of your initiative and how much you have to spend, it might be possible to rely only on organic and shared. But sometimes, bringing paid assets like sponsored and influencer media into the mix will pay dividends. In the next section, we'll take a look at a variety of campaign possibilities that use different combinations of these assets to distribute social media content.

Deciding on Social Media Marketing Campaigns

Now that you have evaluated your media assets, the next step is to coordinate these assets and plan your campaign. Depending on your goals, audience, and budget, you can consider three general types of social marketing campaigns: (1) on-platform, (2) cross-platform, and (3) trans-media. It is important to note that all media assets—organic, shared, sponsor, and influencer—are relevant and can be used with each campaign type. Let's look at the three campaign possibilities in more detail.

On-Platform Campaigns

On-platform is a campaign executed primarily on a single social media platform. It leverages a combination of organic, shared, sponsored, and influencer media assets to increase the reach and engagement of content within the platform.

One example of an on-platform campaign is The Signal Tumblr page by Lexus.[19] According to its market research, the Lexus brand had become too stodgy and not edgy enough for its target customers, upscale Generation X and Generation Y buyers. To help shift their target's perceptions of the brand, Lexus turned to Tumblr, a blog-meets-social-network platform to reach and engage their target. In doing so, they launched The Signal Tumblr page. Importantly, the focus of the page was not about the new 2014 Lexus IS, which was the end product, but about the lifestyle surrounding the car. It was a fashion magazine that emphasized style and design, two core characteristics that Lexus believed their target valued.

The brand took advantage of organic, shared, sponsored, and influencer assets to drive awareness and interest in the campaign. For starters, the brand posted its lifestyle-based content regularly to the Tumblr page, organically reaching its existing followers. Because the content was more entertaining and useful than car advertisements, it stimulated shared media among its audience. In addition, it amplified its organic and shared efforts with sponsored posts on Tumblr. These ads were displayed on the Tumblr homepage and resulted in millions of impressions, which helped contribute to more than 85,000 notes (e.g., the combination of likes and reblogs) for the campaign overall. Finally, they leveraged influencer media, as fashion model and blogger Coco Rocha reblogged to her followers The Signal's content featuring her.[20]

The Signal by Lexus is one example of a company using all four media assets on a single platform. With every post they send daily, social media managers are applying a more scaled-down approach of the on-platform campaign, relying on organic and shared media to increase reach and engagement. Whether it's the sophisticated campaign like Lexus or the daily distribution of social content, the on-platform campaign is the most frequent campaign type. The potential limitation is campaign reach, which is why for certain goals and initiatives, you might consider a cross-platform campaign.

Cross-Platform Campaigns

Cross-platform campaigns refer to marketing efforts that use multiple social platforms in the ecosystem to distribute content. For example, a brand uses its Facebook page, Pinterest page, and YouTube channel to promote a campaign. Combining assets across platforms can be particularly useful in reinforcing key messages in such a cluttered marketplace.

As an example of a car company taking a different approach, Mercedes-Benz capitalized on the cross-platform possibilities with a Facebook and Instagram collaboration. (To be fair, Facebook owns Instagram, and the two platforms are intended to work seamlessly together.) When launching the GLA SUV, the Mercedes Benz team sought to drive awareness, purchase consideration, and website traffic among a Millennial audience. To do so, taking inspiration from the popular #ThingsOrganizedNeatly hashtag on Instagram, they worked with several Instagram photographers to create their own versions of what they would pack in their GLA, otherwise known as #GLApacked. One of the Instagrammers was influencer Theron Humphrey of @ThisWildIdea, who posted on his own account.

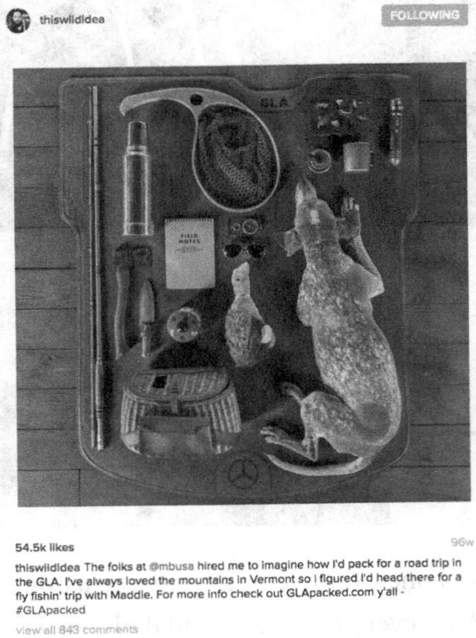
thiswildidea
FOLLOWING
54.5k likes
96w
thiswildidea The folks at @mbusa hired me to imagine how I'd pack for a road trip in the GLA. I've always loved the mountains in Vermont so I figured I'd head there for a fly fishin' trip with Maddie. For more info check out GLApacked.com y'all - #GLApacked
view all 843 comments

●●●●○ AT&T
6:31 AM
97%
mbusa
Sponsored
19433 likes
mbusa @ThisWildIdea took the all-new GLA and his dog Maddie to VT for some fly fishing and acrobatics. Where would you take the GLA? #GLApacked
view all 343 comments
Like
Comment

Mercedes also posted organically and sponsored this same content on its own Instagram feed, and they used their Facebook page to help amplify the story as well. As a result, the Mercedes Benz team reported significant increases in website visits to the GLA SUV product page, where customers could explore the product further.[21]

Cross-platform campaigns sometimes do not need paid components to them. Another way of executing cross-media campaigns is relying simply on the organic assets. The shoe company Vans offers a simple, but instructive example. Vans has multiple social platforms: Tumblr page, Facebook page, Twitter feed, Instagram feed, and YouTube channel. When they announced their new product collaboration with Disney and the 101 Dalmatian shoes, they coordinated it across all their social channels. The core content was, naturally, actual Dalmatians with shoes, and the brand adapted this content for each platform. For example, Tumblr featured an animated gif of a puppy playing in the shoes, Instagram included a photo with the #DisneyAndVans hasthag, YouTube hosted a 15-second video of the puppies playing in the shoes, and one of the posts on the Vans Facebook page drove fans to the online store. Importantly, each post was slightly different and tailored specifically to the platform.

Vans
October 27, 2015 ·
The Disney and Vans 101 Dalmatians collection has arrived just in time for the holidays. Shop now online or find a store near you.
Disney and Vans | 101 Dalmatians
VANS.COM
284 Likes 30 Comments 45 Shares
Share

Cross-platform campaigns can bring to bear all four types of media assets: organic, shared, sponsored, and influencer. They can work across a couple platforms (as in the Mercedes Benz example) or across a variety of platforms (as in the Vans example). And they can also be executed with or without paid support in the form of sponsored posts or influencer media. The final type of campaign is the trans-media campaign, which usually is a step up from cross-platform campaigns in reach, engagement, and, especially, budget.

Trans-Media Campaigns

Trans-media campaigns integrate other media platforms (e.g., TV, digital, audio, out of home) into the marketing mix to increase reach and engagement. Of course, the budget required for this type of campaign may likely be more than the other two campaigns. But particularly for larger initiatives, employing a trans-media approach could be critical to achieving major goals.

Why are trans-media campaigns relevant? In a media environment where information overload is a persistent challenge, campaigns that reach audiences in multiple channels and at the right time tend to work more effectively than others.[22] As a result, the marketing mix has expanded beyond just television and digital to include social media elements. The challenge then is coordinating all these elements into a coherent and effective campaign, in which each component of the campaign reinforces and supports one another.

One example of a trans-media campaign is the Coca-Cola "Share a Coke" campaign. It originated in Australia in 2011 as a strategy to increase sales, particularly among young people. Coke started printing people's names on cans of Coke and selling them in stores. After the campaign had success in Australia, it expanded to the United States and other markets. At this point the company also created a website that enabled people to create their own virtual personalized coke and share it with their social networks. When people found their own personalized bottle, they also took to social media to post the evidence on platforms using the #shareacoke hashtag. All told, the campaign was a significant success for Coca-Cola across multiple platforms and helped the company reverse the downward trend of sales—at least temporarily—and actually increase sales by 2% in the United States.[23]

Another trans-media campaign example is from the beer company Newcastle and its Band of Brands Super Bowl commercial initiative. Although their campaign is lower budget than Coca Cola's, it was no less noteworthy. Because Newcastle is a beer company, the Super Bowl was an ideal advertising opportunity. The problem was that they couldn't afford it. In 2014, the brand released the "If We Made It"

campaign that imagined what their Super Bowl ad would have been if they had the money to create it.[24] Then, in 2015, the brand decided to actually make an ad for the big game. Invoking the ethos of the "sharing economy," Newcastle reached out to brands like them that would be interested in splitting the cost of the $4.5 million ad. To do so, they created a video to convince other brands to join the cause starring actress Aubrey Plaza from NBC's *Parks and Recreation*. They released it on Facebook and it was shared across social media. As a result, 400 brands reportedly asked to be included. Newcastle finally settled on thirty-seven brands and created the commercial, calling it the band of brands. It ran regionally during the Super Bowl as well as online. The campaign generated millions of shared media impressions, making the stunt more efficient and potentially more effective than if Newcastle bought a Super Bowl spot by themselves.[25]

Cross-platform campaigns can be big budget like Coca Cola, or they can be smaller budget creative options that start in social media like Newcastle's. The key is that both traditional media platforms and social media work together to break through and engage an audience.

The three main categories of social marketing campaigns—on-platform, cross-platform, and trans-media—might also be called small, medium, and large campaigns. When you'll use each depends on your goals and budget, among other factors. Regardless, you will inevitably be employing at least one of these campaign types on a daily basis. Most frequent are on-platform and cross-platform, but a trans-media campaign can also be necessary. Distributing for impact in social media is an ongoing process that requires attention to execution, which is the subject matter of the next section.

Implementing a Social Media Marketing Campaign

In the first part of this chapter, we explored the various media assets you can leverage for a social media marketing campaign. Then we discussed how you can combine various media assets in three different campaign types. Once you have selected the assets and campaign, the final key consideration is implementation.

Implementing a social media marketing campaign is increasingly a real-time activity. Because feedback on social content is instantaneous, social marketers must be prepared to adjust on the fly. This is why the "social media command center" has become a popular physical space within some companies, as it allows key decision makers to monitor campaigns and deploy additional content and resources (like sponsored posts) if the situation calls for it.[26] Whether you have a command center or not, make sure you have easy access to real-time information during the campaign and are nimble enough to adapt on the fly.

To help bring some order to the chaos, implementation for social media marketing campaigns can be summarized into three key phases: the launch phase, the expansion phase, and the iteration phase.

- *Launch phase*—Who starts the campaign? Often the brand or communicator that launches the content can make or break it.
- *Expansion phase*—After the initial push, call upon additional assets in this phase to expand the reach and engagement of the campaign.
- *Iteration phase*—Once you've launched the campaign and used other assets to intensify it, you will gain insights about what platforms and content are working. In this phase you begin to make more substantive adjustments to the campaign.

Let's look at each phase in more detail.

Launch Phase

Who starts the campaign and in what platform is an important consideration, as the authenticity and credibility of the launch can spell the difference between a successful campaign and one that falls flat. With this particular decision, organic, shared, sponsored, and influencer assets are all possibilities. Note that you do not need to only rely on one asset to launch. Multiple assets can serve that function.

- *Organic launch*—Sometimes the best (and only) launch possibility is your brand presence. In the case of GoldieBlox, an engineering-inspired toy company for girls, the organic channel proved to be all that was necessary. They created a YouTube video to introduce people to the idea and help galvanize their Kickstarter campaign. Set to the Beastie Boys anthem "Girls,"[27] the Rube Goldberg–inspired video used stereotypical girl toys, mostly in pink, to demonstrate girls' potential as engineers. Striking a chord on gender equality, shared media propelled the distribution of the video, as both prospective customers and the media shared the content to support the fundamental idea.[28]
- *Shared launch*—You can also consider a shared media approach to initiate your messaging. However, this only works if your content is inherently social. Sleep No More, the immersive theater experience in New York City relied primarily on word-of-mouth, accelerated and amplified through social media, to drive awareness of its show at launch. The show is based on Shakespeare's MacBeth and takes place in the sprawling, five-story McKittrick Hotel. It is an individualized, choose-your-own-adventure experience, and you can follow different characters as the story unfolds. For example, you can be alongside Lady MacBeth when she realizes things can't be undone. No matter how many times you attend, you will have a different experience—and, importantly, a different story to tell your friends.[29] Tapping into the talk value of the show, the Sleep No More team embraced and launched a hashtag #MySleepNoMore to encourage people to share their own experience. Because everyone has a different and remarkable individual story to tell, the audience is initiating and spreading the message on behalf of Sleep No More.
- *Sponsored launch*—Under this model, brands lead with the sponsored media first, just as they would buy advertising space on another medium. Interestingly, when Heineken USA came out with a new Heineken Light ad campaign that featured Neil Patrick Harris, they initially went with a traditional launch on television. Then, a few months later, they decided to relaunch the same exact ads on Facebook first. Heineken found that the Facebook relaunch was more successful than the previous TV campaign.[30] Because of the scale of some social platforms, distributing on social first is an increasingly viable approach, even for larger trans-media campaigns.
- *Influencer launch*—Finally, a company may choose to initiate messaging through an influencer. The music video for #Selfie by the Chainsmokers was one of the most effective influencer campaigns in history. The video

includes cameos by numerous social media influencers, who shared the video with their followers when it was time to launch. It was a significant built-in distribution network that put the video in a position to accumulate more than 400 million views on YouTube.[31]

Whether it's organic, shared, sponsored, or influencer, the launch decision is a key consideration. But it's not the only one. How you will build on and expand the buzz you create from the initial messaging is also an important strategic consideration.

Expansion Phase

Once you've created momentum, how do you keep it going? How should the rest of the messaging be coordinated? In the ideal situation, the launch content that you develop will be strong enough to carry attention for weeks. Unfortunately, this is the exception, not the rule. To distribute for impact, follow-up tactics to intensify the campaign on a consistent basis are also important. Considerations include the following:

- *New content*—To keep a campaign fresh, introduce new content. Although it should be from the same theme, it should be a different creative execution.
- *Additional assets*—Capitalize on ancillary organic, shared, sponsored, or influencer assets that may not have been used in the campaign thus far.
- *Complementary platforms*—If appropriate to your long-term strategy, launch the campaign on other complementary social platforms.
- *Incentives for participation*—Add incentives to encourage participation. This can include contests, giveaways, or a simple recognition and amplification of user-generated content people contribute.
- *Media coverage*—Pitch public relations contacts from traditional and digital media outlets to cover your campaign.

Iteration Phase

In the final phase of iteration, you should have enough quantitative and qualitative data to make decisions on what to do with the campaign. We will spend the next chapter discussing measurement strategies in depth, but within the context of campaign iteration, asking the following questions will inform how you might iterate on your campaign:

- *Reach*—Has the campaign reached the target audience?
- *Engagement*—Is the target audience engaging with the campaign?

- *Sentiment*—How is the target audience responding to the campaign? Positively or negatively?

Based on the answers to these questions, you'll have several options:

- *Maintain*—If you are achieving reach, engagement, and sentiment at the levels you expected, continue the campaign as is.
- *Adjust strategy*—If you have not met expectations on any of these metrics, adjusting your platform, asset, and content mix will be necessary.
- *Add new resources*—It may be that a certain asset type is performing better than you expected, but it could benefit from additional support. For example, an organic post is gaining traction and boosting it with a sponsored media buy could help put it over the top.
- *Introduce a new creative execution*—The campaign may be so successful that a derivative of the same creative theme will be warranted and appreciated by the audience.
- *Conclude*—If all performance metrics are not meeting your expectations, it would be better to cut your losses and move on, applying the lessons to your next campaign.

The launch, expansion, and iteration phases of a social media marketing campaign are fluid and constant. They may take place within minutes of a campaign or across multiple weeks, like in the case of this Old Spice campaign.

CASE STUDY: THE MAN YOUR MAN COULD SMELL LIKE

Facing a heated competitive landscape for men's body wash, Old Spice needed to refresh its marketing strategy. In collaboration with their agency Wieden+Kennedy, they started with the insight that both men and women should be targeted for this product. They invented "The Man Your Man Could Smell Like" (TMYMCSL), a shirtless heartthrob that promised a consolation prize to any woman who bought Old Spice—although she could not trade in her man for the Old Spice guy, at least her man could smell like him. Not only were the strategy sound and the content creative and breakthrough, but the campaign implementation across launch, expansion, and iteration phases was executed in textbook fashion.

The first advertisement, which consisted of TMYMCSL making his pitch on a boat and a horse, initially launched on YouTube to much fanfare. The brand bought sponsored media to help build buzz and also benefited from significant shared media. Then, once it was released on television, the campaign expanded and became an even more powerful cultural sensation, in part because of the media coverage of the character, numerous fans creating their own videos imitating him online, and celebrities (such as Oprah Winfrey and Ellen DeGeneres) singing his praises.

Clearly a success, the Wieden+Kennedy team sought to iterate and extend the life of the campaign. They developed the Response campaign, in which the team would answer questions and comments from fans to TMYMCSL and create short, personalized YouTube videos for individual users in "response." For instance, per Twitter user @Jsbeals' request, TMYMCSL asked his girlfriend to marry him on his behalf.

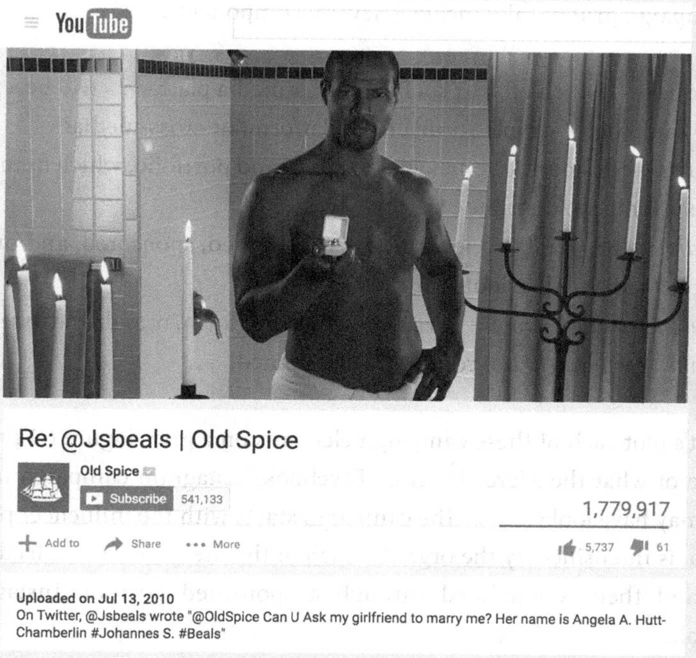
YouTube
Re: @Jsbeals | Old Spice
Old Spice
Subscribe 541,133
1,779,917
Add to
Share
More
5,737
61
Uploaded on Jul 13, 2010
On Twitter, @Jsbeals wrote "@OldSpice Can U Ask my girlfriend to marry me? Her name is Angela A. Hutt-Chamberlin #Johannes S. #Beals"

CONTINUED

CASE STUDY: THE MAN YOUR MAN COULD SMELL LIKE *CONTINUED*

In sum, the Response campaign was one of the more successful YouTube creations ever. And the TMYMCSL campaign overall helped increase sales and move Old Spice into a new position in the marketplace.[32] It is a first-rate example of how goal, audience, platform, brand, content, and distribution work together to achieve strong business results.

Sample Social Media Campaign Grid

From big campaigns like Old Spice's The Man Your Man Could Smell Like to your daily social content efforts, having a social media campaign grid can help organize your distribution plans and thus execute effectively. With so many platforms and content types, this grid can be helpful in keeping your team on track. Let the one shown here be a template to build on and/or modify. You can adjust it to suit your needs on a per project basis.

A campaign grid usually includes several components:

- *Platforms*—which of your social or other media platforms will be a part of the campaign—on-platform, cross-platform, or cross-media?
- *Brands*—considering your social media brand portfolio, which brands will you leverage to distribute the message?
- *Media Assets*—will you leverage organic, shared, sponsored, and/or influencer media to distribute the message?
- *Content*—which content goes with which platform, brand, and asset?
- *Timing*—when will the content be distributed?

Now, let's plot each of these campaign elements on a grid. Figure 6.1 provides an example of what the Mercedes GLA Facebook/Instagram campaign mentioned earlier may have looked like. The campaign starts with the influencer post on Instagram, is intensified by the organic reach of the Mercedes brand feed on Instagram, and then is amplified through a sponsored post on Instagram and Facebook.

Platform	Brand	Asset	Content	Timing
Instagram	@ThisWildIdea	Influencer	#GLApacked	10/5 at 10:00am
Instagram	@mbusa	Organic	Share of @ThisWildIdea #GLApacked	10/5 at 11:00am
Instagram	@mbusa	Sponsored	Sponsored post of @ThisWildIdea #GLApacked	10/5 at 12:00pm
Facebook	Mercedes-Benz USA	Sponsored	Share post of @ThisWildIdea #GLApacked	10/5 at 12:00pm

FIGURE 6.1 **Mercedes GLA's Social Media Campaign**

This is just one example of a campaign grid. The key is ensuring all the pieces are accounted for in one document and organized accordingly. Social media marketing campaigns require significant coordination, especially when it is trans-media in nature. The more organized your team is, the more efficient your execution will be.

Recap: Ready, Set, Go Viral

One of the major myths of the social media industry is going viral. All you need to do is post a video on YouTube and link to it on Facebook and the social media universe will collectively watch, share, and comment on it. Unfortunately, for social media managers everywhere, this is more of a dream than anything else. To ensure your content is seen and engaged with, developing marketing plans like you would for other channels is equally important, if not more so, in the highly cluttered social media space.

In this chapter we examined a wide variety of strategic distribution choices. First, we reviewed the four types of assets that you can use in a social media marketing campaign: organic, shared, sponsored, and influencer. Then we looked at the three campaign possibilities: an on-platform campaign, a cross-platform campaign, and a cross-media campaign. Finally, we examined the considerations in implementation of a social media campaign and the key phases of launch, expand, and iterate.

In the next chapter, we'll pull all the elements of the social media management framework together and discuss measurement to help organizations answer this question: what does social media mean to my business?

Your Turn: Develop a Social Media Marketing Plan for Fidelity

You and your team oversee social media for Fidelity Investments. As part of their company's overall strategy to acquire and retain Millennial customers, your ad agency helped you create a slick new YouTube video on financial literacy and diversification. The thought is that if Fidelity becomes a brand Millennials trust, they will be more likely to do business with the firm.

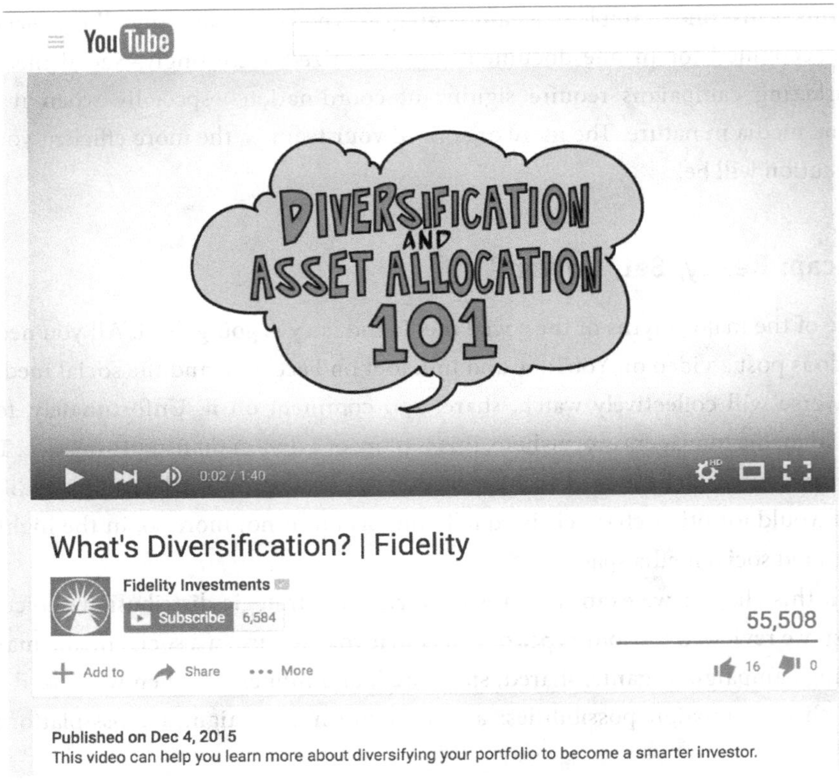

Your executive team thinks the video will go viral automatically. After all, it's on YouTube! You know better. The way to generate the views your executives expect is to put together a distribution plan. You also have a budget of $50,000 to deploy for this effort, if necessary. If not, you could apply that to other social marketing initiatives in the future (e.g., like creating additional social content).

In this exercise, watch the video.[33] Then apply the principles of this chapter to develop a distribution plan. Focus on the following three steps:

1. *Inventory your assets.* Examine possible organic, shared, sponsored, and influencer media assets.
2. *Select a campaign type.* For this video, decide whether to pursue an on-platform, cross-platform, or trans-media campaign.
3. *Determine an implementation plan.* Determine what will initiate the campaign, what assets you will use to expand the conversation, and how you will iterate on the campaign going forward.

Your deliverable is to develop a campaign grid similar to the one discussed in this chapter. Each team will present their recommendation at the end of this exercise to the senior executive team of Fidelity. Good luck.

Notes

1. LastWeekTonight, *Last Week Tonight with John Oliver: Tobacco (HBO)*, February 15, 2015, https://www.youtube.com/watch?v=6UsHHOCH4q8.
2. The YouTube clip accumulated more than 2 million views in the first week. As of July 24, 2016, it had more than 9 million views.
3. During the television segment, John Oliver also revealed that his team had put Jeff on an actual billboard in Uruguay and produced Jeff-branded t-shirts and sent them to Togo for several of its citizens to wear. The segment concluded (naturally) with a real-life Jeff mascot coming onto the set.
4. Mentions tracked via topsy.com.
5. Sarene Leeds, "John Oliver Pitches 'Jeff the Diseased Lung' to Promote Cigarettes," *WSJ Blogs - Speakeasy*, February 16, 2015, http://blogs.wsj.com/speakeasy/2015/02/16/john-oliver-pitches-jeff-the-diseased-lung-to-promote-cigarettes/; Lori Grisham, "John Oliver's Marlboro Mascot Idea? 'Jeff the Diseased Lung,'" *USA Today*, February 18, 2015, http://www.usatoday.com/story/news/nation-now/2015/02/17/john-oliver-marlboro-diseased-lung/23572447/.
6. Sean Corcoran, "Defining Earned, Owned and Paid Media," *Forrester Sean Corcoran's Blog*, December 16, 2009, http://blogs.forrester.com/interactive_marketing/2009/12/defining-earned-owned-and-paid-media.html.
7. Mike Isaac and Sydney Ember, "Facebook to Change News Feed to Focus on Friends and Family," *The New York Times*, June 29, 2016, http://www.nytimes.com/2016/06/30/technology/facebook-to-change-news-feed-to-focus-on-friends-and-family.html.
8. Nielsen, "Global Trust in Advertising—2015," *Nielsen.com*, September 28, 2015, http://www.nielsen.com/us/en/insights/reports/2015/global-trust-in-advertising-2015.html.

9. Josh Constine, "Facebook Messenger Adds Music, Starting with Spotify Song Sharing," *TechCrunch*, March 3, 2016, http://social.techcrunch.com/2016/03/03/facebook-messenger-spotify/.
10. "Edelman Trust Barometer Data Reveals Employee Trust Divide," *Edelman*, accessed July 25, 2016, http://www.edelman.com/insights/intellectual-property/2016-edelman-trust-barometer/state-of-trust/employee-trust-divide/.
11. eMarketer, "US Ad Blocking to Jump by Double Digits This Year," *eMarketer*, June 21, 2016, http://www.emarketer.com/Article/US-Ad-Blocking-Jump-by-Double-Digits-This-Year/1014111.
12. "Blurred Lines: Advertising or Content?—An FTC Workshop on Native Advertising | Federal Trade Commission," accessed October 31, 2015, https://www.ftc.gov/news-events/events-calendar/2013/12/blurred-lines-advertising-or-content-ftc-workshop-native.
13. Tad Friend, "Hollywood and Vine," *The New Yorker*, December 15, 2014, http://www.newyorker.com/magazine/2014/12/15/hollywood-vine.
14. Christopher Heine, "Selena Gomez's Social Media Posts Are Evidently Worth $550,000 Apiece," *AdWeek*, July 19, 2016, http://www.adweek.com/news/technology/selena-gomezs-social-media-posts-are-evidently-worth-550000-apiece-172552.
15. Samantha Worgull, "Sizing Up Marriott's Bold Snapchat Move," *Hotel News Now*, January 21, 2015, http://www.hotelnewsnow.com/Article/15100/Sizing-up-Marriotts-bold-Snapchat-move.
16. Jillian Goodman, "This Brand-Creator Partnership Is How Snapchat's CEO Should Have Tried to Make Money," *Fast Company*, October 20, 2014, http://www.fastcompany.com/3037309/this-brand-creator-collaboration-on-snapchat-is-how-ceo-evan-spiegel-should-have-tried-to-ma.
17. Taffy Brodesser-Akner, "Turning Microcelebrity into a Big Business," *The New York Times*, September 19, 2014, http://www.nytimes.com/2014/09/21/magazine/turning-microcelebrity-into-a-big-business.html?_r=0.
18. Nathalie Tadena, "Lord & Taylor Reaches Settlement with FTC over Native Ad Disclosures," *Wall Street Journal*, March 15, 2016, http://www.wsj.com/articles/lord-taylor-reaches-settlement-with-ftc-over-native-ad-disclosures-1458061427.
19. "The Signal," accessed October 31, 2015, http://sendthemasignal.tumblr.com/.
20. "'The Signal' Lexus Tumblr Is up for a Shorty Award!" accessed October 31, 2015, http://industry.shortyawards.com/nominee/6th_annual/qs/the-signal-lexus-tumblr.
21. "Photoset," *Instagram for Business*, accessed October 31, 2015, http://blog.business.instagram.com/post/98901450706/mercedes-benz-usa-turns-to-facebook-and-instagram.
22. Joon Soo Lim, Sung Yoon Ri, Beth Donnelly Egan, and Frank A. Biocca, "The Cross-Platform Synergies of Digital Video Advertising: Implications for Cross-Media Campaigns in Television, Internet and Mobile TV," *Computers in Human Behavior* 48 (July 2015): 463–472.
23. Mike Esterl, "'Share a Coke' Credited With a Pop in Sales," *Wall Street Journal*, September 25, 2014, http://www.wsj.com/articles/share-a-coke-credited-with-a-pop-in-sales-1411661519.
24. Gabriel Beltrone, "The Best Ad of 2014 Was Brilliant and Subversive, and It Wasn't Even Real," Adweek, November 30, 2014, http://www.adweek.com/news/advertising-branding/best-ad-2014-was-brilliant-and-subversive-and-it-wasnt-even-real-161665.
25. Jeff Beer, "Newcastle's Band of Brands Super Bowl Ad Is a Logotastic Adstravaganza," *Co. Create*, accessed October 31, 2015, http://www.fastcocreate.com/3041491/super-bowl-xlix/newcastles-band-of-brands-super-bowl-ad-is-a-logotastic-adstravaganza.
26. Scott Gulbransen, "Taking Back the Social-Media Command Center," *Forbes*, January 22, 2014, http://www.forbes.com/sites/onmarketing/2014/01/22/taking-back-the-social-media-command-center/.
27. The Beastie Boys ended up suing GoldieBlox for illegally using "Girls," a protracted legal battle that ended in GoldieBlox apologizing to the band and donating to "one or more charities selected by Beastie Boys that support science, technology, engineering, and mathematics education for girls." See Jill Bilstein, "Beastie Boys Settle Lawsuit Over 'Girls' Toy Ad," *Rolling Stone*, March 18, 2014, http://www.rollingstone.com/music/news/beastie-boys-settle-lawsuit-over-girls-toy-commercial-20140318.
28. Catherine Clifford, "GoldieBlox CEO: How I Went from Kickstarter to the Macy's Day Parade in Two Years," *Entrepreneur*, December 3, 2014, http://www.entrepreneur.com/video/240370.

29. Hollie Slade, "Meet Emursive, the Company Behind 'Sleep No More,' The Off-Broadway Production That's Been Sold Out for Three Years," *Forbes*, March 19, 2014, http://www.forbes.com/sites/hollieslade/2014/03/19/meet-emursive-the-company-behind-sleep-no-more-the-off-broadway-production-thats-been-sold-out-for-three-years/.
30. Alison Griswold, "Are Facebook Video Ads a Threat to YouTube?" *Slate*, December 5, 2014, http://www.slate.com/blogs/moneybox/2014/12/05/heineken_facebook_traffic_the_two_video_platforms_are_equal_players_to_heineken.html.
31. Brodesser-Akner, Microcelebrity into a Big Business.
32. "Old Spice: Responses Case Study," *Creativity Online*, August 4, 2010, http://creativity-online.com/work/old-spice-responses-case-study/20896.
33. Fidelity Investments, *What's Diversification?*, December 4, 2015, https://www.youtube.com/watch?v=LU8tubkz_Fg.

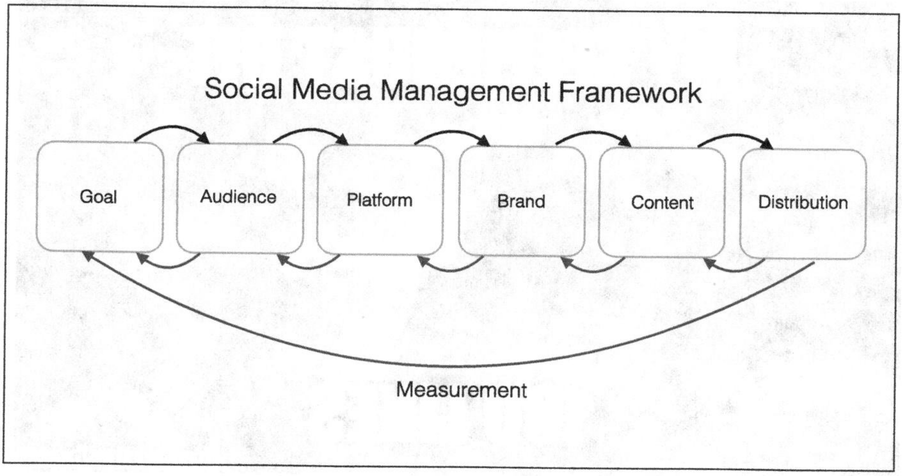

7 Measuring Social Media Results

In 2014, AT&T released a commercial entitled "Selfie."[1] It was part of an "AT&T Network Experts" advertising campaign centered on two engineers, Frank and Charlie, and their travels across the United States. Frank, the veteran, and Charlie, the rookie, were an odd couple of sorts, but their work together helped demonstrate the breadth and quality of AT&T's wireless service.

In the Selfie spot, they are on their latest road trip, with time to kill during the seemingly interminable itinerary. Making conversation, the younger, more impressionable Charlie marvels at the revolutionary nature of the mobile Internet:

CHARLIE: "I can't imagine living without it. It's a place where people can come share knowledge and ideas. It's beautiful."

FRANK: "That's deep, Charlie."

Pause

CHARLIE: "My selfie just hit 100 likes. A hundred!"

Charlie's jubilation is a familiar refrain for active social media users. Not everyone can claim 100 likes on every selfie (and for those of you who can, well done). But the instant gratification of positive feedback is a key driver of the selfie phenomenon—and social media use in general. If people did not want engagement and feedback, why would they share in the first place?

But what exactly does 100 likes or, for that matter, 1,000,000 followers mean? Although the answer is important to a degree for our personal social media use, it's a question that businesses have been struggling with for the better part of a decade. Executives all over the world have asked some version of this question: "We have 50,000 fans on Facebook. Is that good?" In general, the answer is not straightforward. Indeed, measuring the business impact of social media has been a defining challenge for organizations of all types and sizes.[2]

Why is that? Ever since the nascent days of the social media industry, organizations have been focused largely on platform metrics such as fans/likes and followers. Take Skittles, which was a first mover in the social media space. They launched a Facebook page and infused it with a quirky and humorous brand personality. It was as if the "rainbow" (Skittles' mascot) had come to life and started posting random thoughts and musings to its followers such as this one:

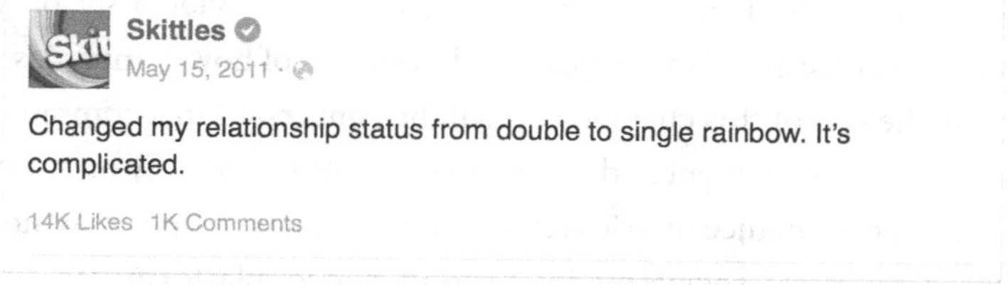
Skittles
May 15, 2011
Changed my relationship status from double to single rainbow. It's complicated.
14K Likes 1K Comments

Over time, the Skittles brand amassed more than 20 million Facebook fans, a hefty number, especially compared to other brands in the space.

Now what? What does having all these fans do for Skittles? Circa 2010, agencies and consulting firms started placing a value on fans. Companies like Vitrue and others developed methodologies to show how much a fan was worth to your business.[3] It did not matter who the fan actually was—their demographics, behaviors, affinity for your product, and so on—if you had a sizable fan base, you were having "success" in social media.

The problem with this platform-driven model is that it obscures your business goals. If you have 20 million Facebook fans, but they are not helping you drive value, what purpose do they serve? Moreover, gaining 1,000 likes on an Instagram post may seem like it's "good," but what does it actually mean to your business? For too long, social media success metrics have been defined by platform metrics.

• • •

As discussed in chapter 1, the key to social media management is flipping the paradigm from platform-driven thinking to a goal-centered social media strategy. With every component of the social media management framework, you have considered key questions of goal, audience, platform, brand, content, and distribution. Now, the final component of the framework is to measure success in relation to your business goals—and not the platform's goals.

In this chapter, we will discuss best practices and cases to inform how you can measure the results of your social media strategy going forward. First, because effective measurement in social media is tied to the goals you identified at the outset of your strategy, we'll revisit the four key business benefits of social media—brand, revenue, operational, and cultural value—that we described in chapter 1.

Then, within each of the four quadrants, we will provide a set of "metrics that matter" that correspond to key goals and examples of how companies can measure them. By the end of this chapter, you will be conversant in a common language of social media measurement and be able to translate the activity on social media networks into performance metrics relative to your goals. As you may notice, the objective is to move social media beyond siloed platform measurement and integrate it into your organization's overall business analytics approach.

Dimensionalizing the Business Value of Social Media

To ground our discussion of social media measurement, think back to chapter 1's discussion of social business value, which can come in a variety of forms: brand, revenue, operational, and cultural. Each of these forms is set up on a grid as in figure 7.1, where the x-axis spans the continuum of financial value and relational value, the nonmonetary benefits to an organization. The y-axis is external and internal, referring specifically to the audiences that are the key stakeholders for these forms of business value.

Not all organizations will be able to achieve value in each of these areas. For some organizations, direct revenue may not be possible, but operational cost savings and brand value could come into play. Moreover, for the organizations that do have direct revenue opportunities, perhaps cultural value is of less short-term

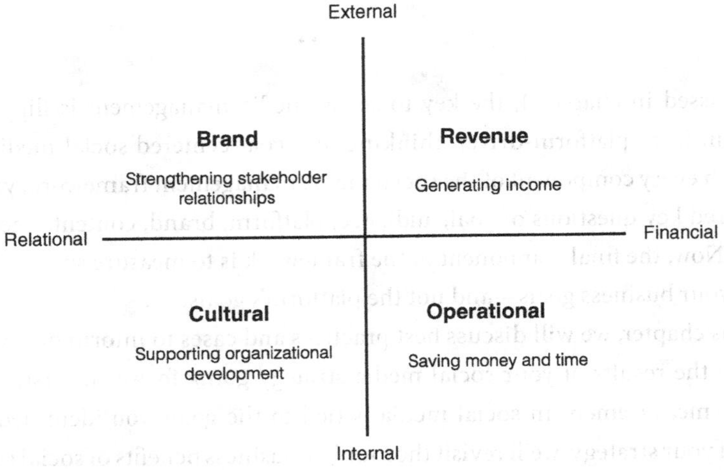

FIGURE 7.1 **Value Can Come in a Variety of Forms**

importance. To fully maximize the business potential of social media, thinking more broadly about value is critical to this process.

With this as a backdrop, let's look at measurement approaches in all four quadrants. For each we will examine potential goals, the metrics that matter related to those goals, and possible methodologies to use to collect the data. To be clear, the measurement of business value will be specific to a firm and its goals. Our discussion here is about possible approaches, which inevitably can be refined and customized to any given situation. Let's first start with brand.

Measuring Brand Value

Brand value is about building and strengthening relationships with your key stakeholders. Although organizations track many different brand goals, social media platforms are particularly well suited to deliver results on whether the target audience is aware of the brand (awareness), what the audience thinks of the brand (perception), and ultimately whether the audience will refer or recommend the brand (advocacy). Given these brand goals, what are the metrics that matter in tracking the performance against each?

Metrics That Matter

Goal: Brand awareness—What audiences are familiar with my brand and its products and services?

Metrics: There are two metrics to help answer this question. The first and most important is engagement. The second is reach.

- *Engagement*—these metrics refer to any action a person takes on the content you post from your social media presences (either via organic media or sponsored media), including but not limited to liking, viewing, commenting, clicking, and sharing. Depending on the platform, you can also assign different weights to these actions. For example, a share is typically more valuable than a like on Facebook. On Snapchat, views are important, but for your purposes, perhaps measuring how many people complete your story, also known as a completion rate, is a more significant metric.
- *Reach*—the number of people who see your content. Important: focus on *actual* reach, not potential reach. Potential reach is a usually misleading number that some social media analytics offer. For example, if

your Twitter account has 10,000 followers, your potential reach is 10,000. In reality, your organic tweets will reach less than that number, as all 10,000 of your followers would have to be on Twitter at the same time in order to see it (a very unlikely occurrence even despite Twitter's gradual move to a Facebook-like Edgerank algorithm). The safer and sounder bet is actual reach.

Methods: There are two possible tools to leverage in your brand awareness tracking. Both can be used in concert to gain a clearer insight into brand awareness.

- Social platform analytics (second-party data) will be a helpful source of engagement and reach numbers for the content posted in your social presences/accounts (e.g., your Instagram or Twitter account).
- Social listening tools can also help measure the shared media and the number of people talking about your brand (engagement) and the number of people who see their posts or tweets (reach).

Let's pause for a moment to emphasize the importance of engagement in measuring brand awareness. Although reach (and impressions) are still an important currency in advertising, engagement is the metric that matters most in brand awareness. Why?

1. Engagement is a truer measure of familiarity than reach and impressions (how many times your content is seen). People seeing a post or tweet does not mean they are familiar with it or can recall it. Social media feeds are inundated with content and distractions. If they choose to actively consume and interact with your content, this engagement is a stronger indicator of awareness than the exposure metrics of impressions and reach. Engagement is in part why video advertising has become a critical content strategy for both Facebook and Snapchat, as voluntarily watching a video is a more telling indicator of awareness than if a person is exposed to a banner ad.
2. Engagement leads to reach and impressions in social media. The more engagement your content receives, the greater number of people it will reach, given the network effects of social media platforms. Reach and impressions are by-products of driving engagement; thus, emphasizing engagement in both content creation and measurement should be the priority.

Goal: Brand perception—Of those who are familiar with my brand, how do they perceive it?

Metrics: There are two metrics that matter for brand perception: sentiment and volume.

- *Sentiment*—what people say about your brand, products, services, and intended points of differentiation. You can classify sentiment according to positive, negative, or neutral and do a close textual analysis to identify key trends, pain points, or causes for celebration.
- *Volume*—to place sentiment into context, also quantify how many people share the same sentiment, relative to your overall audience.

Methods: Leverage social media listening tools to search all publicly available conversations and filter according to specific keywords related to your brand.

Goal: Brand advocacy—Of those who perceive the brand positively, do they recommend it to someone they know?

Metrics: Referrals—identify the people who recommend your brand to others.

Methods: There are at least three methodological tools to help in this process.

- Track recommenders through social listening tools. Use keyword searches (e.g., find people who say "highly recommend" in social posts about your brand) and other indicators to determine who and how many people are giving your brand positive reviews.
- Track people who create content on behalf of your brand also through social listening tools. Use searches for hashtags and other media content to find those who are actively promoting your brand to their networks.
- Some companies prefer Net Promoter Score surveys, which typically involve asking people directly whether they would recommend the brand to their friends. Integrate these surveys at the end of the user experience for your social media campaign.

With these three metrics as background, how might an organization evaluate the brand value of a social media strategy? Let's look at the example of Primark and its efforts to generate awareness in the United States through its first store opening in Boston.

CASE STUDY: #PRIMANIA HITS BOSTON

Primark is a European clothing retailer owned by the Association of British Foods. It launched its first store in 2009 in Spain and has since grown into one of the most successful retailers in Europe. Over the 5-year period between 2009 and 2014, for example, sales increased 150%.[4] Meanwhile, to keep costs down, they maintain a small marketing budget and do not even run an e-commerce business. They are the rare twenty-first century retailer that operates only out of brick-and-mortar stores.[5]

To grow the business beyond Europe, Primark looked to the US market. It launched its first store in Boston in September 2015. Sticking to its principles, the launch was not accompanied by a multimillion-dollar multimedia marketing campaign. Somewhat paradoxically, although the company does not operate an e-commerce business, they have been aggressive in leveraging social media to drive awareness and foot traffic into the store. Their approach to the Boston market was similar, as they relied heavily on social media to spread the message of their arrival.

As a standard operating procedure, Primark leveraged platforms in its social media portfolio such as Twitter, Facebook, and Snapchat to promote the opening, as in the tweet shown here. Using organic media was a cost-effective and easy way to generate awareness.

But the magic in their approach is how they activate customers to advocate on their behalf in social media. Primark's 2015 annual report articulated their philosophy well: "Social media plays an important part in the way our customers live their lives and is an increasingly effective way of broadcasting the excitement of the Primark brand far and wide, thereby enticing more customers into our stores more frequently."[6]

Primark's social brand advocacy strategy had three prongs: (1) the low-priced, fashion-forward product; (2) the in-store experience; and (3) the social media experience. First, Primark products are so cheap, yet trendy that customers can't help but talk about them. A concept Jonah Berger discusses in *Contagious* is relevant here. Shareable products and experiences often have "inner remarkability."[7] The inner remarkability of Primark is the price relative to the perceived fashion value of the product. The prices are so low that some Twitter users have been compelled to say things like this:[8]

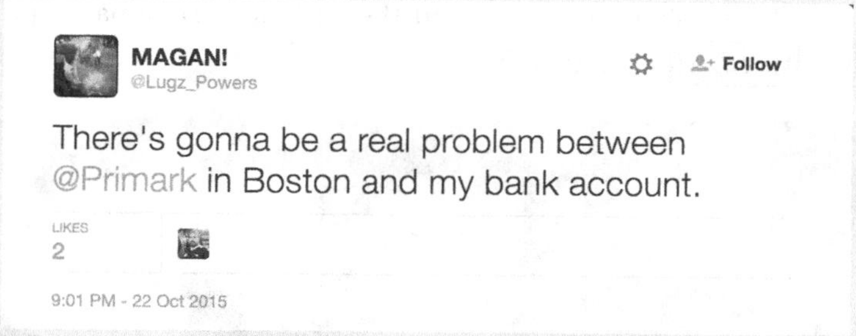

In addition to the bargain pricing, the products are also known as "fashion forward," meaning they're of the trendiest variety. The combination of low prices and high fashion plays into the key social media trend driving consumption: the Instagram effect. Because younger-skewing customers

CONTINUED

CASE STUDY: #PRIMANIA HITS BOSTON *CONTINUED*

take so many selfies and do not want to be seen in the same outfit every time, they're more likely to buy cheap clothing (at places like Primark) and then discard it once they've worn it.[9] In this sense, the low-priced, fashion-forward products are optimized for word of mouth and sharing. Put another way, when Primark sells you a nice-looking pair of jeans for $12, they are betting you will tell your friends about the steal of a deal you just got.

The second component of Primark's social brand awareness strategy is the in-store experience, which encourages customers to take photos while wearing Primark clothing and share them across a variety of social media networks. Meanwhile, other retails tend to prohibit this behavior. The store offers free Wi-Fi and charging stations. The dressing rooms are large enough to accommodate groups of friends, maximizing the number of possible selfies taken and shared on social. Here's one example of the in-store signage that can be found across the store. As you can see, the call to action is "Wear. Share. Inspire." And the hashtag "Primania" is prominently featured. More on this shortly.

Finally, the social media experience complements the product and the in-store experience. As mentioned, instead of an e-commerce site, Primark has channeled all sales to the stores themselves. This helps them keep operating costs and thus prices low. In lieu of an e-commerce site, they've launched their own social media platform that highlights customers and their various fashions that they submit via #Primania. Other users can give photos "Primarks," their version of a thumbs-up. Those that get the most Primarks can receive store credit.[10] This is a way of Primark showing customers that they are listening and rewarding them for their efforts on behalf of the brand. Moreover, Primark benefits from a constant stream of new content, which not only keeps the destination fresh and exciting but also features real-life product testimonials from actual customers wearing their clothes.

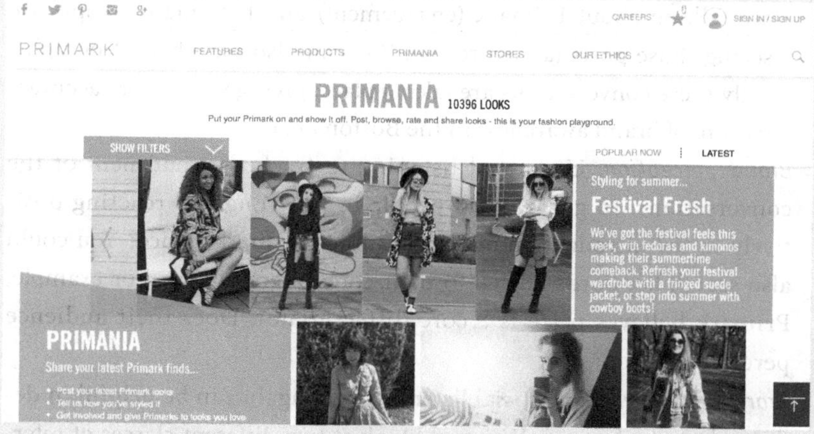

Taken together, the low-cost, fashion-forward product, in-store experience, and the social experience leverage their customers to generate shared media. Now, put yourself in Primark's shoes. If you're expanding into the US market for the first time, what are the types of metrics you should be examining (and pushing social media platforms to provide)? Let's break down each component of brand value:

- *Brand awareness.* We can measure brand awareness in two different forms: awareness generated from organic media (Primark's social accounts) and from shared media (consumers' social accounts).
  - *Awareness from Primark's social posts.* In this analysis, you would examine the performance of any Boston-related post sent from Primark's brand accounts on Instagram, Twitter, Facebook, etc. Calculate two metrics: engagement and reach. For engagement, determine the

CONTINUED

CASE STUDY: #PRIMANIA HITS BOSTON *CONTINUED*

unique number of people who have engaged with the posts. For reach, define the unique number of people who have seen the posts. For more specific engagement and reach numbers related to Primark's U.S. expansion, parse out the unique number of people engaged and reached who live in the greater Boston or New England areas.

- *Awareness from customers' social posts.* You can also look at the universe of conversations that customers start about Primark on their own, not prompted by a Primark tweet or Facebook post. For this method, leverage a social listening tool to find out how many people are talking about Primark (engagement) and how many people are seeing those posts (actual reach). You can also see where geographically these conversations are taking place, giving you a more accurate picture of brand awareness in the Boston area.

- *Brand perception.* Use social listening to track the sentiment of the conversations. In general, are people in New England reacting positively to the introduction of Primark into the marketplace? You could also search keywords related to their core differentiators. For example, Primark believes price is a core differentiator. Does their audience perceive this, too?
- *Brand advocacy.* Using social listening tools again can be helpful in defining brand advocacy. You could look at two different classes of referrers. The first referrers are people who write a positive review of Primark on social media. The second could be content creators that share their own #Primania outfit bought from the store, which then makes it onto the website.

Now to the age-old question of return on investment (ROI). If you needed to make a business case back to your senior executive team about the value of this effort, relative to the level of investment, explain that the engagement and reach you have achieved from this consumer advocacy campaign is much less expensive than a traditional marketing communications campaign. One tactic to prove this is equivalent advertising value. Take the average cost per thousand impressions (CPM) that you might use to buy impressions in other media and price out what the impressions you achieved in social media would cost if you had to pay for them (which you didn't). To calculate the impressions, pull the impressions from both the organic and shared media sources discussed earlier. From here, you could assign a simple ROI formula, (return – investment / investment × 100). Taking the value of the impressions, subtract it by the dollar amount of internal resources expended, and then divide that total by the internal resources.

For example, let's say your social media campaign achieved 10 million total impressions. To buy that same amount of impressions for, say, digital banners ads would cost you $100,000 at a $10 CPM. If the internal costs to manage and execute the Boston launch campaign via organic and shared media were, say, $20,000, then you would be operating with an ROI of 400%.

In the Primark example, they are achieving brand value in a number of ways. By encouraging customers to post and celebrate their Primark purchases, they are generating more awareness, positive perception, and stronger advocacy as a result; these customers are in a position to become more loyal customers to Primark over the long term. In addition, they are seeing operational benefits. Through the shared media created, the organization can operate without the massive marketing budget that other competitors may use and thus see a healthier ROI compared to other marketing tactics. Social media in this sense is the de facto branding tool at a far lower cost than traditional advertising.

Brand value is not the only value source for social media. Let's look at the second type of business value—revenue—and how you can better understand the revenue impact of your social media strategy.

Measuring Revenue Value

While some organizations have seen and measured increased brand value as a result of social media, direct revenue has been more elusive for others.[11] There are at least two reasons for this: one, an organization's products or services may not lend themselves well to direct revenue through social media. (If your organization falls into this category, perhaps looking at other ways to drive value through social media would be a more efficient use of your time.) Second, the social media tools to drive direct sales have not advanced to the point where direct causation between social media and revenue can be proved.

However, change is happening. Increasingly, organizations are finding ways to translate social media initiatives into revenue. In the early days, it was difficult to tie social media activity directly to sales. Now, with the advent of more sophisticated big data collection and warehousing initiatives, companies have a more complete picture of their customers and how they interact with their products and services, which enable them to track the effectiveness of social media strategies on driving sales.

To be clear, effective and definitive understanding of social media value of customers, from a revenue standpoint, rests largely on the ability of organizations to develop a stronger profile of each customer. This means having a detailed customer relationship management (CRM) database that also includes social media profile information such as a Facebook page and Twitter handle. With this information in tow, organizations will be more granular in their analysis of specific effects of social media on revenue.

How? The answer in part is digitizing and tracking the sales cycle, which can encompass a wide variety of components to measure. And in many organizations, detailed metrics about every stage of the cycle are essential. Naturally, bottom-line sales (e.g., how much new revenue is coming into the company) are the most important metric of all. But there are also more granular metrics that can be helpful in attributing cause and effect to social media efforts. For the purposes of our work together, and in light of the bottom-line needs of organizations,[12] we'll focus on these three critical goals: whether your organization is generating leads (acquisition), converting these leads (sales), and driving repeat loyalty (purchases). Let's first look at the metrics that matter related to these goals.

Metrics That Matter

Goal: Acquisition—is your organization creating a need and attracting prospective customers?
Metrics: Leads—customers that have expressed interest in your product or services. Interest can come in a variety of forms: connecting with your brand on LinkedIn, Twitter, Facebook, and other social media platforms; visiting your website; tweeting about your brand; signing up for an email list.
Methods: Leverage CRM technology to pull in leads from a variety of platforms and channels to a central database

Goal: Sales—is your organization converting leads into sales?
Metrics: Conversions—of the leads generated in social media, the percentage of those that converted into direct sales revenue.
Methods: Using CRM tools, track leads throughout the sales cycle and then note when the deal is closed and for what dollar amount.

Goal: Loyalty—are your existing customers spending more with your organization?
Metrics: Repeat purchases—after acquiring and converting the customer, track the number of customers that buy products and services. Seek to understand whether customers acquired and converted via social media are more or less valuable than customers acquired from other parts of your marketing mix.
Methods: Like your other revenue goals, the CRM database can again be a helpful resource in monitoring repeat purchases among customers.

How does an organization monitor these metrics that matter? Let's look at how the National Basketball Association is driving direct revenue through social media.

CASE STUDY: THE NATIONAL BASKETBALL ASSOCIATION MONETIZES SOCIAL MEDIA

The National Basketball Association was a first mover in social media, starting its Facebook page and Twitter feeds way back in 2007. The league ran out to the early lead among other professional sports leagues in terms of sheer audience size. Yet like many other businesses across industries, it started to turn its attention to driving revenue via social media platforms. The league has seen success in this area through a number of revenue streams, most notably through ticketing and merchandise. Let's discuss both in more detail and examine the metrics that matter in each.

Ticketing through LinkedIn Sales Navigator

The NBA has leveraged LinkedIn's Sales Navigator tool in creative ways to increase ticket sales. The LinkedIn Sales Navigator, in effect, digitizes the sales process. Whereas in the past, salespeople would need to rely on the rolodex and other old-fashioned networking tools, LinkedIn has created a product that aims to eliminate the cold call and take advantage of online networking to help salespeople and buyers connect. Moreover, it helps organizations speed up response times, which is increasingly an important component of success in the sales discipline.[13]

CONTINUED

CASE STUDY: THE NATIONAL BASKETBALL ASSOCIATION MONETIZES SOCIAL MEDIA *CONTINUED*

Selling tickets in the NBA (and most leagues) comprises both season tickets and individual tickets. Season tickets, of course, are critical to an organization because it is guaranteed revenue for each game. Teams also often sell season ticket packages to other businesses, thus taking a B2B approach. In doing so, the NBA increasingly leveraged the LinkedIn Sales Navigator to generate leads and track conversions. This knowledge also helped them monitor and convert renewals.

Attendance has been at an all-time high for the league, and the league's efforts on LinkedIn have played an important role. Executive Vice President Amy Brooks has attributed the high renewal rates of 80%–85% from the 2014–2015 season in part to the influence of LinkedIn Sales Navigator, which she said also contributed to suite sales and sponsorships.[14] Meanwhile, some teams like the Sacramento Kings have also reported operational benefits from the tool, saving them time in their sales efforts.[15]

Merchandise on Facebook

The NBA is also using social media to help drive merchandise sales. The master brand NBA page on Facebook does not typically inundate its fans with merchandise sales posts, but it selects the relevant times to do so, such as this share from the NBAStore.com Facebook page (which has a following of over 200,000 likes). Given the Golden State Warriors' historic seventy-three win regular season, making fans aware of the new product available to commemorate it was a logical use of the platform.

How can the NBA measure the success of this post? In it is a unique URL that can track what referral traffic to the NBAStore.com website comes from Facebook. This tracking technology can also follow the customer from start to finish, so each customer coming in gets qualified as a lead; they can also track how many convert, and then if they do convert, they are added to the CRM database, which will be updated if the customer makes purchases again. This is a basic, but powerful way to track the revenue coming from Facebook and other social platforms, and it's a key approach that can help the NBA understand the degree to which its merchandise sales are impacted through Facebook.

Driving ticket sales through LinkedIn and merchandise sales through Facebook are two examples of how the NBA is using social media to generate direct revenue. For both, a simple leads, conversions, and repeat purchases measurement model applies. The NBA has monetized social media in other ways; for example, it receives a share of the advertising revenue from Google/YouTube on its highlight content. It has also been suggested that the NBA's global social media footprint contributed to the increase in value of its media rights,[16] which will bring in a total $24 billion in revenue from 2016–2025.[17] In many ways, the NBA is an avatar in deriving real revenue from its social media efforts. And undoubtedly as new social platforms emerge, the league will innovate new ways to not only enhance the fan and customer experience but also monetize the platforms along the way.

Indeed, in both the B2C and B2B contexts, the movement is toward measuring direct causation between social media communications and purchases. With more sales activity happening online, these causal relationships will increasingly be clear. For example, social commerce initiatives will be instrumental in this effort. In 2015, Pinterest launched buyable pins, enabling customers to make product purchases directly through Pinterest. This gives Pinterest the ability to understand when a user pinned a product in the first place and when the product was purchased.[18] In turn, advertisers and brands will have visibility into the sales cycle for B2C products and services and the corresponding metrics. As the industry matures, the causation between liking or pinning a product on social media and then purchasing that item will become clearer than ever before. With this new world of social commerce, a host of measurement approaches become possible.

Revenue from social media is a goal organizations have pursued with mixed results. As technology continues to advance, achieving this goal will be increasingly realistic. In this section, we've seen examples of revenue possibilities from the NBA's B2B and B2C efforts. But it's not the only way to impact the bottom line for an organization. As we'll see in the next section, operational cost savings are another way an organization can derive value from social media.

Measuring Operational Value

Social media can also impact the bottom line of an organization through operational efficiencies. If deployed appropriately, it can help an organization streamline and improve the way it does business. Importantly, achieving operational efficiencies is relevant to disciplines across the enterprise, whether it's product development, customer service, IT, or anything in between.

From this perspective, measurement of operational impact of social media on how an organization functions comes down to saving money and saving time. Let's look at metrics that matter for both.

Metrics That Matter

Goal: Save money—how can we decrease the financial resources required to accomplish tasks within an organization?

Metrics: Operational costs—the amount of cost savings as a result of social media use.

Methods: Benchmark the typical amount of money your organization spends to complete a task. Then introduce social media into the process to determine the impact on costs.

Goal: Save time—how can we decrease the time it takes to accomplish tasks within an organization?
Metrics: Productivity—the ratio of outputs to inputs.
Methods: Benchmark the typical amount of time your organization takes to complete a task. Then introduce social media into the process to determine the impact on productivity.

With more information about our customers (either B2B or B2C), employees, clients, and other audiences via social media, organizations can become more cost efficient and productive. Let's look at examples from the customer service and supply chain functions to see how organizations are impacting the bottom line through operational savings.

Customer Service Optimization at JetBlue

The use of social media in customer service is growing for a number of reasons: it's more efficient, it costs less, and customers tend to prefer it.[19] Although some leaders might be hesitant to move forward with social media customer service, due to the potential volume that companies might need to handle, the benefits in terms of costs savings and productivity are difficult to ignore. Plus, if you do it right, you could be in a position to actually strengthen customer relationships, rather than always being on the defensive. These potential benefits are relevant to organizations large and small and in a variety of sectors.

Let's look at an example of the airline JetBlue. Air passengers can be especially vociferous if their flight is late or cancelled, their baggage is lost, or the flight attendants run out of their favorite snacks. And since they have a public outlet to express this frustration via social media, they do not hesitate to let the airline and the rest of the world know.

JetBlue recognized this shift in consumer behavior as early as 2007, when an employee began experimenting with @JetBlue on Twitter. The company shortly thereafter made the decision to embrace social media to better serve its customers. Since then, the brand has become an avatar of social media customer service. They have evolved and expanded their customer service team in an efficient manner, optimizing the amount of money and time they spend to deliver high quality service on social media. In doing so, JetBlue also drives brand value with strong customer satisfaction and low complaints.

In 2010, JetBlue committed financial resources to launching a dedicated social media team that would handle customer relationships around the clock. They staffed a seventeen-person team with in-house professionals who embodied the brand's values and personalities. By 2014, the team grew to twenty-five highly qualified people, all of whom worked from home.[20] Compared to other staffing approaches, like hiring a third-party agency or building a state-of-the-art social media command center, JetBlue's move to establish a remote social media team at the outset kept operating costs down and employee satisfaction up, while also enabling them to deliver a consistent brand experience to customers. Despite many different people operating @JetBlue, the team strives to deliver a consistent brand personality, which seeks to bring humanity back to air travel, in all interactions with customers, even when they express frustration.

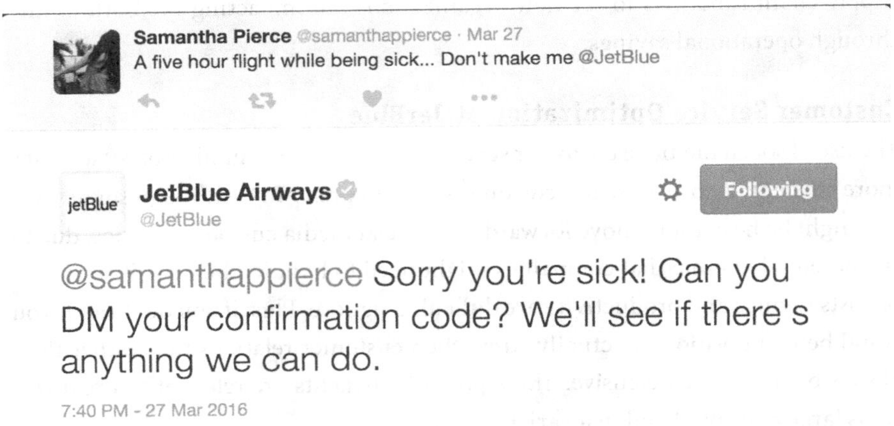

Samantha Pierce @samanthappierce · Mar 27
A five hour flight while being sick... Don't make me @JetBlue
jetBlue
JetBlue Airways
@JetBlue
Following
@samanthappierce Sorry you're sick! Can you DM your confirmation code? We'll see if there's anything we can do.
7:40 PM - 27 Mar 2016

JetBlue's social media customer service efforts are also time efficient. The team's average response time is ten minutes.[21] Let's compare that to an airline's traditional call center. Whether real or perceived, wait times to get through to a "representative" are notoriously long, not to mention the pre-human menu of options that ostensibly route your call to the right place. In contrast, when a customer tweets @JetBlue, he must articulate the issue in 140 characters or fewer, which helps the customer service professional get to the heart of the matter more quickly. And if the customer is responded to within ten minutes, he may leave the interaction more satisfied as well. On both sides of the interaction, customers and agents can save time versus other modes of communication like phone or email.

Because JetBlue's social media customer service team is optimized to deliver excellent experiences to its customers, they are seeing high levels of customer satisfaction. In fact, the brand is so efficient at creating satisfaction that they have achieved a customer complaint rate of 0.79 out of every 1,000 customers.[22] This customer satisfaction can extend to customers' overall perception of the brand, which can help justify JetBlue's investment in social customer service as well. And it can also leave the team, in collaboration with other JetBlue employees, more time to surprise and delight its customers, as in the example shown here.[23]

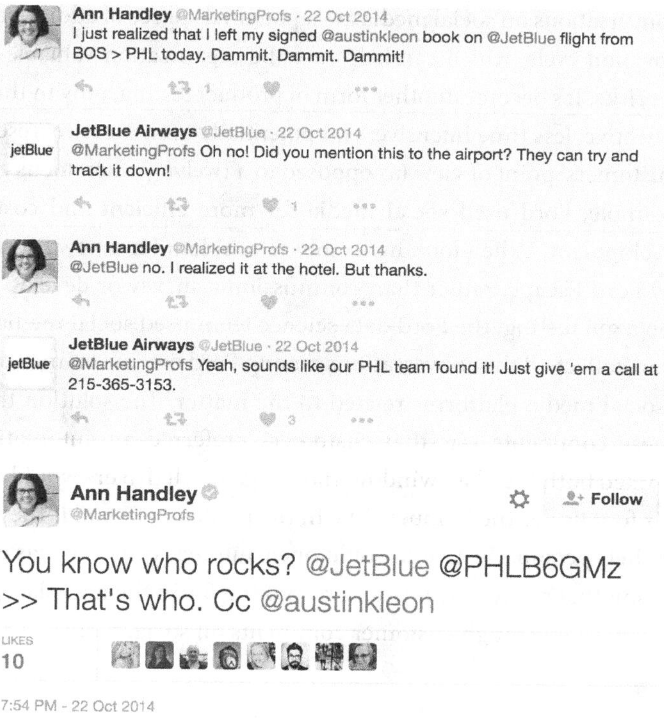

The shift from snail mail and call centers to social media is an operational advantage for many organizations. And it also helps position these organizations to create stronger connections with their audiences, as social media tools uniquely enable these two-way conversations. All the while, JetBlue and numerous other companies are handling more work and using internal resources efficiently, a fact that is improving customer satisfaction and the bottom line of those organizations.

Supply Chain Optimization at Ford

Another function within organizations that can derive operational benefits from social media is the supply chain. For example, product development budgets have historically been critical to the innovation process within the supply chain. Companies need the money to do market research on what customers want and to develop prototypes. This research and development process is a necessary, but often expensive cost of doing business. Yet it does not guarantee success. The success rate of product launches is historically very low. How can social media help organizations achieve more certainty in the products they develop?

Although research and development is still a critical element in any organization, customer conversations on social media are a potential source of additional insights for the innovation cycle, which can help save the organization valuable resources and mitigate risks. It's become another form of product testing, only in this way it is more cost effective, less time intensive, and potentially even more representative of the target customers' point of view (as opposed to a twelve-person focus group).

As an example, Ford used social media for more efficient and cost-effective product development. When looking to solve a problem for a new liftgate for the sport-utility Ford Escape, rather than commission a survey or develop the product based on a gut feeling, the Ford data science team used social media listening technology to collect all the conversations among Ford owners on message boards and other social media platforms related to the matter. The solution they culled from all these comments was that customers preferred an automatic liftgate, which combined both the glass window and the gate. All drivers would need to do is wave their foot under the bumper (like in the photo here), and if they had their car keys on their person, the trunk would open automatically.[24] It was exactly the type of solution that many customers were looking for in the first place, and Ford found it by combing through customer comments on social media.

Tri-State Ford
@TriStateFord
Follow
Tuesdays are a handful -- use your feet. Ford's available hands-free liftgate opens w/ just a kick under the bumper.
LIKES
11
5:00 PM - 8 Dec 2015

What is the value of this approach to product development? For starters, the speed to market can be faster than a more traditional research and development pace. Moreover, considering the amount of internal time and resources dedicated by Ford to find this solution, it is likely much cheaper than the traditional big budget approach to figuring out exactly what customers want. By listening to customers via social media, they eliminated this process and saved money and time as a result. Most important, they delivered a better end product to their customers.

The operational efficiencies that can be gained from the use of social media in the customer service and supply chain disciplines are just two examples of how social media can lead to savings in costs and time spent. There is similar potential in other disciplines as well. Indeed, compared to brand and revenue value, firms have only scratched the surface of what's possible in achieving operational efficiencies through social media. And in many respects, the metrics that matter in this value quadrant are straightforward and enduring—how can the organization reduce costs and be more productive using social media? If you're looking for a promotion, come up with an answer to that question and prove it to your executive team.

Measuring Cultural Value

Successful chief executives often cite the importance of culture to the effectiveness of their companies. It is a competitive advantage, a brand differentiator, and most of all, the key to creating and maintaining a productive and energetic workforce. Naturally, given its importance, the question of how to create a vibrant employee culture is increasingly critical, and some companies are turning to social media to do so, whether it's by attracting top talent (recruiting), empowering employees (engagement), or retaining the best and brightest (retention), all through social media.

But how do you know these efforts are working? Similar to the other sections of this chapter, let's identify the metrics that matter and then discuss an applied case.

Metrics That Matter

Goal: Employee recruitment—how can the organization attract high-quality talent that fits the organization?

Metrics: There are two metrics that matter. One is acquisition; the second is conversion.

- *Acquisition*—number of qualified candidates applying for jobs through social media
- *Conversion*—number and rate of hired employees coming from social media referrals

Methods: Measure the referral traffic to your organization's jobs website coming from social media posts. Track applicants with a CRM tool as they move through the hiring cycle.

Goal: Employee engagement—how active are your employees on company-wide social media initiatives?
Metrics: Engagement rate—the number of employees that participated relative to the total target
Methods: Leverage metrics from your owned or rented platforms to identify the number of employee participants. To get the rate, divide that number by total targeted employees.

Goal: Employee retention—How can you keep talented employees through a social media strategy?
Metrics: Satisfaction—the impact of company's social media strategy on employee happiness and fulfillment at work.
Methods: In a routine employee survey, ask employees for their feedback on the company's social media efforts and how it impacts their pride and satisfaction in working for the company.

Of course, culture can also be measured through qualitative methods and anecdotal evidence. Indeed, these more qualitatively based data points help add texture to an organization's culture. But the metrics that matter identified here are quantifiable and can relate directly to some of the social media initiatives companies are undertaking to build a strong culture. L'Oreal is an example of an organization that is emphasizing culture building internally and communicating that culture externally, both through social media.

CASE STUDY: LIVING #LIFEATLOREAL

Whereas some companies might put limits on social media use, others are actively encouraging their employees to share with the outside world a view from inside the firm. L'Oreal, the beauty brand, is one of those companies. Capitalizing on a hashtag that was initially intended mostly for internal purposes, the #LifeatLoreal campaign asked its global employee base to post on social media what it's like to work at the company.[25] An example of an employee-generated post is shown here. The brand also created its own original content highlighting its employees, as the second post shows.

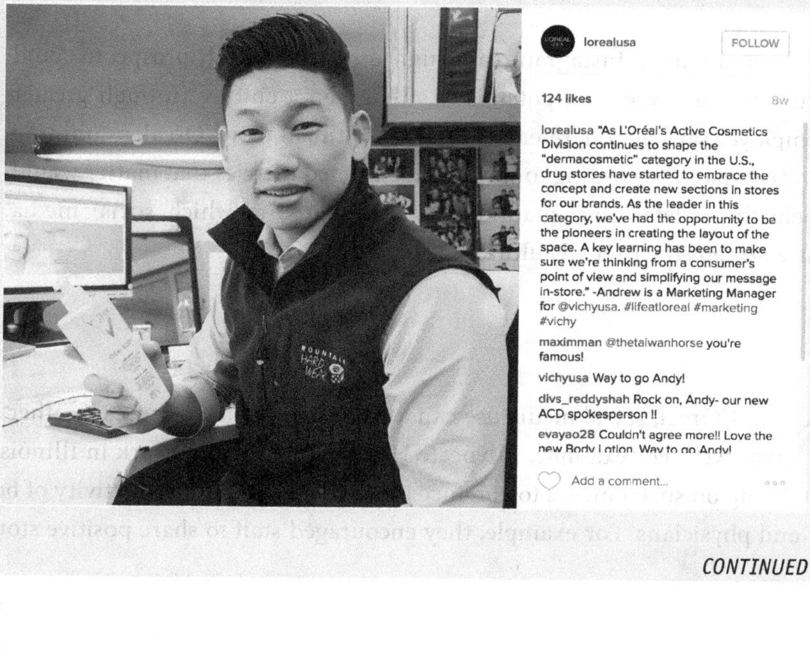

CONTINUED

CASE STUDY: LIVING #LIFEATLOREAL *CONTINUED*

How might the company think about measurement of the campaign? Let's break this question down according to the three metrics that matter:

- *Employee recruitment.* The initiative could invite applications at L'Oreal's jobs website, which can enable the company to track how many and what type of applicants resulted from the social media campaign. This referral traffic and subsequent applications can be attributed directly to the social media campaign.
- *Employee engagement.* The campaign can help position L'Oreal as a desirable place to work, which is important for prospective employees but also enhances the perception of the organization among the employees that work there. To measure this, the company could (1) count the number of employees who participated in the campaign and divide them by the total number of employees at the company and (2) conduct an internal survey gauging reactions to this initiative.
- *Employee retention.* Included in that survey, the company could also probe on retention issues. For example, it could ask about the reasons employees like working at the company and include a section on social media activity and campaigns to determine their effect on employee satisfaction and ultimately retention.

Even a simple Instagram campaign directed to both prospective and current employees can potentially strengthen a culture through greater employee satisfaction, retention, and recruitment. For L'Oreal, examining the campaign according to the aforementioned metrics that matter would help them determine quantitatively the degree to which social media strengthens the L'Oreal culture.

Beyond L'Oreal, social media use can measurably impact cultures in other industries as well. For example, Advocate Health, a hospital network in Illinois, is capitalizing on social media to enhance the satisfaction and productivity of both staff and physicians. For example, they encouraged staff to share positive stories about patients via internal social networks, creating a culture of celebrating success and feedback. Moreover, they implemented secure and private Twitter feeds for emergency situations, improving the ways in which hospitals can communicate in real time. As a result, the organization saw positive changes in how its employees work together and serve patients.[26]

Going forward, the use of social media as it relates to recruitment, engagement, and retention will be a key strategic consideration for many firms, given the Millennial generation's role in the workforce. One study found that an organization's social media policies can influence whether a Millennial wants to work for the company.[27] Given the importance of social media use to this new generation of the workforce, it's not a question of whether social media should be allowed, but how. And in doing so, testing how social media initiatives affect employee culture will be a critical organization building routine.

Recap: Measuring Results Is Not Easy

In social media's brief history, measurement has made executives' heads spin countless times. But as the platforms and tools evolve, there is newfound hope for quantitative data to show the value (or not) of social media initiatives. As the pressure mounts for social platforms to grow their own businesses, data and measurement tools will only become more available to the business world.

To position ourselves for this measurement reality, we examined a number of measurement approaches in this chapter. We revisited the key business benefits of social media: brand, revenue, operational, and cultural. Then we examined each within the measurement context, identifying metrics that matter and exploring how different organizations have approached the measurement process. In the end, for social media to be a real driver of business impact, it must be translated into a firm's overall business intelligence program. It's not just about likes and tweets, but converting this unit of analysis into the current business analytics approaches that organizations use to build brands, drive revenue, operate more efficiently, and cultivate culture.

With our work on the social media management framework completed, let's now turn our attention over the next three chapters to three special topics—crisis management, internal social media, and personal social media strategy. We will apply the framework to the specific topic to help you think through effective social media strategies in each case. First up is crisis.

Your Turn: Devising a Measurement Plan for Sanergy

You are the social media director of Sanergy, a hybrid profit/for-profit organization in Nairobi, Kenya.[28] With smartphone adoption accelerating and corresponding use of social media increasing exponentially, your CEO is interested in how social media can deliver business value to the organization. Your job is to develop a social media strategy that will achieve the organization's objectives with a recommendation on measurement approaches.

The recommendation should be about Sanergy's new brand, Farm Star, which is a low-cost fertilizer for farmers. Prior to launching Farm Star, Sanergy launched Fresh Life, which is a line of hygienic, no-water toilets that communities throughout Kenya now use. With the waste from the Fresh Life toilets, Sanergy creates the by-product of fertilizer, which is then packaged and sold under the Farm Star brand. Not only are they helping Kenyan communities with more hygienic toilets, they are doing right by the environment and helping farmers yield more crops.

The team is putting in place a social media strategy centered on Facebook and WhatsApp. Sanergy's sales team is seeking to connect with farmers via both platforms to ultimately drive sales of the fertilizer. In light of this social media plan, consider the following two questions for your recommendation:

- What business goals should Sanergy social media consider for the Farm Star product?
- What measurement plan should you put in place to track the organization's progress against those goals?

You will be presenting this recommendation to your CEO, who is open to using social media for the Farm Star brand but is not convinced of its value and wants to understand how you will measure the success. Good luck.

Notes

1. AT&T, *Video—AT&T Network Experts: "Selfie" | AT&T*, 2014, https://www.youtube.com/watch?v=dO64FvfZSW4.
2. Kevin Shively, "60% of Social Marketers Say Measuring ROI Is a Top Challenge in Trust Radius Survey," *The Simply Measured Blog*, June 2, 2015, http://simplymeasured.com/blog/60-of-marketers-say-measuring-roi-is-top-challenge-in-trustradius-survey/#i.66cuzs1ouvfhfx.
3. Christina Warren, "Facebook Fans Valued at $3.60 Each [STATS]," *Mashable*, April 14, 2010, http://mashable.com/2010/04/14/facebook-fan-valuation/.

4. "Faster, Cheaper Fashion," *The Economist*, September 5, 2015, http://www.economist.com/news/business/21663221-rapidly-rising-super-cheap-irish-clothes-retailer-prepares-conquer-america-rivals-should.
5. Courtney Reagan, "Retailers Get Ready: Primark Is on the Move," *CNBC*, September 24, 2015, http://www.cnbc.com/2015/09/21/primark-could-change-the-game-for-us-retailers.html.
6. Associated British Foods, "2015 Annual Report and Accounts" (Associated British Foods, 2015), http://www.abf.co.uk/documents/pdfs/2015/abf-annual-report%202015.pdf.
7. Jonah Berger, *Contagious: Why Things Catch on* (New York: Simon & Schuster, 2013), 37–44.
8. Zoe Szathmary and Erica Tempesta, "Americans Go Wild as British Retailer Primark Opens First in Boston," *DailyMail.com*, October 23, 2015, http://www.dailymail.co.uk/femail/article-3286834/I-felt-like-kid-candy-store-Americans-wild-loved-British-retailer-Primark-fast-fashion-brand-opens-store-Boston.html.
9. Andrea Felsted and Hannah Kuchler, "Instagram: Retail's Holy Grail," *Financial Times*, July 27, 2015, http://www.ft.com/intl/cms/s/0/bef817ae-31f1-11e5-91ac-a5e17d9b4cff.html#axzz3quZBWSVD.
10. Hilary Milnes, "On Social, 'Primania' Looks to Fill Primark's E-Commerce Void," *Digiday*, December 22, 2015, http://digiday.com/brands/social-primania-looks-fill-primarks-e-commerce-void/.
11. Jack Loechner, "Social Media Creates Brand Awareness for Marketers," *MediaPost*, July 22, 2015, http://www.mediapost.com/publications/article/254309/social-media-creates-brand-awareness-for-marketers.html.
12. Frank V. Cespedes, "Is Social Media Actually Helping Your Company's Bottom Line?" *Harvard Business Review*, March 3, 2015, https://hbr.org/2015/03/is-social-media-actually-helping-your-companys-bottom-line.
13. James B. Oldroyd, Kristina McElheran, and David Elkington, "The Short Life of Online Sales Leads," *Harvard Business Review*, March 2011, https://hbr.org/2011/03/the-short-life-of-online-sales-leads.
14. "NBA to Set Record in Full-Season-Ticket Sales," *Sports Busines Journal*, October 27, 2014, http://www.sportsbusinessdaily.com/Journal/Issues/2014/10/27/Leagues-and-Governing-Bodies/NBA-meetings.aspx.
15. Kim Davis, "LinkedIn Ups Seat Sales for the Sacramento Kings," *TheHubComms*, July 27, 2015, http://www.thehubcomms.com/social-media/linkedin-ups-seat-sales-for-the-sacramento-kings/article/428775/.
16. Eillie Anzilotti, "How the NBA's Progressivism Is Helping It Thrive," *The Atlantic*, June 19, 2016, http://www.theatlantic.com/business/archive/2016/06/nba-progressivism/487610/.
17. "ESPN, Turner Will Pay A Combined $24B In New Nine-Year NBA Media Rights Deal," *Sports Business Daily*, October 6, 2014, http://www.sportsbusinessdaily.com/Daily/Issues/2014/10/06/Media/NBA-media.aspx.
18. Alexandra Samuel, "How Pinterest's Buy Buttons Can Change E-Commerce," *Harvard Business Review*, June 9, 2015, https://hbr.org/2015/06/how-pinterests-buy-buttons-can-change-e-commerce.
19. Gadi BenMark, "Why the COO Should Lead Social-Media Customer Service | McKinsey & Company," *McKinsey Quarterly*, January 2014, http://www.mckinsey.com/insights/marketing_sales/why_the_coo_should_lead_social_media_customer_service.
20. Jo Piazza, "The Secret of JetBlue's Social Media Success? Stay at Home Moms, Cat Memes—and a Sense of Humor," *Yahoo Style*, July 29, 2014, https://www.yahoo.com/style/the-secrets-of-jetblues-social-media-success-93024204957.html.
21. Lindsay Kolowich, "Delighting People in 140 Characters: An Inside Look at JetBlue's Customer Service Success," *Hubspot*, July 28, 2014, http://blog.hubspot.com/marketing/jetblue-customer-service-twitter.
22. Kerry O'Shea Gorgone, "True Blue Customer Devotion: JetBlue's Marty St. George on Marketing Smarts [Podcast]," *MarketingProfs*, February 25, 2015, http://www.marketingprofs.com/podcasts/2015/27092/social-media-JetBlue-Marty-StGeorge-MarketingSmarts.
23. Ibid.
24. Derrick Harris, "How Data Is Changing the Car Game for Ford," *Gigaom*, April 26, 2013, https://gigaom.com/2013/04/26/how-data-is-changing-the-car-game-for-ford/.

25. Jack Simpson, "How L'Oréal Uses Social Media to Increase Employee Engagement," *Econsultancy*, October 22, 2015, https://econsultancy.com/blog/67091-how-l-oreal-uses-social-media-to-increase-employee-engagement/?utm_campaign=bloglikes&utm_medium=socialnetwork&utm_source=facebook.
26. Christina Beach Thielst, "Engaging Staff with Social Media: Using These Tools Can Help Increase Customer, Physician and Employee Satisfaction," *Healthcare Executive* 26, no. 6 (December 11, 2011): 52.
27. Jaehee Cho, Dong Jin Park, and Zoa Ordonez, "Communication-Oriented Person-Organization Fit as a Key Factor of Job-Seeking Behaviors: Millennials' Social Media Use and Attitudes toward Organizational Social Media Policies," *Cyberpsychology, Behavior And Social Networking* 16, no. 11 (November 2013): 794–799.
28. This case is adapted from the MIT Sloan case series on Sanergy Edward Ruehle and I wrote. For the full case, please see: https://mitsloan.mit.edu/LearningEdge/strategy/Sanergy/Pages/default.aspx.

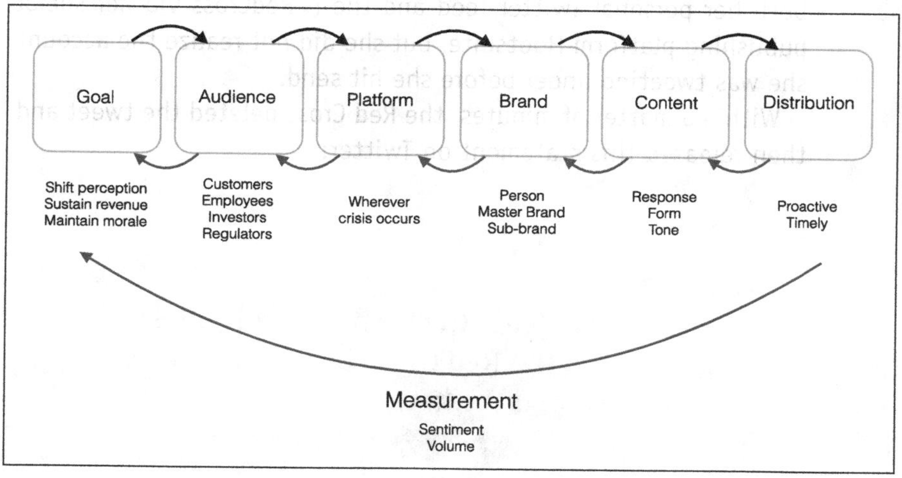

8 Managing Crisis in Social Media

One winter evening the Red Cross tweeted the following:

American Red Cross
@RedCross
Ryan found two more 4 bottle packs of Dogfish Head's Midas Touch beer.... when we drink we do it right #gettngslizzerd
HootSuite · 2/15/11 11:24 PM

#Gettngslizzerd was not the humanitarian organization's new mission. It was the unfortunate punctuation on this classic errant tweet. The Red Cross social media manager, Gloria Huang, managed both her personal Twitter feed and the @RedCross via her social publishing platform Hootsuite, but she did not realize the account she was tweeting under before she hit send.

Within a matter of minutes, the Red Cross deleted the tweet and then released this statement on Twitter:

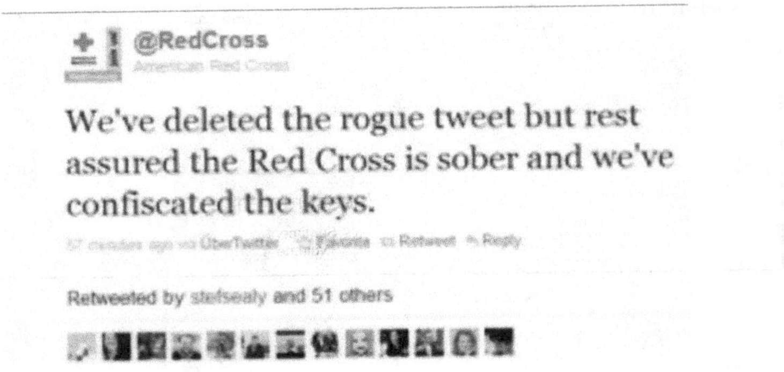

@RedCross
We've deleted the rogue tweet but rest assured the Red Cross is sober and we've confiscated the keys.
Retweeted by stefsealy and 51 others

A couple best practices are operating here. First, the speed with which Red Cross reacted was noteworthy. They stopped the conversation before it got too far out of hand. Second, the tone and manner in which they handled it were also noteworthy. They took the rogue tweet seriously because it was a mistake after all, but they did so with a wink and a nod, making light of the situation.

Soon after, Gloria also responded in kind with a similar tone. It was fair and honest, although who knows about the #gettingslizzard part (note the different spelling). She acknowledged the mistake quickly and effectively.

Rogue tweet frm @RedCross due to my inability to use hootsuite... I wasn't actually #gettingslizzard but just excited! #nowembarassing

Finally, in an effort to capitalize on the conversation, Dogfish Head Brewery got in on the act, turning the potentially negative situation for Red Cross into a "shared media" opportunity.

Dogfish Head Brewery
@dogfishbeer
Follow
RT @Michael_Hayek: #craftbeer @dogfishbeer fans, donate 2 @redcross 2day. Tweet with #gettngslizzerd. Donate here http://tinyurl.com/5s72obb
RETWEETS 28
LIKES 4
9:19 AM - 16 Feb 2011

Because of the Red Cross's swift action and self-deprecating response, Gloria's mea culpa, and Dogfish Head Brewery's inspired cross-promotional idea, the crisis not only was managed, but it turned into an opportunity for all involved, bringing surprisingly positive attention to the Red Cross and Dogfish Head accounts on Twitter.

• • •

To be clear, not all crises will end as successfully as this one. Justine Sacco, a public relations representative for IAC (InterActiveCorp), sent a tweet to her 170 followers shortly before turning off her phone for a flight from London to South Africa. She did not think anything of it and presumably flew in peace. Unfortunately for Justine, who thought she was making a humorous statement, the tweet turned out to be highly inappropriate and racially offensive. When she landed in Cape Town 11 hours later, she found out her tweet and name had been trending worldwide, she had lost her job, and her reputation was besmirched for the foreseeable future.[1]

In today's social media environment, crisis is the new normal. As Steven Fink, crisis management expert and author once wrote, "A crisis in business is as inevitable as death and taxes; it is not a question of if, but rather when."[2] And no matter what, social media will now be a part of the equation, for better or for worse.

It can both be the cause of a crisis as well as a critical communication tool to help manage it.

How can you manage crises in this new social media–driven dynamic? Using the social media management framework as a guide, this chapter will help you develop a social media crisis management blueprint to help you respond when a crisis hits. First, we'll further define crisis in social media. Second, we'll discuss approaches to evaluating the crisis. Third, we'll discuss management and response strategies. Finally, we'll consider executional components of crisis management. By the end of this chapter, you will be equipped with possible strategies and approaches for handling a crisis when it hits.

Crisis in Social Media

Let's start with a common understanding of crisis. Steven Fink offers three definitions that frame his approach to the topic.

- *Crisis*—"an unstable time or state of affairs in which a decisive change is impending."[3]
- *Crisis management*—"deals with the reality of the crisis. It is the actual management of the precarious situation that is rapidly unfolding."[4]
- *Crisis communication*—"managing the perception of that same reality."[5]

For our work together in this chapter, managing perception through social media crisis communication strategies is our critical focus. Here's why: the reality of the crisis can matter little in the social media space. Because everyone has a voice and messages can spread rapidly and unchecked, what audiences *perceive* as the reality is often the challenge to address first and foremost.

Because of social media, crises are more frequent, immediate, and ubiquitous. So how do crises originate? As figure 8.1 illustrates, crises can come from both online and offline spheres. Invariably, social media can amplify a crisis in either sphere. It can turn a crisis originating offline into a major situation. Or, if a crisis starts online, it can provoke enough conversation to spread the crisis offline. Let's look at each category in more detail.

The first and most obvious social media crisis is the one that originates online in social media. Within this category of online social media crises, there are two types: the brand-created social media #fails and the customer complaint. Regarding the brand #fails, the Red Cross errant tweet crisis mentioned earlier is a primary

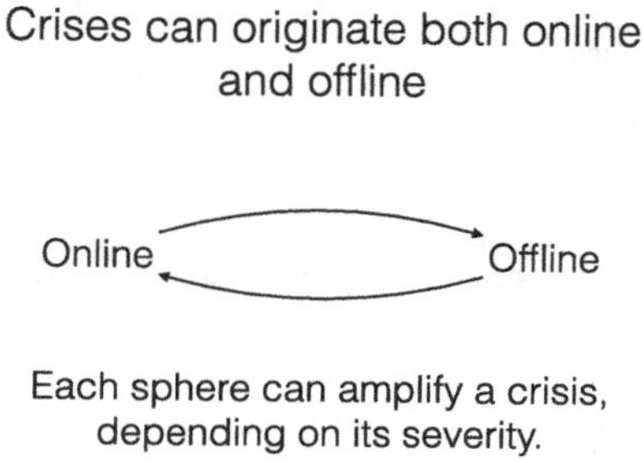
Crises can originate both online and offline
Online
Offline
Each sphere can amplify a crisis, depending on its severity.

FIGURE 8.1 **Where Crises Originate**

example. This type of crisis occurs as a direct result of an organization's social media presences—an inappropriate Facebook post, a tweet taken out of context, an ill-conceived YouTube video, and so on.

The other key source of social media crisis is the customer complaint. Bank of America is one firm that faced a combination of the customer complaint and #brandfail crisis. Outside one of its Manhattan branches, an activist used chalk to create an antiforeclosure sign on the sidewalk. When the police allegedly forced him to leave, he tweeted with the message here and tagged @bankofamerica:

darthmarkh
@darthmarkh
Follow
Just got chased away by #NYPD 4 'obstructing sidewalk' while #chalkupy-ing with @CyMadD0x outside @bankofamerica HQ
BUS
ILLEGAL FORECLOSURES
FRAUD
THEFT
RETWEETS
258
LIKES
132
3:52 PM - 6 Jul 2013

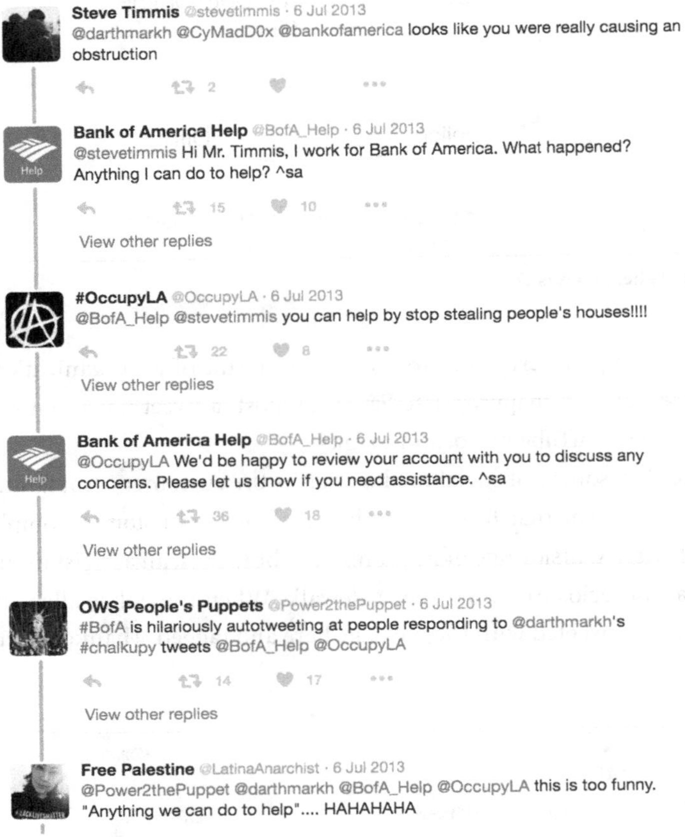

Steve Timmis @stevetimmis · 6 Jul 2013
@darthmarkh @CyMadD0x @bankofamerica looks like you were really causing an obstruction
2
Bank of America Help @BofA_Help · 6 Jul 2013
@stevetimmis Hi Mr. Timmis, I work for Bank of America. What happened? Anything I can do to help? ^sa
15 10
View other replies
#OccupyLA @OccupyLA · 6 Jul 2013
@BofA_Help @stevetimmis you can help by stop stealing people's houses!!!!
22 8
View other replies
Bank of America Help @BofA_Help · 6 Jul 2013
@OccupyLA We'd be happy to review your account with you to discuss any concerns. Please let us know if you need assistance. ^sa
36 18
View other replies
OWS People's Puppets @Power2thePuppet · 6 Jul 2013
#BofA is hilariously autotweeting at people responding to @darthmarkh's #chalkupy tweets @BofA_Help @OccupyLA
14 17
View other replies
Free Palestine @LatinaAnarchist · 6 Jul 2013
@Power2thePuppet @darthmarkh @BofA_Help @OccupyLA this is too funny. "Anything we can do to help".... HAHAHAHA

The bank then responded with boilerplate language asking whether they could help with his account, an undeniably awkward response that made it seem like autobots ran their Twitter feed (although Bank of America publicly denied this was the case).[6] Then @darthmarkh's tweet and @BofA_Help's responses were picked up by other Twitter users, as the screenshot here shows, calling attention to what Bank of America may have hoped was only a one-to-one communication. Raising the visibility of the situation even more, a variety of publications wrote about the customer service interaction gone awry.[7]

In a previous media era, the disgruntled protester may have called Bank of America on its customer service telephone line to vent his frustrations and the response would only be his to hear. Under these circumstances, perhaps the incident could have been contained. Instead, the exchange played out in full public view, and Twitter users and the media magnified Bank of America's faux pas as a result.

Whereas crises now develop in social media (either through a brand's #fail or a customer's actions), crises also originate in the offline world but are then influenced by social media. In this respect, social media can have an impact in a couple different ways: igniting a crisis and amplifying it. First, in terms of igniting a crisis, an organization could make a decision that in a pre-social world may be confined to its local market or employee base. But with the advent of social media, the potential for broader reach can be significant. For example, the British music retailer HMV announced mass layoffs for its company in 2013. Although the decision was controversial and heartbreaking to those involved, it was not the first time that a company has announced layoffs. However, because of social media, the decision became a globally reported crisis for the company. An employee logged into the HMV official Twitter account and began live tweeting the firings, using a hashtag #hmvXFactorFiring.[8] A sampling of those tweets is shown here.

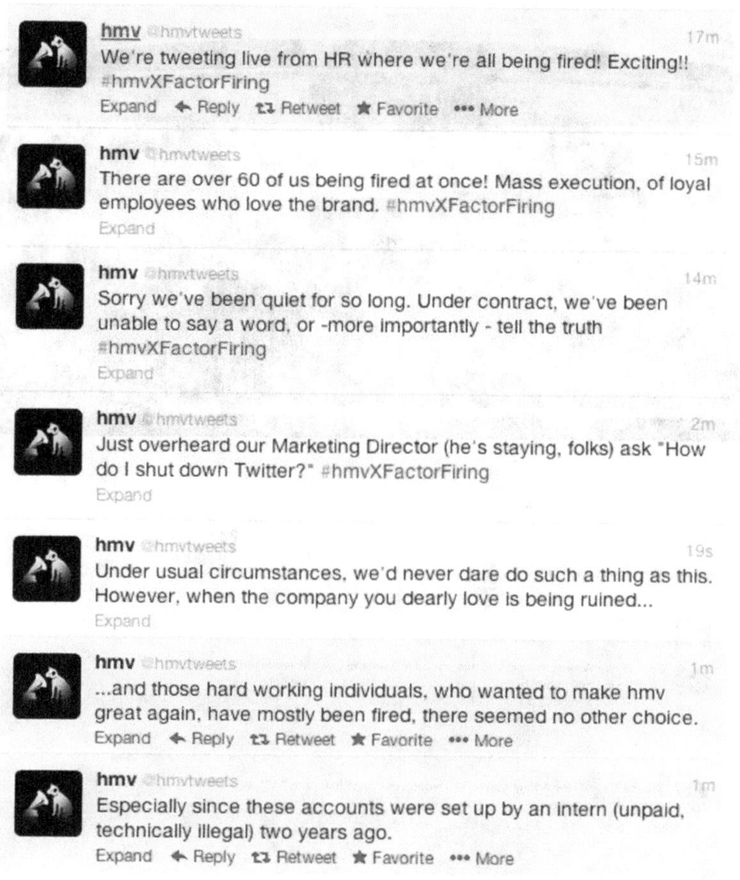

This Twitter takeover was a wake-up call for the HMV executive team to put in place better social media policies and procedures. It was also an example of how social media can ignite a crisis from an offline event that would likely have gone unnoticed in another media era. Thinking about the social media implications and response must now be a component of most major decision making at organizations large and small.

In the offline world, social media can not only ignite a crisis but also amplify and sustain it. The global crisis Volkswagen found itself in is a case in point. When the allegations broke in 2015 that Volkswagen had cheated on the emissions tests of its diesel vehicles, the public outcry via social media exploded.[9] Volkswagen was immediately put on the defensive, and disgruntled customers took to Twitter and Facebook to vent their frustrations. The post here was Volkswagen's last update on its Facebook page before the scandal. Notice the comments.

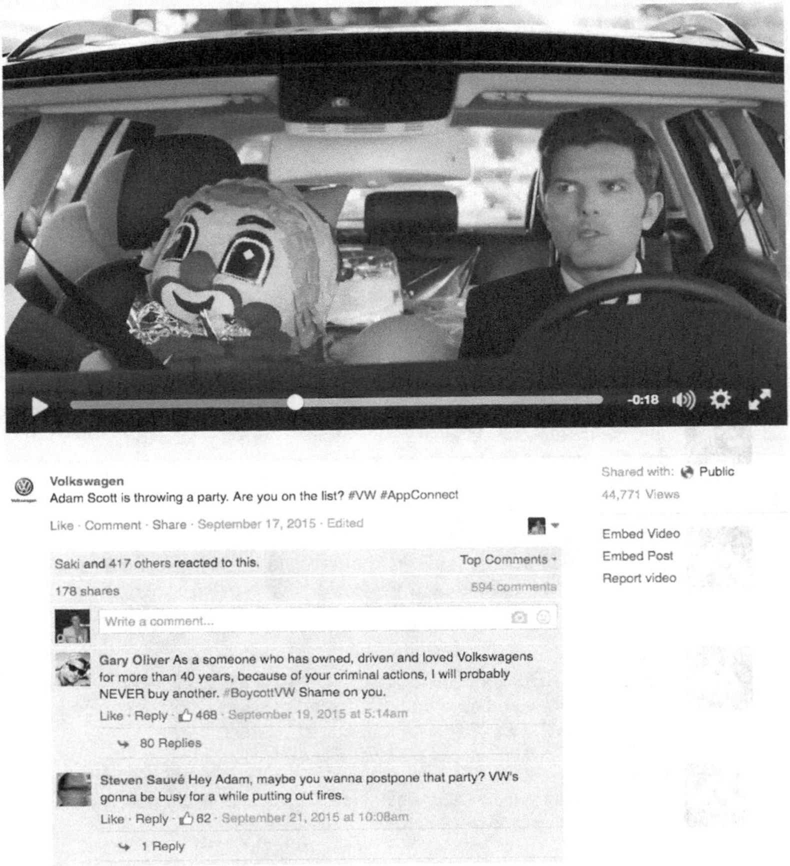

With the crisis accelerating in social media, the company was now forced to develop a cross-platform response strategy. After the Adam Scott party post, Volkswagen did not post on its Facebook page again for another week, when the president and CEO of the American division offered his apology in the post here.[10]

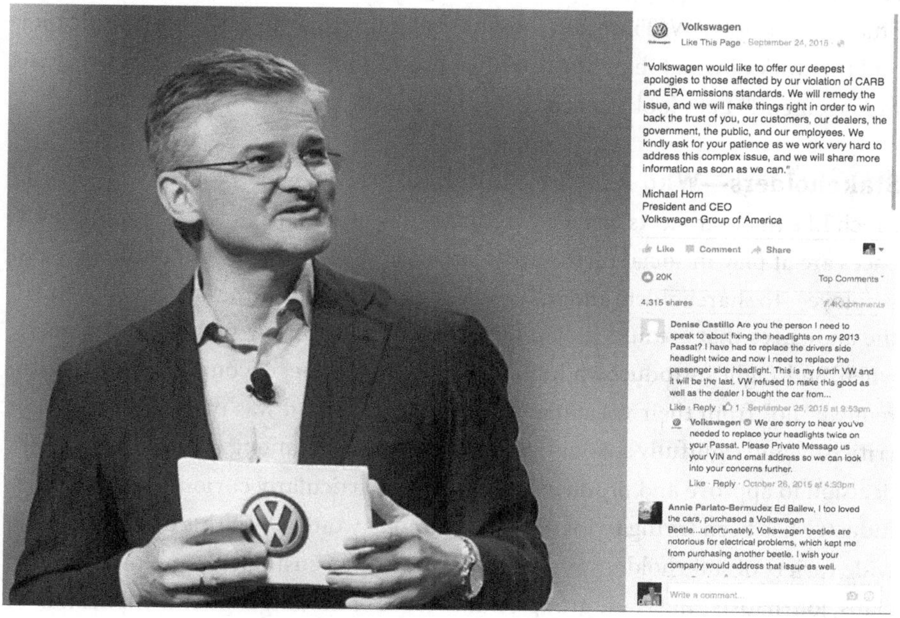

Over time, the brand started to use social media to communicate information and solutions to the problem, but their initial response (or lack thereof) only instigated a difficult situation. As we will discuss shortly, transparency and timing are key guiding principles in social media crisis response. For now, let the Volkswagen case serve as a reminder that crises originating offline can and will accelerate in social media, and companies must now be prepared for it. As we've seen, social media crises can originate from a number of different sources. Online, they can be stimulated by the brand and/or customers. Offline, they can be ignited or amplified by powerful social media communication tools. The bottom line is this: crisis management now requires constant monitoring of all potential sources of crises. Of course, the best crisis management strategy is to avoid the crisis altogether. Knowing where to look and how to avoid it will help significantly. But after the crisis occurs, how should you react? In the next section, we'll address a key first step: evaluating the crisis.

Evaluating a Social Media Crisis

When a crisis in social media hits, analyze the situation to determine if and how you should respond. To help in your analysis, consider five key factors to better understand the reality and perception of the situation: stakeholders, type, truth, severity, and credibility (summarized in figure 8.2). This situation analysis combines both scholar W. Timothy Coombs's seminal work on crisis communication and the work of Gita Johar, Matthias Birk, and Sabine Einwiller on effective crisis management.[11] Let's look at each component of the analysis in more detail.

Stakeholders—Who Are the Stakeholders?

Much like in other facets of social media, as discussed in chapter 2, multiple audiences are at play in social media crisis situations. They range from customers and employees to shareholders and the government. A good routine is to account for all the audiences that are affected and then prioritize your key targets. For example, when Bud Light introduced a highly objectionable label encouraging drinkers to remove "no" from their vocabulary while out at night, it was met with significant criticism (and rightfully so) on social media, especially among women. The brand's decision to approve and produce this label was particularly curious, since the beer industry has been trying to increase sales among women.[12] In this circumstance, a wide variety of stakeholders were involved, including customers, employees, politicians, journalists, and trade groups. But because of the language and implication of the label, the brand needed to design a response that primarily addressed the concerns of women and women's rights activists, regardless of whether they were

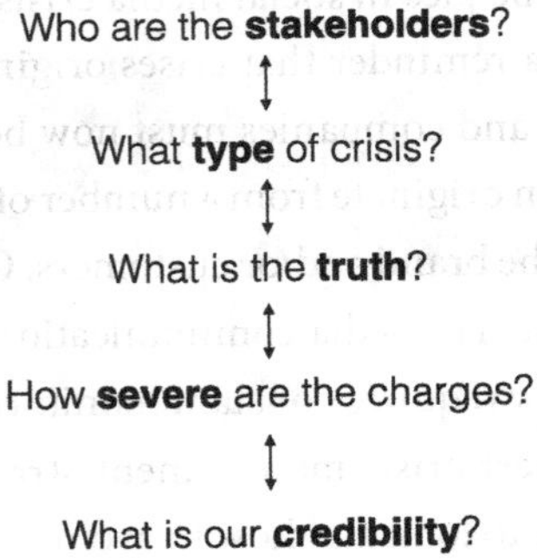

Who are the **stakeholders**?
What **type** of crisis?
What is the **truth**?
How **severe** are the charges?
What is our **credibility**?

FIGURE 8.2 **Crisis Situation Analysis**

consumers of Bud Light. The company reacted swiftly to admit fault and stated, "We would never condone disrespectful or irresponsible behavior."[13] They also halted production on additional bottles with the label. It is unclear if this response fully mitigated the situation, but it was clearly directed to those audiences who were justifiably offended. On the other hand, if a crisis threatened the stock price of parent company Anheuser-Busch InBev, then the choice of primary target would likely be shareholders, and the response strategy would be different as well. In general, having a strong understanding of stakeholders—and who needs to be addressed—will be critical in your response strategy.

Type—What Type of Crisis?

The next factor to consider is the type of crisis. Depending on the type of crisis your organization is facing, you will likely respond differently. To help categorize the types, Coombs identifies three general categories: victim, accident, and preventable.[14]

The victim crisis usually refers to situations outside of an organization's control. For example, Commonwealth Edison, the electricity utility in Chicago, found itself in a crisis when severe thunderstorms resulted in power outages across the Chicagoland area. Clearly, customers were not happy to be without power—and often the electric utility is not necessarily the most well-liked organization in a city. But because it was a victim crisis and ComEd effectively used social media to communicate key information about their efforts to restore power, the utility navigated the situation as effectively as it could, given the circumstances.[15]

The accident crisis is a situation where an organization is involved but might not be fully responsible for the situation. When Dell laptop computers were spontaneously imploding due to faulty batteries, the company positioned itself—along with its customers—as the bystander to this accidental crisis. The maker of the batteries, Sony, bore the brunt of the criticism.[16] Whether Dell deserves some of the responsibility is a legitimate question, but they recognized early that emphasizing Sony's role in this accidental crisis was a viable strategy, and that helped them shape the perception of the crisis accordingly.

The preventable crisis occurs, however, when the mistake or mishap could have been avoided. A number of examples fall into this category. For instance, seeking to capitalize on the Twitter conversation about protests in Egypt, Kenneth Cole tweeted an insensitive message suggesting that "rumor is they heard our new spring collection is now available online."[17] This tweet was entirely preventable. Moreover, offline crises such as the BP Deepwater Horizon oil spill can also be categorized as preventable. Indeed, a key reason why BP dealt with the crisis for so long was the mounting evidence suggesting BP was liable for and could have prevented the damage.[18]

Why does the type of crisis matter? It will inform the scope of response your organization develops. Being in the position of the victim, an organization faces a unique set of opportunities and challenges, as some stakeholders will be sympathetic to your cause, whereas others may not be. Meanwhile, the accidental crisis can be particularly difficult depending on the impact of the crisis event. Again, some stakeholders will withhold blame, but others may not. Finally, preventable crises usually require the most sophisticated and strategic response, since organizations are usually the target of significant blame. No matter the crisis type, once you identify it (and quickly), identifying the truth is the next step in evaluating the situation.

Truth—What Is the Truth?

It may seem like an obvious point, but getting a handle on the truth of the matter is arguably the most important component of the situation analysis. If the charges against your organization are true, a strategy of denial may not serve you well over the long term. However, if the allegations are false, taking a more aggressive stance against your critics will be justified. For example, Taco Bell was once accused in a lawsuit of using only 36% beef in its "seasoned beef" recipe. The company categorically denied those claims and ramped up a cross-platform crisis communication response to refute the allegations, which emphasized the 88% real beef and 12% "signature recipe" ratio.[19] By most measures, the company weathered the storm and benefited from support from its customers on social media as well. In short, the truth (as well as what your stakeholders perceive it to be) will be a key factor in your response strategy.

Severity—How Severe Are the Charges?

The severity of the charges also will inform your response strategy. As a general rule, the more severe the charges, the more substantial your crisis communication response should be. For example, let's say you're running social media for the Hilton Hotel chain. If a customer complains on your Facebook page that their room wasn't ready until 8 p.m., 5 hours past the documented check-in time, you may have a minor crisis on your hands, but the charge is not too severe. Yes, this particular chain could improve its logistics, but the customer was not inconvenienced too much for the 5-hour delay. Alternatively, your hotel could be hosting a huge conference and serve bad chicken, giving salmonella to hundreds of attendees. This is a more severe crisis and would probably require a national and/or international response to assure customers, employees, and shareholders worldwide that the incident was isolated. As it turned out for Chipotle, news of an outbreak of *E. coli* in a small number of its locations became water cooler conversation on social and traditional media in the United States, which led to a quick and significant drop in its stock price.[20] Severity also has implications for who will speak on behalf of the company, which we'll discuss momentarily.

Credibility—What Is Our Credibility?

The final situation analysis factor is the credibility of your organization. Think of it as a repository of goodwill. Depending on the crisis, if you have a strong bank of goodwill and trust with your stakeholders, they may be more forgiving of your actions. In fact, they may even come to your defense. However, as Coombs also suggests, there are crisis intensifiers such as history of crisis, negative reputation, and low credibility that may make the crisis more difficult to manage.[21] During Toyota's infamous unintended acceleration crisis, the company made many mistakes in the beginning stages—they did not identify the source of the problem or properly acknowledge the severity of the crisis. Moreover, there was a sense (fairly or unfairly) that the truth was being obscured or manipulated. Despite all the troubles, Toyota had built up enough credibility—and had a very minor previous history in these types of crises—that customers eventually came back to the brand.[22] Without high credibility and the track record for quality, Toyota may not have rebounded in the way that it did.

As with any communication challenge, analyzing and evaluating the situation is the critical first step. The factors discussed here—stakeholders, type, truth, severity, and credibility—will inform how you and your organization develop a response strategy. In the next section, let's look at the building blocks of your response.

Responding to a Social Media Crisis

How can you think about responding to a social media crisis? The social media management framework can be helpful in this context as well. By now, the specific elements should be familiar to you, but the ways in which you might apply them to a crisis challenge will be slightly different.

Goal—Focus Your Goal on Mitigating the Crisis

Your overall business goals in a crisis situation will still be the same as in more normal times. It's just that the crisis places your ability to achieve those goals in jeopardy. As such, you'll need to focus your efforts initially on mitigating the crisis. To do so, be specific about your crisis communication goals. Sample goals include the following:

- Shift perception and share of voice to your desired position.
- Direct audiences to a specific action.
- Improve brand health.

Of course, diffusing the crisis is the overarching goal, but by being more specific and targeted in what you're trying to accomplish, you'll position yourself to navigate the uncertainty more successfully and perhaps even earn respect and credibility for your response.

Audience—Identify Your Key Targets

Based on the prioritization of your stakeholders, as discussed in the previous section, identify the key audiences you need to reach. It may be that convincing one or two key audience groups will spell the difference between success and failure in social crisis communication.

Platforms—Engage in Platforms Where the Crisis Is Occurring

Based on your goals and key audiences, you will have more clarity on which platforms to use for your messaging. As a general rule of thumb, if a crisis erupts in a certain social media channel, it would be wise to include that channel as part of your response strategy. A crisis on Instagram will not be fully resolved through a press release on your website. You must engage directly on the platform in question and more often than not employ other platforms where related conversations are happening.

Brand—Select the Communicator That Is Appropriate to the Situation

Brand strategy questions become arguably more complex in social media crisis situations. Who will respond? Will it be the brand itself? A corporate spokesperson? The CEO? Generally speaking, for more severe crises, the CEO or other senior-most leaders should be involved. However, if the crisis is not severe, a senior executive's involvement may unnecessarily exacerbate the situation. Also, in important matters, using the master brand account may not be the appropriate strategy either, as stakeholders may demand to hear directly from the humans running the company.

Content—Develop a Content Strategy in Support of Your Goals

In developing your message content, there are three key considerations: your response strategy, the message format (video, written, etc.), and your tone. Let's look at each in more detail:

Response Strategy. Scholar William Benoit developed the image restoration theory, which includes a number of crisis response strategies.[23] These strategies apply across platforms, not only to traditional forms of media but also the social media space as well. Following are the five key types of responses. Your situation analysis will guide you to the appropriate response.

- *Denial*—when you know the truth and the charges against you are false, your organization can employ the denial strategy with confidence. Conversely, if you deny, but are withholding the truth, the damage can be irreparable.
- *Apologizing and mortification*—if your organization has made a mistake, apologizing and expressing remorse over the situation can be effective, especially if it happens quickly. Severity also plays a role here. If the crisis is not severe, a swift apology, like that from the Red Cross case, is all that's necessary. But with a more severe crisis, such as Volkswagen's emissions violations, other response tactics will be necessary, such as corrective action.
- *Corrective action*—usually paired with an apology, corrective action lays out what you and your organization will do to solve the problem in the future. It communicates to your stakeholders that you are doing everything that you can to move on from the crisis and right whatever wrongs have occurred.
- *Evasion of responsibility*—this response can pair well with the accidental type of crisis. Dell's move to place more of the blame on Sony for the battery malfunctions was a textbook case. For this strategy to work, evasion of responsibility should be grounded in the truth.

- *Reduce the offensiveness of the event*—to manage the perception of a crisis, sometimes organizations can try to make the event seem less severe than it actually is. The risk is making light of a situation. If a natural disaster like a hurricane hits, treating it lightly via social media communications (or other media platforms for that matter) will be a losing strategy.

Format. The second key content consideration is the format your message will take. Your options are as follows: text, video, and/or image. If you go with a text-only response, you have the advantage of tightly controlling the message. However, you may lose some of the emotional appeal of a more visual approach. The video approach can be helpful, especially if you choose a representative from your organization to deliver the message, but that representative must be an effective communicator appropriate to the situation. You also have opportunities to use the video setting to influence the message. For example, an executive at Volkswagen might deliver a message while on the plant floor to show the audience visual evidence of the company following proper procedures with their gas tanks. Finally, the image approach can enable an organization to tell its story quickly and effectively. The con of this approach is that you may lose the human quality of video and message control of text. Regardless of what you choose, prepare for whatever content format to be taken out of context. The phrase in your tweet, 5-second video snippet, and Photoshopped image will inevitably be parsed and reconfigured in the social media age, so be careful as to how your audiences may react to every single snippet of content.

Tone. The third and final message consideration is tone. In general, a positive, human, transparent tone will resonate in social media more than an overly corporate or bureaucratic tone. Organizations, especially large for-profit companies, may face widespread skepticism during the outset of a crisis. Using a more formal tone in any of the messaging may only fuel mistrust along the way. To the extent possible, try to maintain the same brand voice (as discussed in chapter 5 and the JetBlue example in chapter 7) in your social media communications during the crisis situation. Not only what you communicate but the tone in which you do so is critical to effective crisis communications. Maintain your brand voice in these situations and offer that human, positive, and empathetic tone.

In short, the three content considerations are response strategy, format, and tone. Of course, they all work together, as the response strategy will inform the message format and the tone used to communicate it.

Distribution—Act Swiftly and Transparently

The advent of social media has put enormous pressure on organizations to respond in times of crisis. In general, swift action is appreciated in uncertain times. So, if possible, the distribution plan for your social crisis communication strategy should be quick and efficient. The more time that goes by without an answer or response, the more that doubt among your constituents increases. As a result, the crisis may only intensify due to the public demands for answers on social media. That said, an organization should not act without a purpose. If you do not know the truth yet, it is better to be transparent, making clear what you know, what you do not know, and what actions you're taking to fill in the gaps. Because of the demand of the media and customers to know key information in times of crisis, being proactive and "overcommunicating" is typically critical to success.

Measurement—Track Volume and Sentiment of Conversations over Time

Finally, how will you know that you are successful in your social media crisis communication efforts? Here's where social media listening tools can be particularly helpful. Let's say you want to measure the first goal we identified earlier: your ability to shift perception and share of voice to your position. You could track social media posts by customers from the start of the crisis to a certain point in time and correlate your social media efforts to changes in the following: volume of posts and sentiment of posts. Although not a comprehensive measure of your entire crisis communication strategy, looking at the volume of posts and how it increased or decreased will give you a sense of how the crisis communication initiatives are going. Moreover, in your effort to manage the perception of the crisis, examining the sentiment—and whether it has trended positively or negatively during the course of the crisis—will offer insight into whether you are achieving your goal to shift perception. For measurement of crisis communication efforts in social media, social listening is an indispensible measurement tool and should be a key source of ongoing data about the crisis. Moreover, it will help you uncover key learnings that will refine your blueprint for future crises, when needed.

The fundamental concepts of goal, audience, platforms, brand, content, distribution, and measurement still apply in social media crisis situations. To illustrate these concepts, let's look at the efforts of FedEx to reverse the negative of a YouTube video that went viral.

CASE STUDY: FEDEX RIGHTS A WRONG

When you do business with FedEx, your expectation is that the packages will be handled with care. During one delivery in 2011, that wasn't the case. With a new computer monitor in tow, a FedEx delivery person walked up to his final destination, a home. Rather than gently dropping off the monitor in front of the door, the delivery person thought it would be more efficient to toss the monitor over the wall that separated the house from the sidewalk. A surveillance camera caught the whole episode on tape. The owner then decided to upload the video evidence to YouTube, and the video subsequently spread in social media, amassing millions of views within days. Not good for FedEx.

How would FedEx analyze the situation? They knew they were dealing with a preventable type of crisis that primarily affected their customers. The charge was true, due to the video evidence, and it was moderately

YouTube
FedEx
0:11 / 0:20
FedEx Guy Throwing My Computer Monitor
goobie55's channel
Subscribe
1,093
9,604,051
Add to
Share
More
19,398
1,309
Uploaded on Dec 19, 2011
Here is a video of my monitor being "delivered". The sad part is that I was home at the time with the front door wide open. All he would have had to do was ring the bell on the gate. Now I have to return my monitor since it is broken.

severe—no one was hurt, but it did strike at the core of their primary service. Finally, they were operating from a position of strength with credibility. Their history of similar crises was limited.

To FedEx's credit, they activated a social media crisis response strategy that effectively managed the crisis (both the perception and the reality). They did a number of noteworthy things. First, they were clear on their goal—to preserve their reputation as a reliable company and position this incident as isolated. They focused on their customer base and sought to reach them primarily on YouTube, where the video of the delivery mishap first appeared. In terms of content, they wrote a blog post on their corporate blog and embedded a YouTube video they created with the SVP of US Operations communicating a message that apologized, expressed mortification, and offered corrective action (i.e., the employee was fired). They

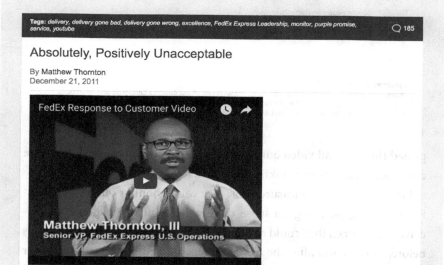

Tags: *delivery, delivery gone bad, delivery gone wrong, excellence, FedEx Express Leadership, monitor, purple promise, service, youtube* 185

Absolutely, Positively Unacceptable

By Matthew Thornton
December 21, 2011

Along with many of you, we've seen the video showing one of our couriers carelessly and improperly delivering a package the other day. As the leader of our pickup and delivery operations across America, I want you to know that I was upset, embarrassed, and very sorry for our customer's poor experience. This goes directly against everything we have always taught our people and expect of them. It was just very disappointing.

However, from the customer's perspective, I am pleased to let you know that the matter has been resolved in a very positive way. We have met with the customer face to face and they already have a replacement monitor at no cost to them. They have accepted our apology and say they are fully satisfied with what we've done in response to this unacceptable delivery. They've made it clear, though, that they prefer not to be identified in any way, and in this case as always with customers, we fully respect their privacy.

CONTINUED

CASE STUDY: FEDEX RIGHTS A WRONG *CONTINUED*

YouTube
Matthew Thornton, III
Senior VP, FedEx Express U.S. Operations
0:04 / 1:42
FedEx Response to Customer Video
Official FedEx YouTube Channel
Subscribe 15,813
596,094
Add to
Share
More
3,403
362
Uploaded on Dec 21, 2011
"Along with many of you, we've seen the video showing one of our couriers carelessly and improperly delivering a package the other day. As the leader of our pickup and delivery operations across America, I want you to know that I was upset, embarrassed, and very sorry for our customer's poor experience. This

posted the blog and video quickly after the crisis first occurred, to assure customers that they were taking swift action.[24]

Finally, in terms of measurement, they could monitor online sentiment from the blog post to get a sense of how the company response was received. Of course, they could also track the number of shipments and sales before, during, and after the crisis. In general, FedEx was applauded for their actions to address the isolated incident and preserve their solid reputation.[25]

The strategy worked not only because it was informed by a keen awareness of the situation but also because their response was tailored to the social media space. Everything from the goal to the platform to the content and distribution strategy was appropriate to the social media space, and they avoided more dire consequences as a result.

Like in other business contexts, the social media management framework is intended to be flexible and a starting point. The same is true when you apply it to social media crises. The timeline may be urgent, but the fundamental issues of the framework are still at play. Of course, an organization may have the best plan on paper to manage a crisis, but if it is not executed effectively, then the crisis will only worsen. In the next section we take a look at best practices of executing social media crisis management.

Executing Social Media Crisis Management

When a crisis hits, the uncertainty and chaos within an organization can be an added and difficult challenge. To help your organization plan for the inevitable social media crisis, consider these invaluable organizational measures to manage crises effectively. Here's the key: *all these decisions should be made prior to when the crisis hits.*

Executive Alignment

At the highest levels of the company, the executive team must be aligned with the strategy and approach. It seems like a simple task, but in times of crisis, getting everyone on the same page, and fast, is critical. Here's why: top executives have the authority to communicate with external audiences. All it takes is one tweet or post from the COO that is different from the overall company's strategy to cause further damage or a setback to the crisis management steps taken thus far. To avoid confusion, set up a clear chain of command that will ensure all parties are operating from the same strategy.

Designated Team with Clear Roles and Responsibilities

The crisis free-for-all can mean many well-intentioned employees will be trying to do their part. Although all hands on deck sounds useful in times of need, it will only create more confusion. Do your organization a favor and designate the crisis communication response team. It should be interdisciplinary—people from communications, product, marketing, technology, and so on, and all of them must be conversant in social media platforms and strategy. Then, once you have the team in place, designate specific roles and lanes for people to operate in. You should also do crisis simulations so that this team can better understand how to work with one another once the real problem occurs.

Appropriate Staffing and Resources

Along with designating the team, ensure that they have the resources, people, and tools to respond effectively. A crisis can make or break a company's reputation. It is wishful thinking that an ad hoc team that only focuses on crisis management when the crisis happens will navigate it successfully.

Constant Monitoring and Reporting

As we discussed in the measurement section, social media listening tools are critical to understanding how stakeholders are perceiving the crisis and your efforts to mitigate it. Along with the resource discussion, your organization should invest in these tools to keep the pulse of the conversation and report to key internal decision makers on a regular basis as to the current state of the crisis.

Mechanism for Iteration and Quick Decision Making

Finally, the time to deliberate actions in the social media crisis age is not long. The committee and executive leadership your organization identifies should be equipped to make decisions quickly based on new data from your social media monitoring efforts. Speed and transparency of communications are now the expectation, and your organization must be set up to deliver on it.

The most beneficial crisis communication work an organization can engage in is precrisis planning. Aligning executives, assigning team members and specific roles, providing appropriate resources, constantly monitoring the conversation and response, and instituting a mechanism for feedback and quick decision making are all best practices for successful execution of crisis communication in social media when the time comes.

Recap: Another Day, Another Potential Crisis

Never before have customers had more direct access to organizations. Social media gives everyone a voice and, as a result, the pressure on organizations to manage crises has only intensified. Crisis is indeed the new normal in the business world. For better or worse, it is now a business routine, and organizations must strategize for it accordingly.

To prepare you for when the time comes, we discussed a variety of topics in this chapter. First, we grounded our discussion in the nature of crisis in social media, as it can originate in both the online and offline world. Then, we introduced and explored three key areas of a crisis management blueprint: (1) the evaluation stage, which includes examining the crisis stakeholders, type, truth, severity, and credibility; (2) the response stage, which leverages the social media management framework to develop your strategy; and (3) the execution stage, which considers the organizational measures, such as executive alignment, cross-functional teams, and monitoring and iteration, that will ensure successful management of the crisis.

The next chapter continues our discussion of how the social media management framework applies to different contexts in business and looks specifically at the use of social media platforms within organizations.

Your Turn: Kashi Crisis Management

Kashi cereals had built a devoted fan base for a number of years. They touted their commitment to "natural" ingredients, which were presumably free of genetically modified organisms (GMOs). However, the Cornucopia Institute, a nonprofit consumer protection and food rights organization, published a study revealing the true definition of natural and that the soy in the Kashi cereals was genetically modified.[26]

When the owner of the Green Grocer in Rhode Island came across this report, he pulled his inventory and replaced it with this note. A customer then took a photo of it, uploaded it onto Facebook, and then a social media crisis erupted.

Growing Organic, Eating Organic with Ghee Keay and 14 others.
Like Page
April 27, 2012 ·
This photo was taken at a supermarket called The Green Grocer in Porthsmouth, RI. Let's encourage all of our grocery stores to tell the truth like this! And also contact Kashi and let them know that you don't want GMO Soy and Pesticides.
The yellow signs read: "You might be wondering where your favorite Kashi cereals have gone. It has recently come to our attention that 100% of the soy used in Kashi is Genetically Modified and that when the USDA tested the grains used there were found to be pesticides that are known carcinogens and hormone disruptors."
WHERE'S MY KASHI?!
Kashi
You might be wondering where your favorite Kashi cereals have gone. It has recently come to our attention that 100% of the soy used in Kashi products is Genetically Modified, and that when the USDA tested the grains used there were found to be pesticides that are known carcinogens and hormone disruptors.
Cranberry Chew

Customers took to the Kashi Facebook page with comments such as these:

Had I known I was buying a product that was like all the others in the "normal" cereal aisle. . . . I would have never purchased it and I certainly would not have paid the high prices!!!!! It disgusts me.

Yours is the only brand cereal I have bought for years. Not anymore! You are despicable. Everything you supposedly stand for is a lie.

This is where you come in. Put yourself in the shoes of the Kashi social media team and develop a crisis management plan. Before you get to work, here are three pieces of additional context on the situation:

1. The charges are true. Kashi uses some GMOs in its foods.
2. According to Kashi General Manager, David DeSouza, "The FDA has chosen not to regulate the term 'natural.'" . . . Kashi's definition of natural was "food that's minimally processed, made with no artificial colors, flavors, preservatives or sweeteners."[27]
3. Finally, because of the irate reaction of avid Kashi customers on social media, mainstream media outlets are beginning to write about the negative posts, bringing even more attention to the crisis.

As you work on your crisis management plan, consider the following steps:

- *Evaluate*—analyze the situation according to crisis stakeholders, type, truth, severity, and credibility
- *Respond*—decide on a goal and develop a response strategy informed by the audience, platforms, brand, content, distribution, and measurement
- *Execute*—create an organizational execution plan. What type of team and structure would you put into place?

You have no restrictions. This crisis is not abating any time soon, and the one thing you know for sure is that doing nothing will not solve it. In your teams you will be asked to report to the general manager on a new plan of action to stem the tide. Good luck.

Notes

1. Jon Ronson, "How One Stupid Tweet Blew Up Justine Sacco's Life—The New York Times," *The New York Times Magazine*, February 12, 2015, http://www.nytimes.com/2015/02/15/magazine/how-one-stupid-tweet-ruined-justine-saccos-life.html?_r=1.
2. Steven Fink, *Crisis Communications: The Definitive Guide to Managing the Message*, 1st ed. (New York: McGraw-Hill Education, 2013).
3. Steven Fink, *Crisis Management: Planning for the Inevitable* (New York, NY: American Management Association, 1986), 15.
4. Fink, *Crisis Communications*, 8.
5. Ibid.
6. Saya Weissman, "Bank of America's Epic Twitter Fail," *Digiday*, July 11, 2013, http://digiday.com/brands/bank-of-americas-epic-twitter-fail/.
7. Ibid; Casey Chan, "Bank of America's Twitter Account Is One Really Really Dumb Robot," *Gizmodo*, July 8, 2013, http://gizmodo.com/bank-of-americas-twitter-account-is-one-really-really-713634226; Gaby Dunn, "Bank of America Twitter Bot Trolls Occupiers," *Salon*, July 8, 2013, http://www.salon.com/2013/07/08/bank_of_america_twitter_bot_glad_to_assist_angry_occupiers_partner/.
8. Emma Rowley, "HMV Staffer Claims Responsibility for Tweeting Mass Sacking," January 31, 2013, http://www.telegraph.co.uk/finance/newsbysector/retailandconsumer/9839855/HMV-staffer-claims-responsibility-for-tweeting-mass-sacking.html.
9. Ben Davis, "Social Media and Crisis Management: A Volkswagen Case Study," *Econsultancy*, September 25, 2015, https://econsultancy.com/blog/66972-social-media-and-crisis-management-a-volkswagen-case-study/?utm_campaign=bloglikes&utm_medium=socialnetwork&utm_source=facebook.
10. Ibid.
11. W. Timothy Coombs, *Ongoing Crisis Communication: Planning, Managing, and Responding* (Thousand Oaks, CA: Sage Publications, 2014); Gita V. Johar, Matthias M. Birk, and Sabine A. Einwiller, "How to Save Your Brand in the Face of Crisis," *MIT Sloan Management Review*, June 11, 2010, http://sloanreview.mit.edu/article/how-to-save-your-brand-in-the-face-of-crisis/.
12. Stephanie Strom, "Bud Light Withdraws Slogan After It Draws Ire Online," *The New York Times*, April 28, 2015, http://www.nytimes.com/2015/04/29/business/bud-light-withdraws-slogan-after-it-draws-ire-online.html.
13. Ibid.
14. W. Timothy Coombs, "Crisis Management and Communications (Updated September 2014)," *Institute for Public Relations*, September 23, 2014, http://www.instituteforpr.org/crisis-management-communications/.
15. Daniel Diermeier and Daniel Petrella, "Commonwealth Edison: The Use of Social Media in Disaster Response," *Kellogg Case Publishing*, 2013, http://www.kellogg.northwestern.edu/kellogg-case-publishing/case-search/case-detail.aspx?caseid=%7Be7174a1e-24d5-4075-8a7b-dcdfabf285b1%7D.
16. Damon Darlin, "Dell Will Recall Batteries in PC's," *The New York Times*, August 15, 2006, http://www.nytimes.com/2006/08/15/technology/15battery.html.
17. Ken Sweet, "Kenneth Cole Egypt Tweets Ignite Firestorm," *CNNMoney*, February 4, 2011, http://money.cnn.com/2011/02/03/news/companies/KennethCole_twitter/.
18. Reuters, "Gulf Oil Spill Could Have Been Prevented By BP Workers Who Weren't Consulted: Report," *The Huffington Post*, May 25, 2011, http://www.huffingtonpost.com/2011/02/17/oil-spill-could-have-been_n_824647.html.
19. Elizabeth Flock, "Taco Bell Says Taco Meat Is Actually Meat; Lawsuit Withdrawn," *Washington Post*, April 19, 2011, https://www.washingtonpost.com/blogs/blogpost/post/taco-bell-meat-is-actually-meat-lawsuit-withdrawn/2011/04/19/AFDiEm4D_blog.html.
20. Sydney Ember, "Chipotle Stock Tumbles after E. Coli Outbreak," *The New York Times*, December 4, 2015, http://www.nytimes.com/2015/12/05/business/chipotle-stock-tumbles-after-e-coli-outbreak.html.

21. W. Timothy Coombs, "Impact of Past Crises on Current Crisis Communication Insights From Situational Crisis Communication Theory," *Journal of Business Communication* 41, no. 3 (July 1, 2004): 265–89.
22. Johar, Birk, and Einwiller, "How to Save Your Brand in the Face of Crisis."
23. William L Benoit, *Accounts, Excuses, and Apologies: A Theory of Image Restoration Strategies*, SUNY series in Communication Studies (Albany: State University of New York Press, 1994), 74–80.
24. Gini Dietrich, "How FedEx Turned a Disaster into a PR Win," *PR Daily*, January 13, 2012, http://www.prdaily.com/Main/Articles/How_FedEx_turned_a_disaster_into_a_PR_win_10539.aspx.
25. Ibid.
26. Cornucopia Institute, *Cereal Crimes*, October 5, 2011, https://www.youtube.com/watch?v=-sw2uEupTwo.
27. Elizabeth Weise, "Kashi Cereal's 'Natural' Claims Stir Anger on Social-Media Sites," *USA TODAY*, April 29, 2012, http://usatoday30.usatoday.com/money/industries/food/story/2012-04-29/kashi-natural-claims/54616576/1.

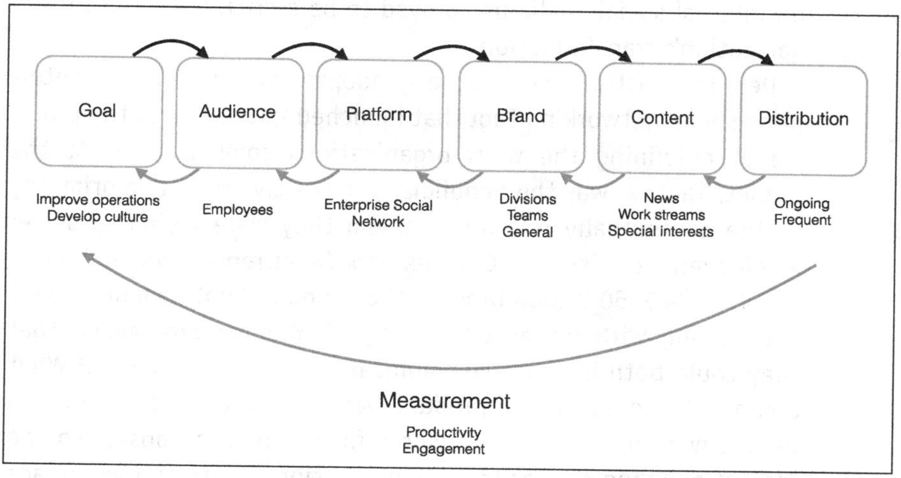

9 Building a Social Culture

In 2003 the Deloitte Australia consulting firm was at an inflection point. Revenues were declining, morale was down, and competitors were outmaneuvering them at seemingly every opportunity. Chief Marketing Officer David Redhill described the situation more bluntly: "I came into this place when we were a $330m business, going south and hemorrhaging money with our reputation in the gutter."[1]

To turn around the company, David and the rest of the senior executive team adeptly identified digital and social media technologies as a catalyst for change. As researchers Kristine Dery, Ina M. Sebastian, and Jeanne W. Ross from the MIT Sloan Center for Information Systems Research (CISR) uncovered, Deloitte adopted social media to help reinvent the organization.[2] Although using social media tools to provide services to clients was part of the equation, the firm looked inward at its employees and thought strategically about how to deploy similar social platforms to create a more transparent, empowered, and innovative workplace. This focus on internal social media use proved to be a critical step in the organization's transformation.

Deloitte Australia was an early adopter of Yammer, the enterprise social networking tool that launched in 2008 with the promise of redefining the ways organizations communicate. At the outset, Yammer was the beneficiary of positive buzz due primarily to the contextually relevant problem they were trying to solve: email overload. Citing a 2007 *New York Times* report, which defined email as "'a $650 Billion Drag on the Economy,' with email inboxes overflowing with unwanted messages," Yammer proclaimed that they could both increase communication and reduce email.[3] What a concept! Moreover, the product was introduced at a time when people were using social networks for personal purposes, so the idea of applying similar tools and functionality to the workplace seemed like a logical extension.

The Deloitte Australia team certainly thought so and deployed Yammer to strong effect. As Dery and her colleagues demonstrate, Yammer helped break down the siloes and traditional hierarchies in the organization; now everyone within the firm could have access to the key conversations. This newly open communication culture also meant that employees could connect with senior executives more easily, something that was not as realistic in the pre-Yammer era. Moreover, employees could also let their voices be heard; if they had an idea, Yammer would be an outlet to share it and get feedback. Conversely, senior executives checked in on the network often to listen to employee ideas and concerns and monitor projects.[4] As a result, the Deloitte Australia team became much more open, collaborative, innovative, and even fun, as they tell us in a Facebook video they created.[5]

Deloitte Australia's embrace of Yammer and other social tools helped the organization realize value in a number of ways. From a brand standpoint, the firm could position itself to clients as a sophisticated organization that is on the cutting edge of technology, which would help with their credibility in a rapidly digitizing marketplace. Operationally, the firm became more innovative, with more ideas coming from more voices. Culturally, Deloitte Australia became one of the most desirable firms to work for in Australia. And finally, from a revenue perspective, the organization picked itself up out of the "gutter" and became a $1 billion business.[6]

Deloitte
Deloitte Australia
February 20, 2011
When someone says 'yam', do you think vegetable or a short online update? With our 3,700th Yammer member just signed up, here's why our people think the latter
-2:28
Like
Comment
Share
9

To be clear, is all of this revenue attributed to Yammer? Of course not. But the smart use of internal social media undoubtedly contributed to the organization's successful transformation.

• • •

Unfortunately for organizations, the Deloitte Australia successful example is the exception, not the rule. Despite the growing number of internal social media tools in the marketplace like Yammer, Slack, Hipchat, Facebook for Work, and others, the list of failed internal social media initiatives is long and growing. As Charlene Li of the consulting firm Altimeter Group concluded in 2015, "Corporate social networks just aren't that popular."[7] The problems facing organizations range from adoption to actual usage. Indeed, according to another Altimeter Group study in 2014, "Only 36% and 25% of respondents have organizations where many employees use their internal collaboration platform and enterprise social network, respectively."[8] In many ways, the question is not about whether the technology has the right functionality, but how it can meaningfully deliver value for an organization.

So if organizations and employees are not using these tools, why should we care? Because when an organization integrates internal social media tools effectively, the benefits can be substantial. By implementing social technologies, McKinsey estimated that organizations could increase the productivity of knowledge workers by 20 to 25 percent.[9] By enhancing operational efficiency through social media, organizations are in a better position to generate additional revenue. Moreover, for employee cultures, reducing email and streamlining communication has the potential to lead to higher employee empowerment and satisfaction.

Deloitte Australia is just one example of the promise of internal social media platforms. Certainly, challenges still remain, but given the potential of these tools to build more engaged workforces and healthier organizations, it is a topic most organizations should pursue strategically, especially as employees continue to use social media networks to communicate in their personal life and generational turnover continues in the workplace.[10]

Applying the social media management framework, our focus in this chapter turns to the internal organization and its employees. We ask the question: How can managers use social media platforms to create a more open, collaborative, productive, and innovative organization? To answer this question, we'll address several key topics in this chapter. First, we'll define internal social media and the different possibilities within the category. Second, we'll delve deeper into the trade-offs of internal social media and the complexities that organizations face in using them. Third, we'll examine internal social media in action through the case of Humana Buzz. Finally, we'll conclude our discussion of internal social media with a review of the key success factors driving usage and adoption. By the end of this chapter, you will have strategies and tools to create a healthier and stronger organization via social media platforms.

Social Media Use within Organizations

To begin our work on internal social media, let's align on a definition. Scholars Paul M. Leonardi, Marleen Huysman, and Charles Steinfield offer a comprehensive starting point. They select the term *enterprise social media* because "it makes less sense to distinguish between tools such as social networking, microblogging, and social tagging, and more sense to treat these individual tools as part of an integrated enterprise social media platform."[11] Indeed, Yammer started out as a microblogging tool, like Twitter for the workplace, but over time introduced more Facebook-like features, such as individual groups. Similarly, Slack, another popular internal social media tool, began as a simple messaging platform, but it has since added other social networking tools. As we see in other social networks, some services adopt similar features over time (e.g., Twitter becoming more like Facebook, and vice versa), so the idea of grouping the various tools under an enterprise social media umbrella stands to reason. We will proceed under this premise for the remainder of this chapter.

So what about that definition? Much like the definition we used in chapter 1, *enterprise social media* are communication technologies that enable employees to share content and collaborate across the organization. Leonardi and colleagues also offer a more detailed version. They define enterprise social media as:

> *Web-based platforms that allow workers to (1) communicate messages with specific coworkers or broadcast messages to everyone in the organization; (2) explicitly indicate or implicitly reveal particular coworkers as communication partners; (3) post, edit, and sort text and files linked to themselves or others; and (4) view the messages, connections, text, and files communicated, posted, edited and sorted by anyone else in the organization at any time of their choosing.*[12]

Types of Enterprise Social Media

What are some examples of enterprise social media? Recalling our renting and buying analogy from chapter 3 on platform selection, enterprise social media platforms can be divided into three main categories: public B2C rental, private B2B co-op, and wholly owned proprietary networks.[13] Let's look at each type in more detail.

- *The rental–public B2C network.* Some organizations have opted to use Facebook or Whatsapp as the de facto enterprise social media solution. Importantly, this is not a special enterprise version of the software but what the rest of the public uses. For example, a startup might launch a Facebook page to disseminate key company news to all internal stakeholders or use a Whatsapp chat group to enhance collaboration among the core team. This enterprise social media possibility is lightweight and easy to manage, but they lack features that a more customized enterprise solution can provide. That's why many organizations, especially large ones, have moved on from this model and into one of the two others discussed next.

- *The co-op–private B2B networks.* Like Yammer, a host of startups have launched to capitalize on the potential market for enterprise social media software. Think of it like business-to-business social media providers, whereas the Facebooks and Twitters of the world are more squarely focused on B2C. A list of the players includes Slack, Google Apps, Hipchat, Facebook for Work, SalesForce Chatter, and others. Invariably, there will be others by the time you read this section. Here's what's important: because they've prioritized the corporate client, they seek to emphasize the safety and security of information. For example, as Slack planned its growth strategy, it saw opportunity in the financial market and thus invested in features and procedures that would ensure its potential clients could easily comply with government regulations.[14] Meeting corporate safety and security needs is a specific competency that the "standard" version of social networks like Facebook, Twitter, and so on are not equipped to handle, at least as they were initially conceived. The downside—and the reason this model can be known as a co-op—is that the ownership of the platform is fundamentally shared. Certainly, companies will have data privacy restrictions in place, but in the end they are still working on a platform created and managed by a third party.
- *The house-owned and -operated proprietary network.* Some of the more technologically inclined organizations have built their own internal social media networks. They could make this decision for a number of reasons. This may be because of the security concerns. It might also be because they know their organization better than a third party and can thus tailor their social solution to the culture more effectively. Or, like the case of IBM's Beehive internal social network, some organizations have built an enterprise social media platform to beta test ideas they might eventually roll out to their customers.[15] Whatever the motivation, the owned and operated model gives the organization a degree of control the third-party solution simply cannot provide. The key consideration is cost and competency. If your organization has the resources and expertise to "buy" and the value proposition is clear, then choosing this direction could be appropriate.

Selecting the Right Platform

In selecting an internal social media platform, what are the key factors in your decision? They should include the following:

- *Size of company*—If your organization is small and nimble, an existing B2C network like Facebook or WhatsApp may be all that's necessary. If it's a medium or large-scale organization, then one of the B2B networks or proprietary platforms will likely be a better choice.
- *Nature of information*—The more regulated your industry is, the more secure your network must be. It would be very difficult for a financial organization to exist solely on a B2C network, but perhaps it could make sense for a business that sells chocolate.
- *Level of technical expertise and resources*—Is it worth your organization building its own internal social network? The trade-off is control. Should you relinquish some control of information and data in return for an easier-to-implement technological solution?

Now that we have a better sense of what an enterprise social media platform is and the range of possible platforms, let's move on to an analysis of the trade-offs of enterprise social media. By understanding the specific issues and complexities of internal social media use, you'll be in a better position to design an effective internal social media strategy.

Trade-offs of Internal Social Media Use

As we discussed earlier in the chapter, the first decade of internal social media tools has yielded mixed results. On the one hand, the sales pitches of the enterprise social media platforms, coupled with the few success stories, paint a picture of organizational utopia through enterprise social media. On the other hand, many organizations large and small have decided to experiment with these technologies, but the repeat usage and promised organizational change have been hard to come by.

Why is the promise of enterprise social media so compelling but organizations have such a difficult time realizing it? The answer is due in large part to the trade-offs organizations must make to fully embrace enterprise social media. Among the trade-offs organizations must consider: hierarchical versus participatory decision making, closed versus open communication, and task oriented versus relationship building. Let's look at each more closely.

Hierarchical versus Participatory Decision Making

A key trade-off organizations must consider in their evaluation of enterprise social media efforts is how decisions get made. In the traditional command-and-control decision-making model, key decisions were made by the top and then cascaded down to the rest of the organization. With enterprise social media tools, the decision-making model becomes more participatory by design.

There are two implications with this shift. First, the organization's leadership must be prepared to listen to ideas from employees on any number of topics, from organizational strategy to improvements to the lunchtime menu. And second—and most importantly—leadership must be willing to act on these ideas. The feedback loop that enterprise social media forces upon organizations is an unavoidable feature of these new tools. If the organization is not prepared to alter its decision-making process by embracing employee feedback from the bottom up, then enterprise social media may not be the best fit for your organization. What's more, if the organization does adopt enterprise social media, but the executive leadership does not listen to and act on employee ideas, then the technology will serve little purpose within the organization and the employee backlash could be considerable.

If your organization is willing to loosen the reins on the hierarchical decision-making model, other issues come in to play. How much involvement is too much? On what decisions should you open to employees? When does wisdom of the crowds prove foolhardy? If the organization does not agree with your decision and voices its displeasure to your ideas, how do you handle it? The answers to these questions are generally on a case-by-case basis, but they do represent the types of trade-offs an organization must make when adopting enterprise social media.

Closed versus Open Communication

Different from email, a key technological shift that enterprise social media facilitates is openness of communication. Although private communications can happen between employees and within teams, the ethos of these platforms prioritizes transparency. Choosing to meaningfully adopt and use an enterprise social media platform forces another trade-off for organizations: do you want to be a more closed or more open organization?

On the surface, most managers when pressed will answer this question with open, but in truth, it can be difficult to open up a historically closed organization. For starters, siloes develop because they are more convenient, controllable, and politically important within the organization. Some may argue that siloes are more efficient than an open communication model. Existing attitudes toward a more siloed and closed organization would need to be addressed head on as part of an internal social media strategy. Moreover, the organization's leadership must be comfortable with information and key business processes becoming more transparent to the rest of the employee base.

This trade-off may seem easy in theory, but in practice, laying bare communication and information of teams and divisions within an organization is a massive shift. It's part of the reason why adoption and usage has stalled, but once managers are realistic about the trade-off and foster norms that support openness, the benefits of using social media internally can finally begin to accrue.

Task Oriented versus Relationship Building

A final trade-off that an organization must be comfortable with is relationship building versus business processes. Some companies have become uncomfortable with allowing social media use in the workplace. The argument is that it takes time and focus away from the task at hand. However, research is starting to show that organizations with more open social media policies that allow employees to use these platforms at work are actually more productive and healthier organizations.[16]

With regard to the decision to adopt an enterprise social media platform, leaders will have to be comfortable with employees building relationships with each other. Invariably, if your organization introduces a new social networking tool, people will likely use it to be social. It's inherent to the platform and how people behave. This may mean that business processes will not be the only topic of conversation on the enterprise social platform, but on the other hand, the relationships within teams and across the enterprise can strengthen as a result. The organization could also become a more fun place to work, which of course has implications for employee satisfaction and retention.

If an organization chooses to avoid enterprise social media tools and/or focus all communication technologies and tools on the task at hand, it may be more efficient as an organization. But trade-offs in employee morale and retention could come into play. Moreover, innovation may suffer. If the processes are rigid and routinized and a mechanism is not in place for the informal water cooler conversations online, then new, unsolicited ideas from the ranks will likely be less frequent.

The reality is that organizations have deeply rooted cultures that the introduction of a technology alone cannot change in one fell swoop. And the trade-offs they must make to fully embrace social media internally, including hierarchical versus participatory decision making, closed versus open communication, and task oriented versus relationship building, make this change process even more difficult. But it's not impossible. So how can organizations overcome the challenges of enterprise social media to realize the significant opportunities? Let's look at how we can apply the social media management framework to the specific situation of internal social media use.

Internal Social Media Use in Action

In applying the social media management framework, there are a few questions to help interpret and define a strategy within the internal social media context. The purpose of these questions is to help you explore the possibilities.

- *Goals*—What operational and cultural goals is your firm working toward? Working more efficiently to save time and money? Improve employee satisfaction and retention?
- *Audience*—Employees are your primary target audience, of course. But go another layer deeper and think about what specific employee groups within the organization may benefit the most from internal social media? Additional social segmentation along the lines of "influence" and other factors discussed in chapter 2 could be at play as well. Also, as with any internal or external social media strategy, what secondary or tertiary audiences like customers, shareholders, or prospective employees could be in the mix?
- *Platform*—Platform selection is a critical choice. Refer to the platform discussion earlier in this chapter for key considerations as to whether you'll choose to pursue a rental, co-op, or wholly owned and operated house.
- *Brand*—An internal social media tool will be competing with the other social media networks your employees invariably use, so how can you develop a brand strategy that can encourage adoption and maximize usage? Additionally, as illustrated by the Deloitte Australia example, adoption of enterprise social media can bolster your brand reputation externally, in which case, designing the brand strategy for secondary and tertiary audiences would be wise as well.
- *Content*—What content will make the internal social media tool sticky? How is it useful? How is it shareable? Many of the concepts of social content creation from chapter 5 apply in this context as well.
- *Distribution*—The rollout of internal social media tools is an indispensable part of the equation. Do you make the tool available to everyone at the same time? Or offer a beta testing period?

- *Measurement*—Informed by your goals, what metrics will your organization track? What are your metrics that matter? Operational measures to save time and money? Cultural measures to enhance employee satisfaction, retention, and recruitment?

With this framework as a backdrop and the employee base as a clear audience, let's now explore how one organization used social media to become more open, collaborative, productive, and innovative.

CASE STUDY: HUMANA BUZZ LEADS THE WAY

The insurance company Humana was a classic case of a hierarchical, top-down culture. Seemingly every nook and cranny of the organization operated in a silo, resulting in inefficiencies across the enterprise. Realizing the marketplace for employees and customers was changing and in light of the opportunities an enterprise social media platform presented organizations, its executive team approved an experimental period to see how this technology could transform the culture more effectively.

Humana first experimented under the radar with Yammer to better understand the opportunities and challenges of enterprise social media. During this beta period, 2,400 employees used Yammer, showing enough potential that the executive team approved a more permanent solution. In 2010, Humana launched a "co-op" private enterprise social network from a company called Socialcast and branded it Buzz, which was crowdsourced among employees. As we've discussed, the technology itself was not the key to the successful culture transformation. It was the strategy the organization used to deploy and shape the Buzz network. Importantly, they not only drove adoptions but also repeat usage. In just five years, the internal social network touted more than 44,000 users.

How did they do it? For starters, they were clear on the business objectives they were trying to achieve. They focused on operational and cultural benefits of social media. Their stated goal with Buzz was to "empower associates to meet Humana's business objectives by fostering communication, cooperation and collaboration."[17] They also embraced the relationship building potential of internal social media. They wanted their associates to connect socially with one another around key interests and passions.

CONTINUED

CASE STUDY: HUMANA BUZZ LEADS THE WAY *CONTINUED*

Within the context of these business and relationship-building goals, Humana put associates at the center of the Buzz platform. They imported the 2,400 employees from the Yammer trial into Buzz, giving the community a solid foundation on which to begin. From there, the usage and rules of the platform were negotiated among its users. For example, they cocreated with the community a ten commandments for Buzz to help govern the network. Buzz also enabled the creation of special interest groups. For example, by 2014 they had more than 1,600 such groups ranging from health and wellness topics to music to parenting.[18]

As the community began to take shape, the Buzz moderators provided content and experiences that emphasized practical information and transparency. Among the tactics the organization used were ask/answer open question forums, where employees could inquire about topics related to the organization or problems they were trying to solve. In line with the more transparent and responsive organization Humana was trying to build, Buzz also included a suggestion box, which ensured that any ideas proposed by the community were shared with the appropriate executives. Finally, speaking of executives, Buzz was a frequent forum for town halls, which not only demonstrated that the executive team supported Buzz but also that they were willing to use it to communicate directly with their employees.

Although the content and experiences the Buzz team facilitated were strategically sound, what really made Buzz stand out as a best practice example were the strategies and tactics the organization put in place to drive usage among the employees. This distribution approach leveraged a number of tactics to integrate Buzz fully into the fabric of the Humana culture. They included the following:

- *Designated a champion influencer.* His name was Jeff Ross, and his primary job was to drive adoption and usage of Buzz. In other organizations that have adopted enterprise social networks, the technology is seemingly dropped into the laps of the employees, but without an advocate or champion to spur on adoption and usage, the initiative goes nowhere. Among his many initiatives, Ross would email employees who haven't been on Buzz in a while encouraging them to come back. He

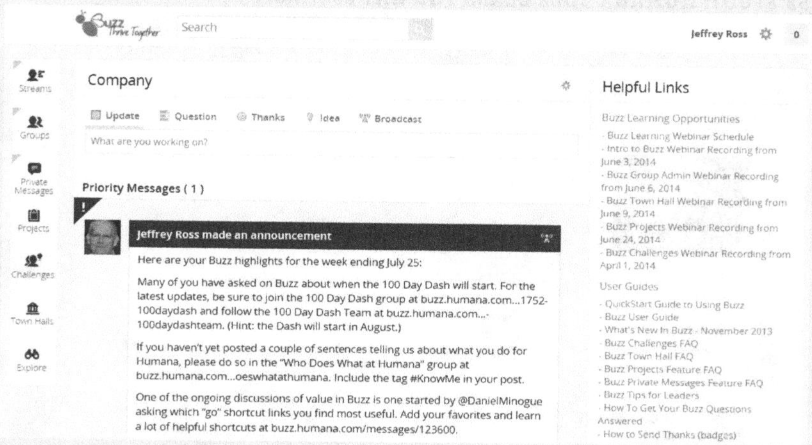

would positively reinforce the best behavior on the platform. And he would publish summaries of the Buzz activity like the one here to keep people up to date on the community and encourage further involvement. His role was critical to the success of the platform.

- *Spread organically.* There was no formal announcement of Buzz. Instead, word about the network spread organically. This fit with the bottom-up approach to adoption and usage. A formal announcement from the corner office would potentially create more pressure on the platform, whereas allowing it to spread informally made it employee-centric and enabled them to shape it in the way that they saw fit.
- *Offered Buzz training sessions.* Ross and his colleagues also developed training materials to teach the organization how to use it. As with any technology, adoption and usage will be much easier if people know what they're doing. And this simple fact was not lost on the Buzz team.
- *Integrated across internal platforms.* Finally, the leadership team acknowledged that Buzz was yet another platform employees were being asked to use. So to reduce the barrier to use, they integrated all the employees' existing tools (e.g., intranet, Sharepoint) into Buzz. This way everything that an employee would need is easily accessible while using Buzz.

As the distribution strategy of the Buzz platform took shape, its popularity internally continued to increase. Perhaps as the critical step in its

CASE STUDY: HUMANA BUZZ LEADS THE WAY ***CONTINUED***

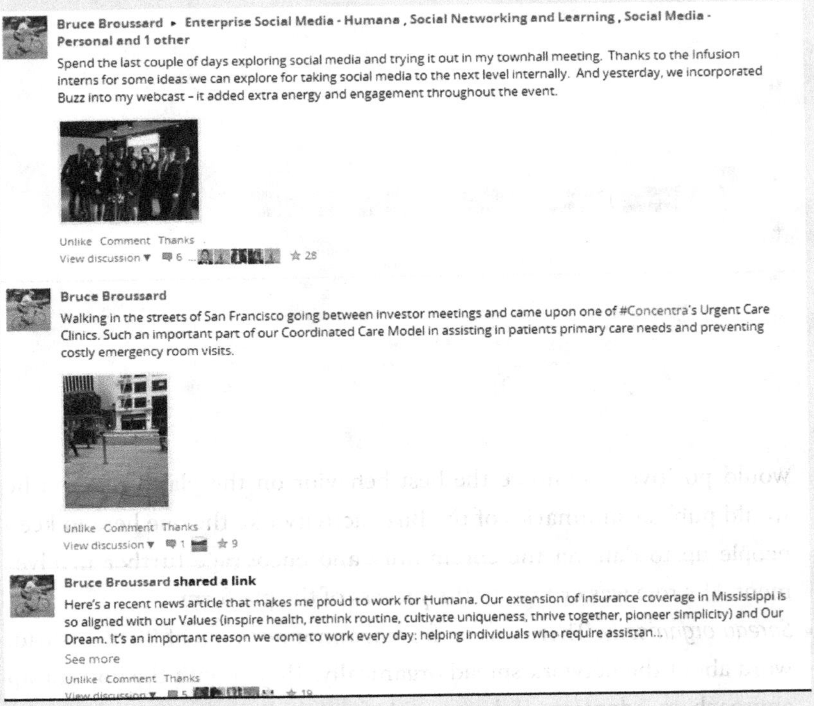

Bruce Broussard ▸ Enterprise Social Media - Humana , Social Networking and Learning , Social Media - Personal and 1 other
Spend the last couple of days exploring social media and trying it out in my townhall meeting. Thanks to the Infusion interns for some ideas we can explore for taking social media to the next level internally. And yesterday, we incorporated Buzz into my webcast - it added extra energy and engagement throughout the event.
Unlike Comment Thanks
View discussion ▼ 6 28
Bruce Broussard
Walking in the streets of San Francisco going between investor meetings and came upon one of #Concentra's Urgent Care Clinics. Such an important part of our Coordinated Care Model in assisting in patients primary care needs and preventing costly emergency room visits.
Unlike Comment Thanks
View discussion ▼ 1 9
Bruce Broussard shared a link
Here's a recent news article that makes me proud to work for Humana. Our extension of insurance coverage in Mississippi is so aligned with our Values (inspire health, rethink routine, cultivate uniqueness, thrive together, pioneer simplicity) and Our Dream. It's an important reason we come to work every day: helping individuals who require assistan...
See more
Unlike Comment Thanks

successful adoption and usage, the executive team began to develop a presence on the platform. The CEO at the time, Bruce Broussard, began using Buzz to document his travels to various Humana offices, share his thoughts, and connect with employees.

With the bottom-up growth plus support from the top, Buzz had become an integral component of the way the Humana organization works. In doing so, they measured their goals to foster communication, collaboration, and cooperation and achieved a number of results: increased workforce productivity, more efficient onboarding and training of new employees, more collaboration across the enterprise, and increased efficiencies in communication and new ideas being shared.[19] Although continued evolution and usage will always be a challenge, the organization successfully built a vibrant community on Buzz that changed the way its employees communicated.

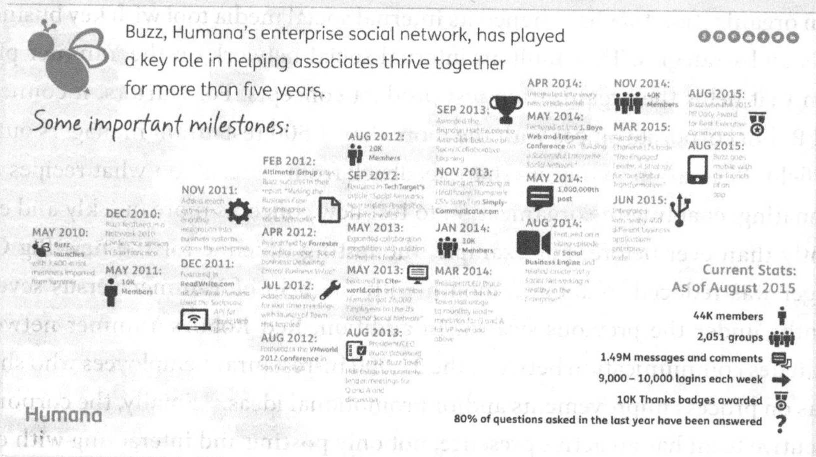

As the Humana Buzz example indicates, it is possible to launch and manage an enterprise social media platform that can meaningfully affect a business. Their success brings to bear the elements of the social media management framework, including clear goals, narrow target audience, strategic platform choice, brand strategy, social content, distribution plans, and measurement tied to business goals. Now, to help synthesize our discussion of enterprise social media, let's examine a few of the key success factors of internal social media use.

Key Success Factors for Adoption and Usage

As we mentioned in the beginning of the chapter, the technology alone is not enough to ensure the success of an internal social media initiative. To implement social media platforms meaningfully within an organization, the following factors will help determine whether your strategy will work. These are comprehensive, but not exhaustive of the possibilities.

Use the Platform for a Purpose

First and foremost, the enterprise social media platform must have a purpose—and that purpose should align with the organization's goals and strategies. This is important for a variety of reasons, but especially from an adoption and usage standpoint, employees must be incentivized to actually engage with it. And that engagement should ultimately help an organization achieve its broader business goals.

Red Robin, the fast food burger joint with over 25,000 employees, is an example of an organization that has aligned its internal social media tool with key business goals and strategies. They built an internal social network on the Yammer platform that helps the organization test product concepts. For starters, it connects Red Robin corporate offices with the more than 1,500 restaurant managers out in the field. Restaurant managers share feedback from "guests" on what recipes are resonating, enabling the organization to test new concepts more quickly and efficiently than ever before. For example, the testing timeline for the new Pig Out burger was reduced to about a month with the help of Yammer versus several months under the previous system. In addition, Red Robin's Yammer network facilitates communication between the 22,000 in-restaurant employees who share ideas on process improvements and/or promotional ideas.[20] Finally, the corporate executive team has an active presence, not only posting and interacting with employees but also listening to what's happening on the front lines.[21] As a result, the organization achieved a number of business benefits, not the least of which was increased cost savings due to the ideas contributed by employees across the enterprise.[22] And it's largely because the platform has a clear purpose within the organization.

Executive Support

Across the board, another key success factor is executive support for the internal social media platform. Imagine a situation where your organization installs a new internal communication tool, which the executive team promises will make the organization run better and result in happier, more engaged employees. That promise might resonate for a short period, but if the executive team is not using the platform, it will ultimately be unsuccessful. The Altimeter Group, which has done a significant amount of work in this area, has suggested that the number-one reason corporate social networks fail is because leadership is not "bought in" to the initiative and is not using the platforms in the way they are intended. The CEO of Telstra, which is an Australian telecommunications company, posted on their internal social network a question: "What processes and technologies should we eliminate?" In the first 60 minutes, more than 700 responses were offered. More to the point, the gesture made clear that the internal social network mattered because the CEO was using it.[23] The bottom line: If you want your platform to be successful, your boss, and your boss's boss, and your boss's boss's boss must be using it as well.

Integrate into Existing Communication Workflow

An enterprise social media platform could be a helpful tool to make your employees' work easier and more efficient, or it could be an additional tool that just piles on to what they already have to do. Of course, successful internal social initiatives will gravitate more toward the former than the latter. For example, the Vox Media's newsroom integrated the internal social network Slack into its workflow. It enables the organization, which has offices and writers all over the world, to monitor deadlines and projects. They've also integrated Slack with their other productivity tools such as Zapier, Trello, and Github that help the team organize projects, workflow, and meet deadlines.[24] All these tools fit seamlessly into their existing processes and tools and also streamline the work for everyone involved, which is a major plus.

Training and Feedback

Making sure employees are trained on the tools is a final key success factor. Of course, trial and error with technology is an important way to learn—and you also want early adopters to shape and adapt the technology in unexpected ways. But once you start to roll out the technology at scale, putting in place a training program that is comprehensive, yet easy is a critical step. Dell has been an industry leader in social media education. Through its SMAC initiative, Dell offers its employees various certificate programs. Depending on the specific job function, it may behoove employees to take a variety of classes on social media. For others, all that's necessary is the basic certification. Dell is an example that may be in the extreme, but because social media is such an organizational priority—it's instrumental to their ability to deliver effective services to clients—a comprehensive training program has been right alongside the growth of Dell Social.

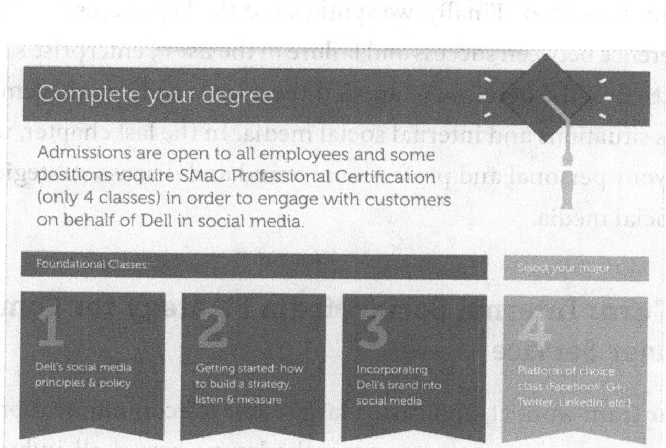

Complete your degree
Admissions are open to all employees and some positions require SMaC Professional Certification (only 4 classes) in order to engage with customers on behalf of Dell in social media.
Foundational Classes:
Select your major:
1
Dell's social media principles & policy
2
Getting started: how to build a strategy, listen & measure
3
Incorporating Dell's brand into social media
4

As you design and implement internal social media tools, success can never be guaranteed. But through the combination of a platform with a purpose, executive support, integration into existing workflow, and appropriate training, your internal social media initiative will be in a better position to help the organization accomplish its goals.

Recap: Thae World's Best Boss

When faced with the decision to implement social media internally, you may relate to character Michael Scott from the sitcom *The Office*, who once said: "And I knew exactly what to do. But in a much more real sense I had no idea what to do." Enterprise social media sounds like a worthy initiative for organizations of all types, as the promise of increased productivity and employee satisfaction is tantalizing for workplaces that often suffer from information overload. But since there have been more failed implementations than successful ones, enterprise social media still has room to grow and evolve.

In this chapter we turned our focus inward and outlined how leaders can use successfully social media to build more effective and healthier organizations. First, we defined enterprise social media and reviewed the three types of platforms in this category: the B2C rental, the B2B co-op, and the wholly owned and operated house. Then, we examined the trade-offs organizations must make when meaningfully adopting enterprise social media, including hierarchical versus participatory decision making, closed versus open communication, and task oriented versus relationship building. Next, we reviewed how the social media management framework could be applied to the specific challenge of internal social media use and examined the case of Humana Buzz. Finally, we synthesized the key success factors that will spell the difference between success and failure in the use of enterprise social media.

In this section of the book we've applied the social media management framework to crisis situations and internal social media. In the last chapter, we turn our attention to your personal and professional brand and discuss strategies to maximize it via social media.

Your Turn: Internal Social Media Strategy for Comcast Customer Service

You and your team work at Comcast, a large cable telecommunication company. Your customer service scores are among the lowest across all industries. Your Executive Committee wants to fix it and is asking you and your team to explore how internal social media tools can help your organization improve internal operations to deliver better customer service.

Your challenge: Devise and articulate an internal social media strategy. Here are some questions to get you started:

- What are the employee engagement challenges your organization faces? (You can make assumptions.)
- How would you define your goal(s)?
- Should all employees be targeted?
- What strategies and tactics will you employ to accomplish your goals (keeping in mind platforms, brand, content, distribution, and measurement)?

Each team will send one representative to present your strategic recommendation to the Executive Committee. Good luck.

Notes

1. Nadia Cameron Cameron, "CMO Interview: A New Brand of Conversation: Deloitte's David Redhill," *CMO*, June 28, 2013, http://www.cmo.com.au/article/466036/cmo_interview_new_brand_conversation_deloitte_david_redhill/.
2. Kristine Dery, Ina M. Sebastian, and Jeanne W. Ross, "The Digital Workplace Transforming Business: The Case of Deloitte Australia," *MIT Sloan Center for Information Systems Research: Research Briefing*, XV, no. 8 (August 2015).
3. Yammer Team, "Welcome to Yammer!" *Office Blogs*, September 8, 2008, https://blogs.office.com/2008/09/08/welcome-to-yammer/.
4. Dery, Sebastian, and Ross, "The Digital Workplace Transforming Business: The Case of Deloitte Australia."
5. "Why Do We Love Yammer at Deloitte?—Deloitte Australia | Facebook," accessed November 29, 2015, https://www.facebook.com/DeloitteAustralia/videos/10150142435224155/.
6. Cameron, "CMO Interview."
7. Charlene Li, "Why No One Uses the Corporate Social Network," *Harvard Business Review*, April 7, 2015, https://hbr.org/2015/04/why-no-one-uses-the-corporate-social-network.
8. Charlene Li, "Employee Engagement: Strengthening Employee Relationships in the Digital Era," *Altimeter Group*, December 14, 2014, http://www.altimetergroup.com/2014/12/strengthening-employee-relationships-in-the-digital-era/.
9. Ibid.
10. Peter W. Cardon and Bryan Marshall, "The Hype and Reality of Social Media Use for Work Collaboration and Team Communication," *Journal of Business Communication* 52, no. 3 (June 2015): 273–293.
11. Paul M. Leonardi, Marleen Huysman, and Charles Steinfield, "Enterprise Social Media: Definition, History, and Prospects for the Study of Social Technologies in Organizations," *Journal of Computer-Mediated Communication* 19, no. 1 (October 2013): 1–19.
12. Ibid.
13. Ibid. These types of enterprise social media platforms are informed by Leonardi et al.
14. Rebecca Greenfield, "Slack Is Getting Ready for Wall Street. But Is Wall Street Ready for Slack?" *Bloomberg.com*, June 23, 2015, http://www.bloomberg.com/news/articles/2015-06-23/slack-is-getting-ready-for-wall-street-but-is-wall-street-ready-for-slack-.

15. "Beehive (SocialBlue)," *IBM*, March 22, 2013, http://researcher.watson.ibm.com/researcher/view_group.php?id=1231.
16. Niran Subramaniam, Joe Nandhakumar, and João Baptista (John), "Exploring Social Network Interactions in Enterprise Systems: The Role of Virtual Co-Presence," *Information Systems Journal* 23, no. 6 (November 2013): 475–499; Toby Wolpe, "Ban Social Media as a Distraction? No, It Boosts Productivity," *TechRepublic*, March 27, 2013, http://www.techrepublic.com/blog/european-technology/ban-social-media-as-a-distraction-no-it-boosts-productivity/.
17. Jeff Ross, "Want an ESN Playbook? Here Is Ours!" *Next Practices*, September 28, 2015, http://jeffrossblog.com/2015/09/28/want-an-esn-playbook-here-is-ours/.
18. Jeff Ross, "Building a 30,000-User Enterprise Social Network by Jeff Ross," May 9, 2014, http://www.slideshare.net/j_boye/building-a-30000user-enterprise-social-network-by-jeff-ross.
19. Ross, "Want an ESN Playbook?"
20. Clint Boulton, "Restaurant Chain Red Robin Socializes Digital Transformation," *The Wall Street Journal CIO Report*, June 4, 2014, http://blogs.wsj.com/cio/2014/06/04/restaurant-chain-red-robin-socializes-digital-transformation/; Yammer Team, "Empowering Employees and Creating Strong Engagement for Better Customer Service," *Office Blogs*, June 18, 2013, https://blogs.office.com/2013/06/18/empowering-employees-and-creating-strong-engagement-for-better-customer-service/.
21. Team, "Empowering Employees and Creating Strong Engagement for Better Customer Service."
22. Ibid.
23. Li, "Why No One Uses the Corporate Social Network."
24. Laura Hazard Owen, "How 7 News Organizations Are Using Slack to Work Better and Differently," *Nieman Lab*, July 30, 2015, http://www.niemanlab.org/2015/07/how-7-news-organizations-are-using-slack-to-work-better-and-differently/.

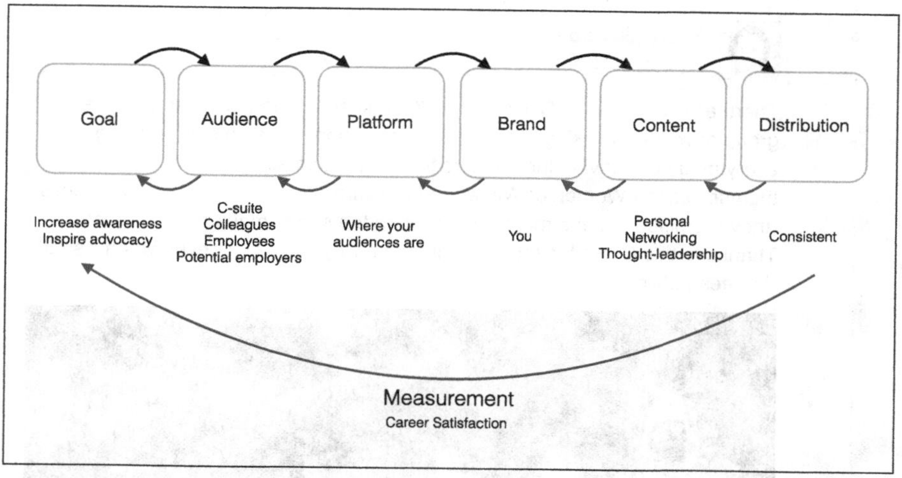

10 Defining Your Personal Brand in Social Media

Sheryl Sandberg, chief operating officer of Facebook, plays multiple roles on her Facebook page of more than 2 million followers.[1] First, consistent with her responsibilities, she is a corporate spokesperson for the most successful social media company in the world.

Second, she is an advocate for social change. Sandberg has used her platform as COO of Facebook to launch a global movement championing gender equality. Through her successful TED Talk encouraging women in the workplace to "lean in" and the subsequent bestselling book she wrote with the same theme, she has become a beacon for this important cause.[2] As a result, her Facebook page is another powerful distribution platform for her to continue communicating her message beyond speeches and books. In this post, she highlights the Lean In Circles, a small group initiative sparked by the Lean In movement, to keep advocating for her message.

Sheryl Sandberg
June 25, 2015 ·

There are now Lean In Circles on all 7 continents! Lean In Antarctica is a group of women working at the McMurdo Station research center, doing everything from driving fuel tankers to coordinating supplies. They call themselves the Women of Winter and are currently living in 24-hour darkness (they promised to send more photos when the sun comes up—in August). Thanks to this Circle for showing you can always #LeanIn...even when it's -20 degrees outside.

Like Comment Share

Tom Stocky, Jerry Maher and 6.9K others Top Comments

195 shares

Third, Sandberg is an internal champion for her employees and their projects. Going beyond the interoffice email, Sandberg often shares congratulatory notes on Facebook, tagging the key leaders of projects or strong performing offices. Through these posts, employees are celebrated publicly for their achievements. Moreover, since Facebook is a multinational company, she physically cannot be in multiple places at one time (although with Facebook's acquisition of virtual reality firm Oculus that may very well be possible one day), so she also commemorates her trips to offices around the world with posts like this one:

Finally, Sandberg is a dedicated family person on her Facebook page. Her husband, notable Silicon Valley entrepreneur Dave Goldberg, died tragically in 2015. Rather than completely closing herself off publicly, she consistently shared on Facebook her feelings of loss and despair and expressed gratitude for all the support from her friends and followers. Even prior to Goldberg's untimely passing, you could find photos and status updates about family times on the weekend, and as she's mourned his death in the months and years afterward, she's still opened up her private family life to a degree to the world of Facebook.

Sheryl Sandberg's Facebook page demonstrates that successful executives can use social media to build a multidimensional leadership brand. She is at once a corporate spokesperson, advocate for social change, internal champion, and dedicated family person. Importantly, this persona is consistent with who she is and what she represents beyond her Facebook page. Whether it's a speech, a book tour, or a meeting, the multiple roles of Sheryl Sandberg are at play in those forums as well.

• • •

Why is the Sandberg example relevant to you? For starters, it highlights the fundamental principle about audience we discussed in chapter 2—*multiple audiences are at play in social media.* Sandberg's Facebook page connects with family, friends, colleagues, current and prospective clients and partners, current and prospective employees, the media, and fans. Each message that she posts may have a primary target—say, her employees—but she keeps in mind how secondary and tertiary audiences may react as well. For example, if she posts about her family, it could endear trust and goodwill among her employees. A post about Lean In might generate media coverage for the movement and motivate fans to get involved. Whatever the case may be, the multiple-audience principle is in full effect with Sandberg's Facebook page.

Second, and just as importantly, the Sandberg case is relevant to you because it demonstrates *the opportunities leaders have to define and shape their personal leadership brand via social media.* In a previous world, leaders were beholden to the controlled corporate speak of a press release and at the whim of the traditional media for an interview or quote, which would almost assuredly be edited, if not completely taken out of context. Social media tools enable people to go directly and more quickly to their audiences with a message about who they are and what they represent.

If the Sandberg best practice still leaves you unconvinced, consider this. Employers are increasingly searching candidates on social media as part of the routine background and skills check. If you've hired for a position and did not Google or search a candidate on LinkedIn, you are likely in the minority. In addition to adding social media searches to background checks, some organizations are even sourcing jobs directly via social media. According to the Society of Human

Resource Professionals, two-thirds of organizations sourced jobs from social media in 2014.[3]

The bottom line: your personal social media presence is now part of your personal and professional brand. You have two choices: embrace it or be left behind. If you choose the former, this chapter will help you devise a personal social media strategy that will position you to achieve your career and leadership goals. First, as we've done in the previous two chapters, we will consider the social media management framework to help inform the development of your personal social media strategy. Second, we'll examine three different approaches to personal social media strategy: the base, standard, and premium models. Third, we'll discuss the risks that you should be aware of in moving forward with a personal social media strategy. Finally, we'll share some tips on execution. By the end of this chapter, you will have possibilities for how to transform your own personal social media presence to align with your goals. But first, if there's one thing you remember from this chapter, please let it be this . . .

Assume Everything You Post Is Public

In today's interconnected world, the "private" message is a quaint notion. There is not enough room in this book to detail the countless cases of mishandled Twitter DM's and content in the cloud going public. Please just let Taylor's faux pas be a not-so-subtle reminder to take great care with anything you post on any social or digital platform.

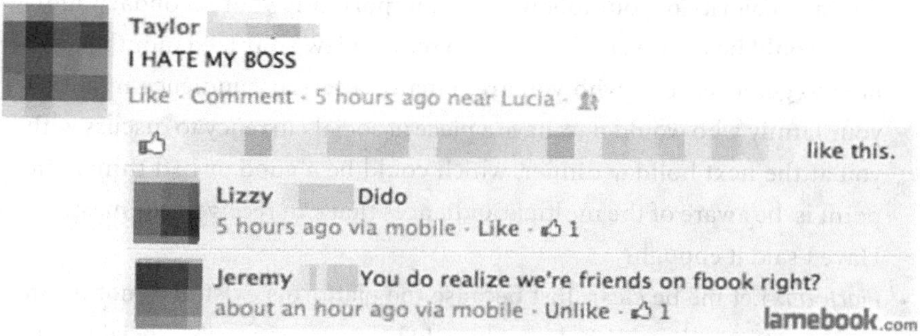

Social Media Management Framework Considerations

By now, you should (I hope) be familiar with how the social media management framework operates. Specific to the challenge of developing a personal social media strategy, here are a few considerations on the most relevant components of the framework.

- *Goals.* Align your social media aspirations with your career aspirations. Are you an MBA student looking to switch careers? If so, how can you use social media to prove to your prospective employers that you have what it takes to succeed in a new industry? Are you an entrepreneur starting a business? If so, how can you use social media to prove to prospective investors, clients, employees, and other interested parties that you are a leader they can believe in? Or are you working toward a promotion within your company? If so, how can you use social media to prove to your managers, team, and colleagues that you have the leadership skills and knowledge to do the job? Or are you a senior executive not looking for a job, but wanting to use social media to enhance the way you lead? If so, social media tools can give you new opportunities to connect with your employees. Whatever your current career situation is, focus your goals and tailor your social media strategy accordingly.
- *Audience.* As we've noted, multiple audiences are at play in social media. This is partly because social media posts can live on if you do not delete them. Always be thinking about primary, secondary, and tertiary audiences. For example, if you are an MBA and post about industry news on Twitter, your primary audience may be your fellow students who make up the vast majority of your followers. But importantly your secondary audience would be future employers, who may review your feed months from now to get a sense of who you are. Finally, a tertiary audience might be your family who would now have a piece of social currency to discuss with you at the next holiday dinner, which could be a good or bad thing. The point is: be aware of the multiple audiences that can receive your message. Have I said it enough?
- *Platform.* Let me be clear. Just because the platforms exist does not mean you have to use them. You do not have to be on every possible social media platform if they do not help you reach your audience and achieve your goals. For most executives, for example, LinkedIn is the most mandatory of all, but it may matter little to prospective employees or employers if you are

on Pinterest. It's better to do a couple of platforms really well than to spread yourself too thin across platforms that will not serve your purpose.

- *Brand.* In most cases you will use your own name to brand your social presences, which is perfectly fine. However, you may run into others that share your same name. I've had some students with the same name as alleged or convicted criminals. To avoid the obvious confusion, being more active in social media will ensure you have more content in the ecosystem reflecting who you are, which can help you draw the distinction between you and the person who is definitely not you. In other cases, you may consider a brand name for yourself. This may make sense if you are in a field where pseudonyms or code names are acceptable, perhaps in the art business. But generally speaking, using your name as you want it to appear on your business card, job application, email signature, and so on is the way to go.
- *Content.* Because content is often the most challenging question for a personal social media strategy, the balance of this chapter will review three content approaches. Stay tuned.
- *Distribution.* Although you'll have organic, shared, sponsored, and maybe even influencer assets at your disposal, most of you will focus on the organic and shared assets to distribute your messages. Remember, organic refers to your own LinkedIn page or Twitter feed, while shared is leveraging your audiences to distribute your message.
- *Measurement.* As usual, measure your success relative to your goals. If you use social media as part of an integrated strategy to switch industries and you get the job you want, you are successful. If you are an entrepreneur seeking to drive awareness of yourself and your company, you can measure your social media efforts according to the brand metrics we discussed in chapter 7. For example, look at your social media content according to reach, engagement, and sentiment. Your social media presence can serve the same function as a brand advertising campaign and should be measured similarly as a result. If you are angling for that promotion at work and use social media to build your leadership brand—and you get the promotion—then you have achieved your goal. Or if you are a senior executive seeking to improve employee morale, you may survey employees on the degree to which your personal social media use affects their perception of working at the company. Within the context of social media for your career, direct causation may be more difficult to come by than in the organizational contexts, as discussed in chapter 7. But pursuing career goals through other strategies and tactics are hard to measure. That coffee chat with a key decision maker at the

company you want to work for? She didn't hire you directly, but she may have put in a good word for you. How can you measure causation in this instance? It's difficult. If you adopt a similar mentality with social media, especially given its growing importance in personal and professional branding, you will stop resisting social media just to resist it and start benefiting from including it as part of your overall career strategy.

These are just considerations. As you use the social media management framework to guide your thinking on your personal social media strategy, other considerations, opportunities, and complications will inevitablly arise. But you now have a place to start. And with that, let's move on to an exploration of the three possible strategic directions for your personal brand in social media.

Possible Strategic Directions

When you walk into a car dealership, you are usually presented with three possible models. The base model is a stripped-down version of the car. All it offers is the necessities—a working engine, some air conditioning, decent seats, secure locks, and so on. Then, one step up is the standard model. Here's where you might get a better engine, an interior with fancy electronic features, maybe even a moon roof if you pay up for it. Finally, at the top of the line is the premium model, where you would be leaving the dealership with a car with as many bells and whistles as possible—leather, heated seats, rear camera to help you park, maybe even some sort of Siri-like character that helps organize your music preferences.

In thinking about your personal social media strategy, the brand hierarchy for automobile classes can be a particularly helpful analogy. In essence, you have three possible strategic models for your personal social media brand:

- *Base*—Having a presence on social media that is consistent across platforms
  - *Primary purpose*—branding and connecting
- *Standard*—Actively engaging with your network
  - *Primary purpose*—sharing and participating
- *Premium*—Developing unique, differentiated thought-leadership content
  - *Primary purpose*—creating and leading

Importantly, when you buy a car and choose to go up from the base to the standard model, you still retain all the basic functionality of the base model; you just add on additional features of the standard model. The same is true for your personal social media presence. If you choose a premium strategy, you will still have elements of the base and standard models.

To help you find the model that's right for you (ok, the egregious car analogies end here), let's look at each of these approaches in more detail.

The Base Model—Branding and Connecting

The base model serves two fundamental purposes. First, it helps you develop your brand on social media. Second, it enables you to connect with current colleagues, prospective employees, friends, and any other audiences that are relevant to your career path.

In tactical terms, the base model simply refers to having a presence on social media that is consistent across platforms. This is important because your social media presence is now inextricably linked to how people may perceive you and your brand in the marketplace.

Look at the profile shown here. Would you hire this person based on their LinkedIn profile?

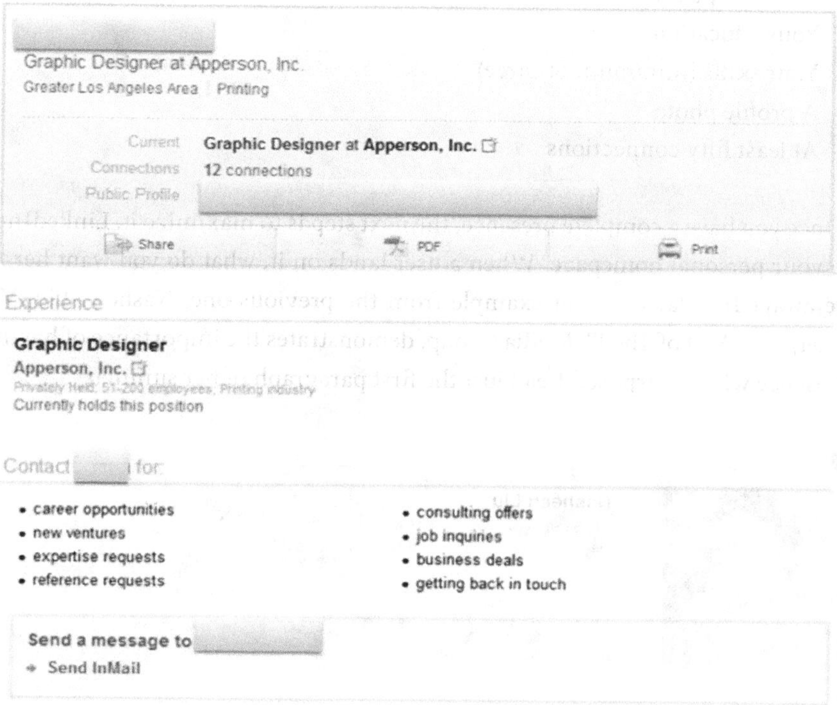

Even if you are the most compassionate and lenient hiring manager, the answer is likely no. There are a number of problems here. For starters, we do not know much about this person's experience. Where have they worked beyond Apperson? Where did they go to school? We also are unclear on their skills. How can this person contribute to our organization? In addition, the twelve connections communicate, whether true or not, that a very small network knows and trusts this person. Influence and credibility may not be critical for every job, but it counts in the business world, and this LinkedIn profile clearly does not reflect either. There are other issues with this profile, but it's probably fair to say this candidate would not make the cut based on their LinkedIn presence.

If your LinkedIn profile looks like this or you do not even have one, strongly consider changing that as soon as you can. The most important step you can take is to complete your profile. According to LinkedIn, these are the indicators of profile completeness:[4]

- Your industry and location
- An up-to-date current position (with a description)
- Two past positions
- Your education
- Your skills (minimum of three)
- A profile photo
- At least fifty connections

Once you have a complete presence, the next step is to maximize it. LinkedIn is like your personal homepage. When a user lands on it, what do you want her to take away? In a far different example from the previous one, Nasheen Liu, VP Strategy & CMO of The IT Media Group, demonstrates the importance of having a presence with a purpose.[5] Read just the first paragraph of her summary.

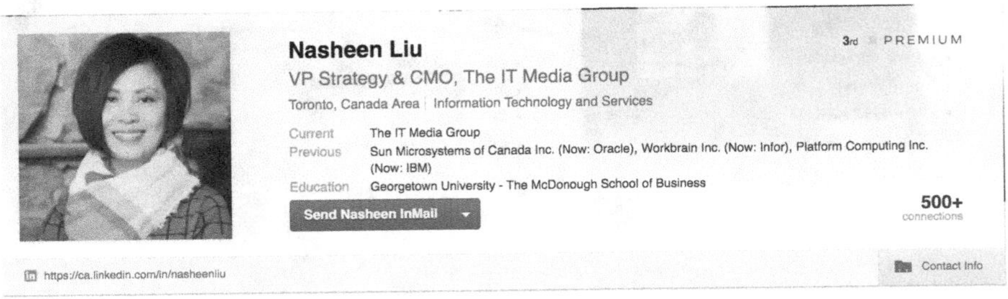

Background

Summary

Technology transforms our reality. Marketing changes our perception. I am a seasoned and curious technology marketer, who believes the #1 objective for marketing is to make every reality our best perception possible. I succeed by using common sense as my sounding board; creating ideas that have wings; delivering more than I promise; connecting with people who are good to me (not just "for" me).

What have we learned about Nasheen? Is she a CPG brand manager? A supply chain management expert? Of course not. She states very clearly that she is a technology marketer. It is reflective of her current role and the roles she may be interested in in the future. Her summary also positions her as a forward thinker, which is critical to her business, and a problem solver. From reading just one paragraph, we have a clear idea of who Nasheen is and what she represents.

The base model is very simple. Have a complete presence on the social media networks that matter to you and your goals. In most cases, that platform will be LinkedIn. If so, you can create a complete profile within an hour. Audiences of all kinds will be searching for you on LinkedIn. Take the opportunity to define and shape that first social media impression.

Now, for those of you looking to take a step up from the base model, let's look at what might be possible in the standard.

The Standard Model—Sharing and Participating

Whereas the base model is more passive, the standard model requires more active engagement on the platforms you choose. It has two primary purposes. First, share content and experiences with your network, whether it is a photo from an event you attended or an article you found interesting. Second, participate with your networks by actively liking/endorsing, commenting, friending, and sharing what your contacts are doing in social media as well. Let's look at two examples of leaders who are active in their social networks.

The first is Stein Ove Fenne, the president of Tupperware U.S. & Canada and former managing director of Tupperware Nordic & Baltic. Fenne is an executive of a global company that also has many employees out in the field. The office stop-by is simply not possible with many of his employees, so he's turned to Facebook to build better relationships between him and his various stakeholders.[6]

Core to his approach is authenticity. He says, "Social media is the extension of who I am. On Facebook, which is the main platform for communicating with consultants, I am Stein Ove—the private person, I am not Tupperware. I have my private inspirations, thoughts and pictures. This builds authenticity and helps consultants feel that the person they see on Facebook is real."[7] He's able to achieve this level of authenticity by sharing and participating in his networks like he would with his friends and family. It sounds elementary, but his content strategy is to be a real person rather than a highly powerful corporate executive. On his Facebook page you'll find numerous photos of his wife and kids, which help humanize him. Interestingly, Stein also allows his employees to post pictures of him and tag him so that they show up on his feed as well. This helps position him as accessible, transparent, and likeable. Here's one from one of his consultants.

All told, Fenne actively manages his Facebook page like anyone else would, and this authentic approach resonates with his employees. For a leader of a multinational firm with many virtual teams, this strategy is helping him achieve his leadership communication goals and steer the company to growth and success.

Salit Kulla is another example of strategically using social media to accomplish career goals. Salit matriculated to the MIT Sloan School of Management to switch careers. She was in finance and accounting, working for several firms, but she identified marketing as the field she wanted to enter. By working hard and doing well in the interview process, she landed a summer internship at Google after her first year of business school. What she did with social media during her time at Google helped her secure her dream job.

Knowing that she needed to prove to Google that she could be an effective marketer, Salit decided to use her own personal social media platforms to demonstrate her skills. She launched a summer internship photo series, which involved her taking selfies of her experience working at Google every day and posting them on social media platforms, including Google's own Google Plus. One particular post, pictured here, was +1'd by Google cofounder Larry Page.

Salit's Google internship selfie initiative helped her demonstrate a number of key skills. First, she understood how social media platforms worked. Second, she could tell a story via digital tools, an increasingly important skill set for marketers. Third, she embodied the Google brand and would be a good cultural fit. All told, she smartly differentiated herself from her competition for the few full-time jobs available.

Salit ended up accepting a full-time job to oversee the marketing of Gmail at Google. Of course, Salit is a talented executive in many ways. But her adoption and strategic use of social media was instrumental to her successfully switching careers. And she did it not just by having a solid LinkedIn profile and Google Plus page, but by sharing her experiences and participating in the platform in ways that communicated her skills.

If you choose the standard model, you will actively engage in social media, posting content that reflects your experiences and interests and engaging with others in your network along the way. If you feel that the base and standard model are too limited for your career goals (e.g., you are trying to become a thought leader in your field), then the premium model will be the way forward for you. Let's explore that possibility further.

The Premium Model—Creating and Leading

The premium model is based on creating and distributing unique, differentiated thought-leadership content. Stein and Salit are sharing content on their networks, but with all due respect to them, it does not position them as thought leaders in their field. Thought leadership usually refers to content that takes a position on current industry trends, news items, and future opportunities.

The advantage of social media is that the barrier to entry to becoming a thought leader is lower than it's been. In the past, you might have to work hard to become a regular op-ed columnist in a local or national paper. Today, blogs, Facebook, Twitter, LinkedIn, and other social media platforms are opportunities for leaders to advance their message and positioning. Let's look at two examples of executives who have used social media for thought leadership.

The first is Marissa Thalberg, who is Taco Bell's chief brand engagement officer. She created the "Executive Moms" blog to share her perspectives on being a senior executive while also raising a family.[8] Why does this strategy work? For starters, Thalberg developed a content strategy that is unique and differentiated. There are thousands of brand- and marketing-related blogs in the social ecosystem. By focusing on a highly relevant and comparatively less discussed topic, Thalberg is able to break through with her message more effectively. Second, becoming a thought leader on this topic helps round out her own personal leadership brand. It sends a message to her employees that she acknowledges the pressures of the workplace and work–life balance. It suggests to her employers and the marketing industry at large that, as a digital marketer, she knows how to use these tools for her own purposes. And, although she may not be looking for a new job right now, her thought leadership in this area is simply another way to keep her name in the discussion as a highly valuable and successful executive. For all these reasons, the Executive Moms initiative is a positive thought leadership effort for Thalberg.

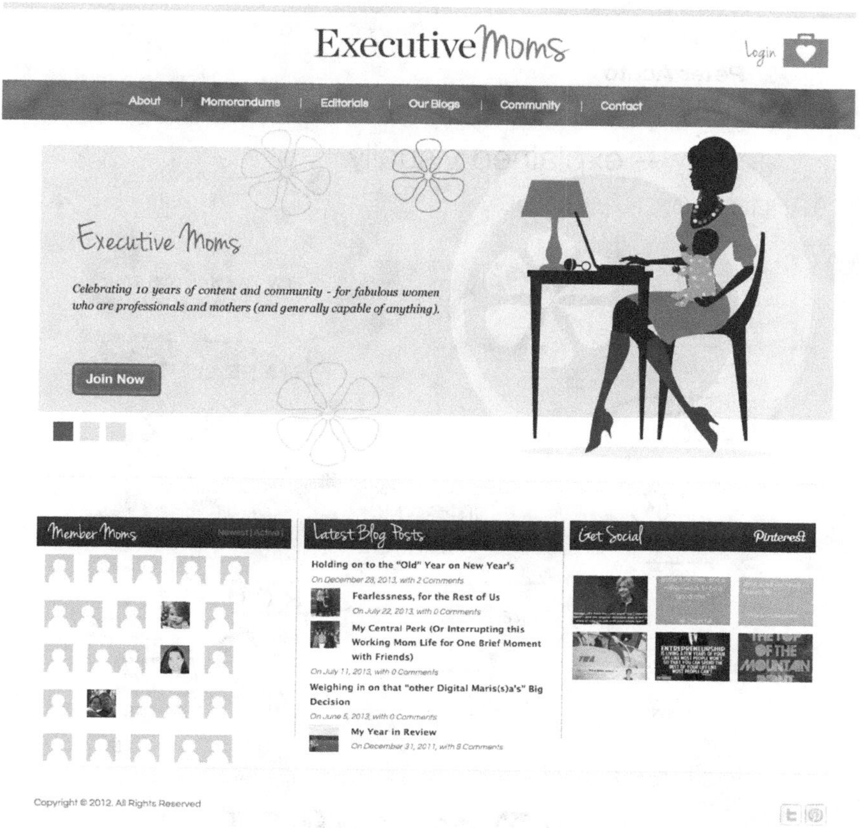

Peter Aceto, CEO of Tangerine Bank in Canada, is another example of an executive who is using social media to become a thought leader. Aceto's been an active user of Twitter for a number of years now, earning the nickname of "The Social Media CEO."[9] What's interesting about his embrace of social media is that he is the CEO of a bank. By law he is restricted from tweeting most any information about the industry. So how could a finance CEO possibly be a fit for social media?

Aceto has used Twitter as a platform to position himself as a thoughtful, credible, and team-oriented leader. In an industry where reputations of CEOs have been sullied at times, Aceto uses Twitter to communicate that he is the antithesis of those characters. His tweets about leadership principles, treating people well, and celebrating his team led him to write a book called *Weology*, which is about the power of we versus I.[10] Because he's built up such a strong audience base, he uses his Twitter feed as an outlet to promote this philosophy as well as sell more books, as in the following example.

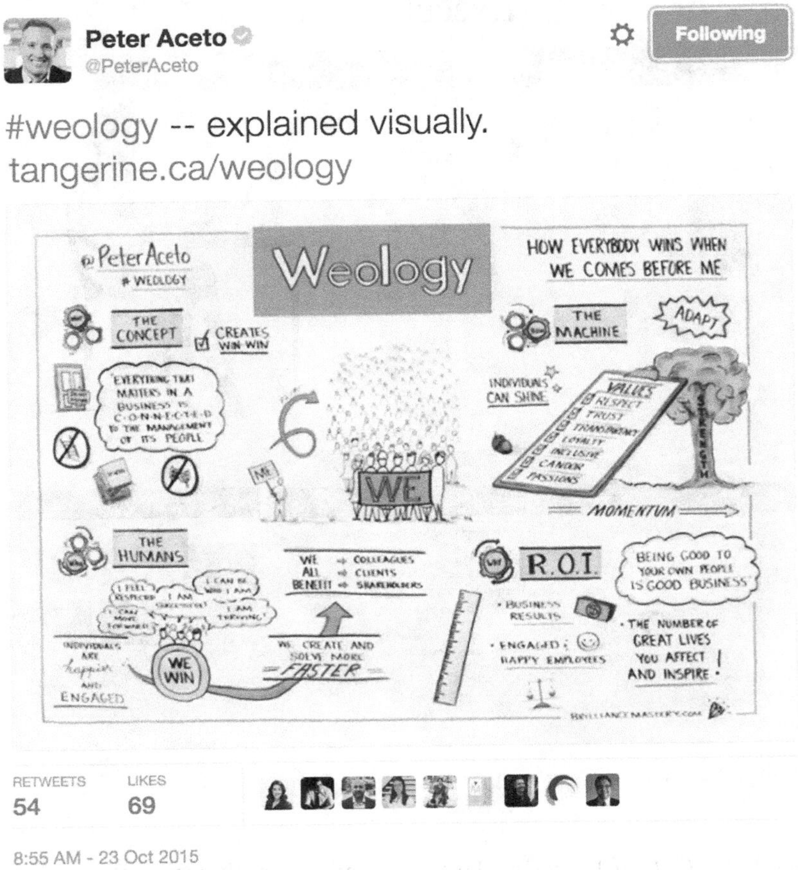

For Aceto, the value of this strategy is wide ranging. In a commoditized industry, he helps put a face on his bank in a way that can differentiate Tangerine to appeal to employees, customers, the media, even government regulators. Interestingly, his Twitter profile has more followers and engagement than Tangerine Bank's official feeds, so he also becomes a valuable asset in the firm's marketing communications. The impressions and engagement he receives are organic and contribute to the overall marketing efforts for the company. In addition, it increases his profile as a CEO. Perhaps he's very happy at Tangerine Bank, but if the call for another opportunity occurred, his Twitter profile and ability to use social media adeptly in a heavily regulated industry may be appealing to other institutions.

In summary, the premium model is where you start creating thought leadership content on a more consistent basis. In Marisa Thalberg's case, she identified a topic that wasn't necessarily core to her day-to-day function as a marketer, but it helped differentiate her and prove that she could walk the walk when it came to digital and social marketing. In Peter Aceto's case, he overcame the inherent barriers to a banking CEO using social media and has emphasized thought leadership content on being an effective manager and creating great teams, which he eventually crystallized into a book. In many ways, the premium model requires the most work—you need to have a unique and different content idea, but it could also provide the most benefits in return—better job, more speaking arrangements, more visibility, and so on.

Increasingly, the question is not whether you should develop your personal brand in social media; it's how you should do so. You now have three strategic directions to consider in this endeavor: the base (branding and networking), the standard (sharing and participating), and the premium (creating and leading). Like any strategic decision, you should also be aware of the risks involved.

Managing the Risks of a Social Media Presence

In a seminal piece on personal social media strategy, Soumitra Dutta identified several critical risks of leaders having a social media presence.[11] They are all important to consider regardless of what strategic model you've chosen or where you are in your social media life cycle, whether you're new to the space or a veteran. The risks include the following:

- *Managing time.* How much time you should devote to social media—or really any task—is an obvious but important question. This is where your personal goals should help inform your approach. If you can meaningfully contribute to your goals by using social media, the time you will devote to it will likely be worth it. If your goals and social media use are not aligned, then simply maintaining your presences may be all that's necessary.
- *Managing social capital.* Who you know matters in the offline world, and it matters in social media as well. This refers primarily to the people you choose to add as connections on LinkedIn or accept as friends on Facebook. To the extent possible, make sure you are connecting with the people in your target audience. And also be aware of who you're posting to when you do decide to share content.

- *Managing intellectual capital.* Regardless of what industry you are in, there will likely be restrictions on the types of topics and information you can discuss in social media. If the wrong type of information is posted, you could face dire consequences. Before actively engaging in social media, know what intellectual property of yours and your organization's is in bounds (or not).

Of course, these are just some of the risks. Other risks specific to you or your industry may be relevant as well. The point is this: assess the risk and make sure you're comfortable moving forward. For some of you, social media may not help you achieve your goals, and that's fine. But for many of you, it can be an advantage for your career, as the examples we've discussed in this chapter suggest. Now that we've assessed the risk, the last topic to discuss is execution.

Tips on Execution

You can have the best strategy in the world, but if you do not execute it well, it will not be effective. To help you with the execution of your personal social media strategy, here are a few tips to consider:

- *Create a posting schedule/content plan.* For those who have chosen the standard or premium model, take 15–20 minutes each day to identify and plan your social media posts. This is easier than having LinkedIn up all day and trying to fit in a post between meetings or a lunch break.
- *Use a content management system.* Once you have a posting schedule in place, leverage a content management system like Buffer or TweetDeck to schedule content to post automatically. The one caution with automatic posting is that you should stay attuned with what the conversation is online. If conversations are affected due to unforeseen events like natural disasters or other tragedies, then put a halt to your posting schedule.
- *Monitor analytics.* Social platforms increasingly offer analytics that show you how many people you reached and how many people engaged via an endorsement, comment, or share. Track what types of content work well and do more of it.
- *Stay in your lane.* It can be tempting to post on everything that comes to mind. But if you've developed a content strategy centered on, say, IT news and trends, stick to it. That way your followers will come to expect

this content, and there's a consistency in your brand positioning and messaging.

Above all else, execute with consistency. These tips and tools are simply in support of that goal. You may have other routines to help you stay consistent. However you do it, execute.

Recap: It's All About You

In this chapter we turned our attention to your personal social media strategy. Today, it's not a question of if you should have one, but what it should be. For some, simply having a presence is all that's necessary, as in the base model. Others will do well by more actively engaging in social media via the standard model. A few might view creating thought leadership content via the premium model as the more appropriate strategic direction. In any case, the social media management framework can help guide your approach as you consider issues such as goal, audience, platform, brand, content, distribution, and measurement. As discussed, you should also be aware of the risks involved in any personal social media strategy. And finally, if you intend to move forward, make sure you execute.

That brings us to the end of our work applying the social media management framework to the specific topics of crisis situations, internal social media, and personal social media. To conclude this book, let's look at one of the defining challenges of the social media era: data privacy.

Your Turn: Personal Social Media Audit

To help you think strategically about your personal social media strategy, let's do a little exercise. Here's how it will work.

- Pair up with one partner.
- Using the following questions, your partner will audit your social media presence. You will also audit your partner's presence.
- Your partner will share findings and feedback from the audit. You will do the same.
- After the audit and feedback process, think about how you might change your social media strategy going forward.

Social Media Audit Questionnaire

Step 1: Inventory your partner's social media presence.

- Google your partner's name. What have you found?
- Is your partner on LinkedIn? Facebook? Twitter? Other social platforms? How easily can you find your partner's profile on various social networks?
- Describe your partner's behavior on social media? Is your partner active or passive? What types of content does your partner post?

Step 2: Summarize your perception of your partner.

- Based on your inventory of your partner's online identity, what assumptions would you make about your partner? Define your perception. Be specific.

Step 3: Provide feedback on your partner's social media strategy.

- In light of chapter concepts and the partner inventory, how can your partner enhance her or his personal social media strategy going forward?

Step 4: Reflect on your personal social media strategy.

- Did your partner's audit of your social media presence reflect your intended social media strategy? What refinements to your strategy will you make going forward?

Notes

1. https://www.facebook.com/sheryl
2. Sheryl Sandberg, *Sheryl Sandberg: Why We Have Too Few Women Leaders | TED Talk | TED.com*, TEDWomen 2010, 2010, http://www.ted.com/talks/sheryl_sandberg_why_we_have_too_few_women_leaders?language=en; Sheryl Sandberg, *Lean In: Women, Work, and the Will to Lead*, 1st ed. (New York: Knopf, 2013).
3. "SHRM/Ascendo Resources: The Importance of Social Media for Recruiters and Job Seekers," *SHRM.org*, September 1, 2015, http://www.shrm.org/research/surveyfindings/articles/pages/2015-shrm-ascendo-resources-social-media-recruitment.aspx.
4. "Profile Completeness | LinkedIn," accessed December 10, 2015, https://www.linkedin.com/static?key=pop%2Fpop_more_profile_completeness.
5. Nasheen Liu, "Growing Your Career with LinkedIn," *LinkedIn Pulse*, October 29, 2014, https://www.linkedin.com/pulse/20141029123748-4473935-growing-your-career-with-linkedin.
6. https://www.facebook.com/steinovefenne

7. Zoe McKay, "How Social Media Can Boost Profits," *Forbes*, October 9, 2012, http://www.forbes.com/sites/insead/2012/10/09/how-social-media-can-boost-profits/.
8. "Executive Moms - Networking, Support and Resources," *Executive Moms*, accessed December 10, 2015, http://executivemoms.com/.
9. Carmine Gallo, "The Bank Executive They Call 'The Social Media CEO,'" *Forbes*, January 30, 2013, http://www.forbes.com/sites/carminegallo/2013/01/30/a-bank-executive-they-call-the-social-media-ceo/.
10. Peter Aceto and Justin Kingsley, *Weology: How Everybody Wins When We Comes Before Me* (New York: HarperCollins, 2015).
11. Soumitra Dutta, "Managing Yourself: What's Your Personal Social Media Strategy?" *Harvard Business Review*, November 2010, https://hbr.org/2010/11/managing-yourself-whats-your-personal-social-media-strategy.

Epilogue: Leadership in Data Privacy

One day a Facebook user opened his Facebook page to find this advertisement:

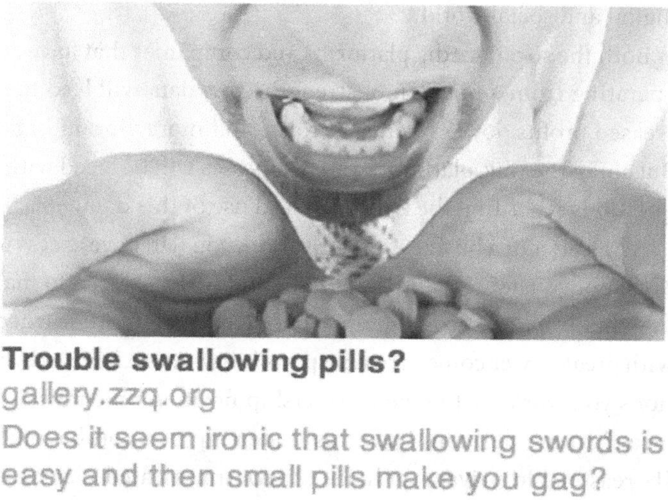

Trouble swallowing pills?
gallery.zzq.org
Does it seem ironic that swallowing swords is easy and then small pills make you gag?

As it happens, this person was a sword swallower who could not swallow pills, which made this particular ad pretty confounding. In truth, he was the only person on Facebook this ad was targeted to, and it was all a prank by his roommate, Brian Swichkow, a social media marketer. Swichkow was launching his own social media consultancy and orchestrated the ruse, which became the subject of a blog post entitled "The Ultimate Retaliation: Pranking My Roommate with Targeted

Facebook Ads," to gain attention for his website and services. (It received more than 25,000 shares.) Although a dramatic example that Brian acknowledged skirted some of Facebook's ad-buying rules, it is a symbol of the potential of today's micro-targeting techniques.

It also represents the complicated line between marketing and privacy that firms must now strike. Most social platforms operate on this arrangement: users provide their information in exchange for free use of the service. It is hardly a quid pro quo. However, it is unlikely the business models for social platforms are going to change any time soon—and arguing for change in this respect is not the purpose of this epilogue.

The charge here is to all firms and leaders to take a stand on data privacy. We just spent ten chapters discussing strategies and tactics that can help your organization realize business value from social media. Informing many of those strategic decisions is the abundant amount of data about audience behavior in today's digital and social world.

Both the social media platforms and companies that have access to this data are operating from a position of strength. This data will lead to stronger brands, increased profits, lower operating costs, and more vibrant organizational cultures. But along the way, platforms and businesses will be faced with a number of ethical questions regarding the treatment and use of this data.

As a leader of a business organization, you will have access to troves of information about customers and employees and will be forced to make decisions involving data privacy at some point in your career. As we learned from *Spider-Man*, with great power comes great responsibility. As such, I urge you and the organizations you work for to take a leadership position on data privacy. What does that mean? In my opinion, I see this leadership position having three key elements: (1) reasonable privacy policies (2) communicated clearly (3) that give people control of their information. Let's look at each in more detail.

Reasonable Privacy Policies . . .

The reality is this: social media platforms build billion-dollar businesses based on user data, and companies need this data to drive profit and operate more effectively. Privacy policies must allow both stakeholders to take advantage of the unique information they are learning about people. At the same time, the line must be drawn somewhere. Policies should acknowledge the enormous importance of customer data to industry but also protect customer rights to privacy.

Communicated Clearly . . .

Landing on a fair and reasonable privacy policy is not enough. It must also be communicated clearly to your key audiences. The thirty-page document that prompts the user to click "agree" after one page scroll is not the ideal solution to this problem. Whether it's through written, visual, or user-experience solutions, privacy policies must be communicated in a way that engages people so that they clearly understand what is being collected about them and what isn't.

That Give People Control of Their Information

Once people understand the terms of a privacy policy and what information about them will be collected, they must also be given the option to control that information. If you are comfortable with your name, email, birthdate, friends, and background being shared, then you should be able to select those options. But if not, and if you are uncomfortable sharing anything else about your online profile, then you should be able to say no. Opting-in and user control must be standard operating procedure for platforms and businesses seeking to capitalize on audience data.

Admittedly, a "reasonable policy communicated clearly that gives people control" might sound achievable, but when you begin to think about specifics, the challenge becomes much more complex. What constitutes a fair and reasonable policy? How can comprehensive policies possibly be distilled into easily understandable messages? What degree of control should people have on the types of personal information that is collected? Questions like these and others can and will be debated for the foreseeable future. And because of the gray area in this complicated topic, even the answers will be imperfect.

The industry must continue to push for fairness in data privacy. I challenge you to take a leadership position on balancing people's privacy and business interests in social media. It could very well be the defining issue of our industry for many years to come.

Index

Page references for figures are indicated by *f* and for boxes are indicated by *b*.

Printed in the USA/Agawam, MA
October 4, 2024

873902.031